Anglais

A Cultural Guide

Françoise Grellet
Agrégée d'anglais

Précis culturel
des pays du monde anglophone

Nathan

Remerciements

Je tiens à remercier Fabien Grenèche et Lynette Vaughan pour leurs suggestions et leur aide.

p. 34, p. 116 : Archives Nathan ; p. 160 : Kevin Kallaugher ; p. 190 : RUE DES ARCHIVES/BCA

Coordination éditoriale : Christine Asin
Édition : Séverine Martineau
Conception graphique de l'intérieur et de la couverture : Courant d'idées
Cartographie et schémas : Légendes cartographie
Mise en pages : Alinéa
Fabrication : Emmanuelle Perrier
Iconographie : Maryse Hubert

ISBN : 978-2-09-160785-6

ISBN : 978-2-09-165201-6

ISBN : 978-2-09-167445-2

AVANT-PROPOS

Ce précis culturel des pays du monde anglophone est destiné aux étudiants de classes préparatoires aux grandes écoles et de premier cycle universitaire, ainsi qu'à tous ceux qui ont besoin de références et de repères culturels clairs et concis pour mieux connaître l'arrière-plan civilisationnel des pays anglo-saxons.

Ce livre est loin d'être exhaustif et ne présente que les aspects institutionnels, sociaux et culturels principaux du Royaume-Uni et de l'Irlande, des États-Unis et de quelques pays du Commonwealth. Son but est de permettre à l'étudiant de redonner un contexte à une œuvre littéraire, à un mouvement d'idées, à un texte de civilisation ou à un article de journal. Il pourra tout particulièrement être utile aux étudiants qui préparent une épreuve orale ou écrite de commentaire d'article de presse.

Chaque chapitre est consacré à un point de civilisation (concernant l'histoire, les institutions, la société, les mentalités ou la culture) et est rédigé en anglais. Il comporte :

– un résumé des faits et informations essentiels accompagné de cartes, schémas, tableaux et liens Internet ;

– la présentation et la discussion, lorsque le sujet s'y prête, d'une ou plusieurs questions d'actualité souvent débattues dans les médias ;

– la traduction du vocabulaire lié au point de civilisation afin de permettre une référence rapide, mais aussi pour faciliter la révision de ce vocabulaire puisqu'il apparaît en liste sous le texte.

Cet ouvrage ne propose donc pas un approfondissement de cours ; son but est de permettre à l'étudiant de combler ses lacunes, de se familiariser avec les problèmes d'actualité des pays anglo-saxons, et d'acquérir le vocabulaire essentiel qui lui permettra de parler de ces problèmes avec rigueur et authenticité.

Sommaire

I THE UK AND IRELAND

II THE COMMONWEALTH

III THE UNITED STATES

I The UK and Ireland

1 A FEW GEOGRAPHICAL, POLITICAL AND CULTURAL DISTINCTIONS

• **The British Isles** = 2 islands: Great Britain + the whole of Ireland = A + B + C + D + E
The British Isles are the islands of Great Britain and Ireland, as well as all the smaller islands around them, such as the Channel Islands (Guernsey, Jersey...), the Orkney Islands, the Shetland Islands, the Hebrides, the Isle of Man, the Isle of Wight.
• **Great Britain:** the larger of the two islands = A (England) + B (Wales) + C (Scotland)
• **The United Kingdom** is the political country: Great Britain + Northern Ireland (also called Ulster) (A, B, C and D)
• **The Republic of Ireland** (E) is another political entity.

Poetic names:
Albion: England (from albus, white in Latin, because of England's white cliffs*)
Caledonia: Scotland
Cambria: Wales
Hibernia: Ireland

| **a cliff:** *une falaise*

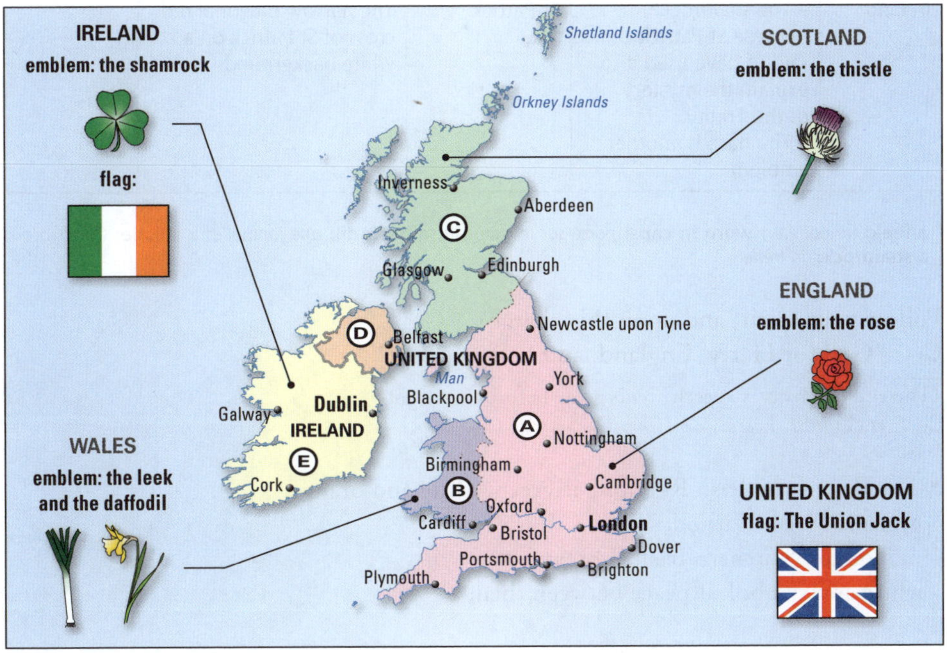

In England, people are mainly of Anglo-Saxon origin, whereas in Scotland, Wales and Ireland, they are of Celtic origin. Thus a Scotsman or a Welshman may well feel more Scottish or Welsh than British and even be offended if he is called English.

EMBLEMS, PATRON SAINTS AND FLAGS

<table>
<tr><th></th><th>Emblems</th><th>Patron saints</th><th colspan="2">Flags</th></tr>
<tr><td>England</td><td>– The rose because it has always been linked to England since the Wars of the Roses.
– The bulldog is another English emblem.</td><td>St George</td><td>The large red cross of St George on a white background (800)</td><td rowspan="4">All united in the Union Jack (a jack is a flag)</td></tr>
<tr><td>Wales</td><td>– The leek* because it was worn in caps* for identification in battle.
– The daffodil*
– The dragon.</td><td>St David</td><td></td></tr>
<tr><td>Scotland</td><td>– The thistle*, because it it said to have helped the Scots in battle.</td><td>St Andrew</td><td>The white diagonal cross of St Andrew on a blue background (1707)</td></tr>
<tr><td>Ireland</td><td>– The shamrock*, because St Patrick is said to have used it to explain the mystery of the Trinity.
– The harp is another emblem.</td><td>St Patrick</td><td>The narrow diagonal red cross of St Patrick on a white background (1801)</td></tr>
</table>

a leek: *un poireau*; **worn in caps:** *porté sur le chapeau*; **a daffodil:** *une jonquille*; **a thistle:** *un chardon*; **a shamrock:** *un trèfle*

Follow your spirit; and upon this charge
Cry, "God for Harry, England, and Saint George!"

(The end of Henry's speech to his army before they fight the French in Shakespeare's *Henry V*, Part III, 1. 33-4)

• The flag of the Irish Republic is green, white and orange:
– green for Irish Catholics
– orange for Northern Irish Protestants
– white as a symbol of peace between them

ROYAL ANTHEM

There is no official national anthem* in the United Kingdom, but the first stanza* of the anthem GOD SAVE THE QUEEN/ KING is sung on official occasions. It is a patriotic song (author unknown), first sung in 1745, when King George II defeated "Bonnie Prince Charlie", the pretender* to the throne.

God save our gracious Queen
Long live our noble Queen,
God save the Queen!
Send her victorious,
Happy and glorious,
Long to reign over us:
God save the Queen!

Rule Britannia is a sort of unofficial national anthem. Written in 1740 by James Thomson and set to music by Arne, it is a hymn to the British empire and its ships, which ruled* the ocean. Here are the first two stanzas:

Rule Britannia

When Britain first at Heav'n*'s command
Arose from out the azure main*;
This was the charter* of the land,
And guardian angels sung* this strain*;

Rule, Britannia! Britannia, rule the waves:
Britons never will be slaves.

The nations not so blest* as thee,
Shall in their turns to tyrants fall;
While thou shalt* flourish* great and free,
The dread* and envy of them all.

Rule, Britannia! Britannia, rule the waves...

Another highly patriotic song is **Jerusalem**, to words by William Blake (→ p. 89). Here is the last stanza of the song:

I will not cease* from mental fight,
Nor shall my sword* sleep in my hand
Till we have built Jerusalem
In England's green and pleasant land.

the national anthem: *l'hymne national*; **a stanza:** *une strophe*; **a pretender:** *un prétendant*; **to rule:** *dominer*; **Heav'n = Heaven:** *le ciel*; **the main:** *l'océan*; **a charter:** *une charte*; **sung:** *sang in modern English*; **a strain:** *un accord, un passage musical*; **blest = blessed:** *béni*; **thou shalt:** *you will*; **to flourish:** *prospérer*; **the dread:** *la terreur*; **to cease:** *cesser*; **a sword:** *une épée*

CONTROVERSIAL ISSUES

Identity politics

With an increasing number of people coming from different backgrounds, British society is changing fast, becoming more and more cosmopolitan and diverse. One of the results is that the very idea of a British identity is under pressure*, as the following 2011 figures show[1]: (2021 census).

In a 2021 survey, almost two-thirds of Scottish people described themselves as 'Scots', while under a third saw themselves as 'British'.

The results of the 2019 general election confirmed this tendency in the Scottish Parliament, with 45% of the votes. In Scotland, the SNP (Scottish National Party, in favour of independence for Scotland) became the largest party in the Scottish Parliament with 63 members (out of 129).

Instead of seeing themselves as British, many people assert their identities in different ways, some see themselves as Muslims first (hence the number of women wearing the veil), others see themselves as belonging to rural England, hence the passionate controversy about fox hunting a few years ago. The celebration of diversity and multiculturalism is perhaps to blame for this lack of national cohesion.

In our attempt to avoid imposing a single British identity and culture, have we ended up with some communities living in isolation of each other, with no common bonds* between them?

Ruth Kelly, Secretary of State for Communities and Local Government, 2006 (in a speech made in the wake of the 2005 terrorist attacks in London).

What new definition of British identity could make sense to a broad spectrum* of people?

In an article published in 2007, Jack Straw, Leader of the House, said that schools should emphasize certain values such as freedom and tolerance, which have contributed to Britain's heroic past (Magna Carta, Britain's role in World War II), and could establish a sense of citizenship based on allegiance* and on shared values.

Would this be enough to act as a cohesive "glue*" for the nation and thus prevent both social tensions and terrorism?

1. The last census took place in 2011; the next one will be in 2021.

under pressure: *sous pression*; **a bond:** *un lien*; **a broad spectrum:** *un large éventail*; **allegiance:** *l'allégeance*; **glue:** *la colle*

2 GEOGRAPHY & ECONOMY

A FEW STATISTICS

Surface: 244 101 km²

Population: (The following figures are mainly estimates as the findings of the 2021 Census of Population will be released in 2022.)
UK: 68,294,438 **(1, September 2021)**

Population density*: 281 inhabitants / km² **(mid-2020)**

Main cities & population (2020):
London: 7,556,900
Birmingham: 984,333
Liverpool: 864,122
Nottingham: 729,977
Sheffied: 685,368
Bristol: 617,280
Glasgow: 591,28
Leicester: 508,916
Edinburgh: 464,990
Leeds: 455,123

Age distribution (2020 estimate): Under 16: 19%
16-65: 62%
Over 65: 18.5%

Life expectancy (2020): 81.8 years
M: 80.2
F: 83.3

Birth rate*: 11.377 per 1,000 **(2021)**

Death rate*: 9.4 per 1,000 **(2020)**

Fertility rate*: 1.8 per woman **(2020)**

Net migration*: 313,000 **(2020)**

Average salary* (2019): £ 36,611 (full-time) / £12,495 (part-time)

Unemployment rate*: 4.7% **(August 2021)**

the population density: *le nombre d'habitants par km²*; **the age distribution:** *la structure de la population par âge*; **life expectancy:** *l'espérance de vie*; **the birth rate:** *le taux de natalité*; **the death rate:** *le taux de mortalité*; **the fertility rate:** *le taux de fertilité*; **net migration:** *le solde migratoire*; **the average salary:** *le salaire moyen*; **the unemployment rate:** *le taux de chômage*

A GEOGRAPHICAL MAP OF THE UNITED KINGDOM

THE COUNTIES OF THE UNITED KINGDOM

The Home Counties*: the counties around London (Kent, Surrey, Berkshire, Buckinghamshire, Hertfordshire, Middlesex, Essex).
The Shires: the counties of the Midlands with names ending in "shire"; they are famous for hunting* (e.g. Leicestershire, Northamptonshire).

| **a county:** *un comté*; **hunting:** *la chasse*

THE MAIN ECONOMIC AREAS OF THE UK

The British economy went through a radical reconversion after World War II. The traditional industries based on coal and iron (in The Midlands, South Wales, Lancashire) have gradually given way to service industries* and to industries linked to the extraction of North Sea Oil*. This has led to an increased North-South divide*. Britain is more geographically unequal than other rich countries.

service industries: *le secteur tertiaire*; **North Sea Oil:** *le pétrole de la mer du Nord*; **North-South divide:** *l'opposition entre le Nord et le Sud*

In London and the south-east (south of a line from the Severn estuary to the Wash) unemployment remains low and house prices are soaring. In the deindustrialised north of England, small cities are struggling with unemployment almost twice the national average. In 2018 productivity per head in London was 77% higher than the British average. But the real gap is not between urban and rural areas; it is between regions, and in the north both rural areas and small and big cities are poor.

ENVIRONMENTAL ISSUES

There is growing awareness about environmental issues and problems such as the degradation of soils and air pollution, the decline of costal and marine habitats (caused by tourism, industry, new housing and rising seawater temperatures), or the need to save endangered species such as the hedgehog* and the red squirrel (because of new predators and destroyed habitat).

The UK is more than ever conscious that sustainability* is essential to stop depleting* natural resources and to reduce the carbon footprint*.

– Carbon emissions (which come from the burning of fossil fuels and the meat we eat since cows produce methane) contribute to global warming and the extinction of many species. Companies are now required to report their carbon emissions, financial incentives* are given to companies that use renewable energy while heavier penalties have been imposed for environmental offences.

– Only a third of the 1.5 million tonnes of recyclable plastic waste produced in the UK is actually being recycled. Since 40% of plastic produced is used for packaging used once only, then thrown away, thus polluting seas and killing fish, efforts are beginning to be made to use more recycled plastic for packaging and manufacturing as well as to use reusable cups and containers.

– Climate change means water supply shortages and both drought* and flooding. People are urged to reduce the amount of water they use since relying on rivers, lakes and reservoirs is unsustainable.

– Deep-sea fishing, particularly when lasers are used, damages marine environments, animal and plants. It is now necessary to fish in a less wasteful way and to rebuild fish populations in order to restore the marine eco-system.

– London and major UK cities exceed air pollution limits, most pollutants coming from road transport. Friends of the Earth have asked for diesel vehicles to be phased out by 2025.

– The UK industry is developing green technology. For instance, it had 10,420 wind turbines*, both onshore and offshore, in 2021.

– Britain has shale* formations containing gas in the north and oil in the south, both of which can be extracted with hydraulic fracturing*. In 2016 the

Cameron government hoped to duplicate the US energy boom thanks to fracking. Exploratory surveys and drilling were carried out in various parts of England. But due to objections from the local population and environmental campaigners (fracking is controversial since it can cause water pollution, seismic activity, air pollution and the process can release methane and contribute to global warming) a moratorium on the technique was announced during the 2019 campaign.

hedgehog: *hérisson*; **sustainable:** *durable*; **deplete:** *réduire, épuiser*; **carbon footprint:** *empreinte carbone*; **incentive:** *récompense, prime*; **drought:** *sécheresse*; **wind turbine:** *éolienne*; **shale:** *shiste*; **hydraulic fracturing:** *fracturation hydraulique*.

(The official National Statistics guide to UK geography)
liennathan.fr/72kj5i

(The official site of the Ministry of Agriculture)
liennathan.fr/3cv6n9

(The official site of HM Treasury)
liennathan.fr/wt93j7

(The official site of the Department for Transport)
liennathan.fr/h45t4m

(The official site of the Environment Agency)
liennathan.fr/z998bp

CONTROVERSIAL ISSUES

Transports

Britain's transport network* is archaic and antiquated*. British Rail was privatised in 1996 and sold to several private operators (hence connection* problems), while the infrastructure (lines, signalling) and some major stations are owned by another operator, Network Rail. This has led to many problems and delays*, as well as criticism following a number of derailments. In 2021, this led the government to publish a proposal for a new state-owned body, Great British Railways (GBR), which would set timetables and prices, sell tickets in England and manage rail infrastructure. Since 1994, the Channel Tunnel has made it possible for trains to link London to Paris or Brussels in about 3 hours, and the time was further reduced in 2007 when the new terminal opened at St Pancras. A shuttle train* service for cars and lorries also uses the tunnel, linking Dover to Folkestone in some 30 minutes. A high-speed rail link between London and northern cities (HS2) is also under study.
With an overloaded* road infrastructure, and the traffic on motorways sometimes

close to gridlock*, what can be done to ease a situation which also has knock-on effects* on pollution and noise? Since 1994, the Channel Tunnel has made it possible for trains to link London to Paris or Brussels in about 3 hours, and the time was further reduced in 2007 when the new terminal opened at St Pancras. A shuttle train* service for cars and lorries also uses the tunnel, linking Dover to Folkestone in some 30 minutes. But with an overloaded* infrastructure, and the traffic on motorways sometimes close to gridlock*, what can be done to ease a situation which also has knock-on effects* on pollution and noise?

– Build more roads to reduce congestion*? But people, and especially environmentalists, object.
– Create pedestrian areas* in large cities?
– Ban* cars from historic centres?
– Have a road-pricing system, such as toll motorways* (as in France)?

In 2003, in London, Ken Livingstone (who was then mayor) introduced a flat-rate congestion* charge*: £5 a day for entering 8 square miles of central London. The revenue goes to the improvement of the bus service. It has proved quite effective in reducing traffic and has led Michael Bloomberg, New York's mayor, to plan a similar congestion charge in Manhattan.

a network: *un réseau*; **antiquated:** *vétuste*; **a connection:** *une correspondance*; **delays:** *retards*; **a shuttle train:** *une navette*; **overloaded:** *surchargé*; **close to gridlock:** *pratiquement bloqué*; **a knock-on effect:** *une réaction en chaîne*; **congestion:** *des encombrements*; **a pedestrian area:** *une zone piétonnière*; **to ban:** *interdire*; **a toll motorway:** *une autoroute à péage*: **a flat rate charge:** *une somme forfaitaire*; **a congestion charge:** *une taxe pour éviter les encombrements*

Are GM crops and food* dangerous?

The debate about the possible advantages and dangers of genetically modified (GM) food is still raging among scientists and politicians. There is no commercial growth of GM crops in Britain, but they can enter the country as animal feed. Here are some arguments for and against:

FOR	AGAINST
– By modifying the genetic composition of a plant, it can be made more resistant to disease and more nutritious. – It would increase production in Third World countries. – If the plants are more resistant, they will not require many pesticides and will be good for the environment. → It is only through a programme of trials* that the effects of such crops* may be assessed*.	– We do not know enough at the moment about the possible effects on human health (on the immune system and on fertility in particular). – If GM crops are grown in a particular field, is there a risk that fields nearby may be contaminated (by water and airborne seeds), thus damaging wildlife and biodiversity? → There should therefore be a moratorium* on all GM crops.

GM crops and food: *des OGM (organismes génétiquement modifiés)*; **a moratorium:** *un moratoire*; **trials:** *des essais*; **a crop:** *une culture*; **to assess:** *évaluer*

A flexible market

With fewer laws and regulations* than in France, the British labour market* is far more flexible than the French one. Business is also low-taxed* and less regulated in order to boost the economy*, and this means less job security*, many low-paid jobs (derogatorily* called "McJobs") including zero-hour contracts (contracts without any particular number of hours of work specified), and a huge gap* between the skilled* and the unskilled, the rich and the poor (the distribution of income is more unequal in Britain than in any other rich country in the world except the United States). But if there is little job security*, it is also easier to find a new job and Britain's unemployment figures have not been as low since the 1970s.
Britain has never, like France, had any doubts about globalisation. With its flexible labour market, foreign investments, deregulated financial markets, imperial past and Commonwealth links, Britain has not seemed very worried about globalisation and there is little protest when jobs go abroad. Following the problems of the 1970s (high inflation, strikes...), the British economy underwent a radical change in the decades that followed, and now mainly specializes in high-tech, service or research sectors, outsourcing* other jobs abroad. One of the consequences of Brexit has been to reduce the number of migrants in the country, which mainly affects businesses that rely on seasonal and low-paid workers. If the tendency is confirmed, more unfulfilled vacancies might mean better wages for low-paid jobs.

a regulation: *une réglementation*; **the labour market:** *le marché du travail*; **low-taxed:** *peu imposé* **(≠heavily taxed); to boost the economy:** *donner du tonus à l'économie*; **job security:** *la sécurité de l'emploi*; **derogatorily:** *de façon méprisante*; **a gap:** *un écart, une différence*; **skilled:** *qualifié*; **to deregulate:** *déréglementer*; **to outsource:** *délocaliser*

3 MAJOR DATES IN BRITISH HISTORY

The Romans

55-54 BC: Julius Caesar first invades England, which was then inhabited by a number of Celtic groups. The Roman occupation lasts for some 400 years, during which many roads and cities such as London (then called Londinium) are built. In 122 AD, Hadrian (the Roman emperor) has a 185-kilometre wall built from coast to coast in the north of England to mark the northern boundary* of the Roman empire and as a protection against tribes* from the north (the Picts in particular).

a boundary: *une frontière*; **a tribe:** *une tribu*

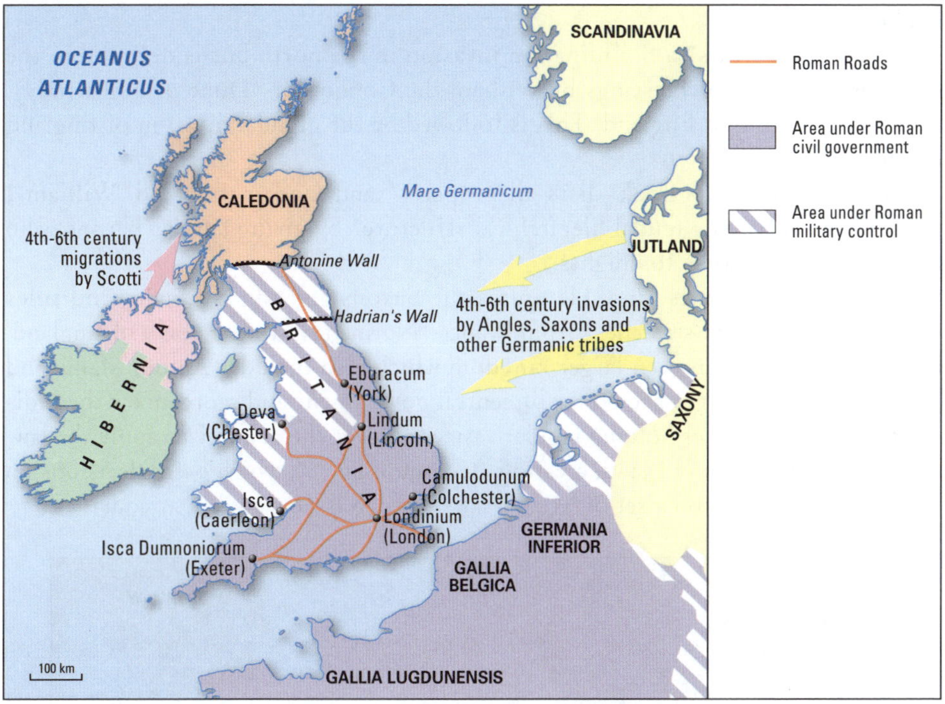

The Saxons

450-550: The Saxon Conquest: it follows the invasion of northern England by Picts and Scots, and the gradual withdrawal* from England of the Romans, who needed to defend Gaul. The new English settlers* come from Germany (the Jutes and the Saxons) and from Denmark (the Angles). They establish the English language, and bring their pagan* religion to England.

597: St Augustine begins converting the English to Christianity. He establishes Canterbury.

865: Danish Vikings invade the north of England.

871: Alfred the Great becomes king of Wessex (the southern part of England). He creates laws, sheriffs, a navy*, encourages the conversion to Christianity and fights off the Vikings. The kingdom is divided into shires*. He also encourages the development of education.

1042: Edward the Confessor is appointed* king of England. When he dies in 1066, another Saxon, Harold, is chosen as king.

(Anglo-Saxons: a brief history)
liennathan.fr/e85t2q

a withdrawal: *un retrait*; **settlers:** *des colons*; **pagan:** *païen*; **the navy:** *la marine*; **shires:** *comtés*; **appointed:** *nommé*

The Normans

1066: Harold defeats* a Scandinavian invasion in the north but is defeated in the south at the Battle of Hastings by William the Conqueror (Duke of Normandy), who becomes King of England. This is followed by the gradual invasion of England by the Normans.

1086: The Domesday Book* lists all property* and land in England. William I gradually establishes a feudal hierarchical structure* by giving land to barons, who themselves grant* some to knights*.

1100: Henry I becomes king. He unites the Saxons and the Normans, and rules over a kingdom which stretches* from France (Normandy) to the north of England. Henry II rules over an even larger kingdom which also includes Anjou, Maine and Touraine. He reinforces the power of central government and reorganizes the judicial system, with judges holding regular assizes all over the country to apply the law. He reforms the system of laws, creating "Common Law"*, which bases decisions on customs* rather than on a set of written laws. French is now spoken at court.

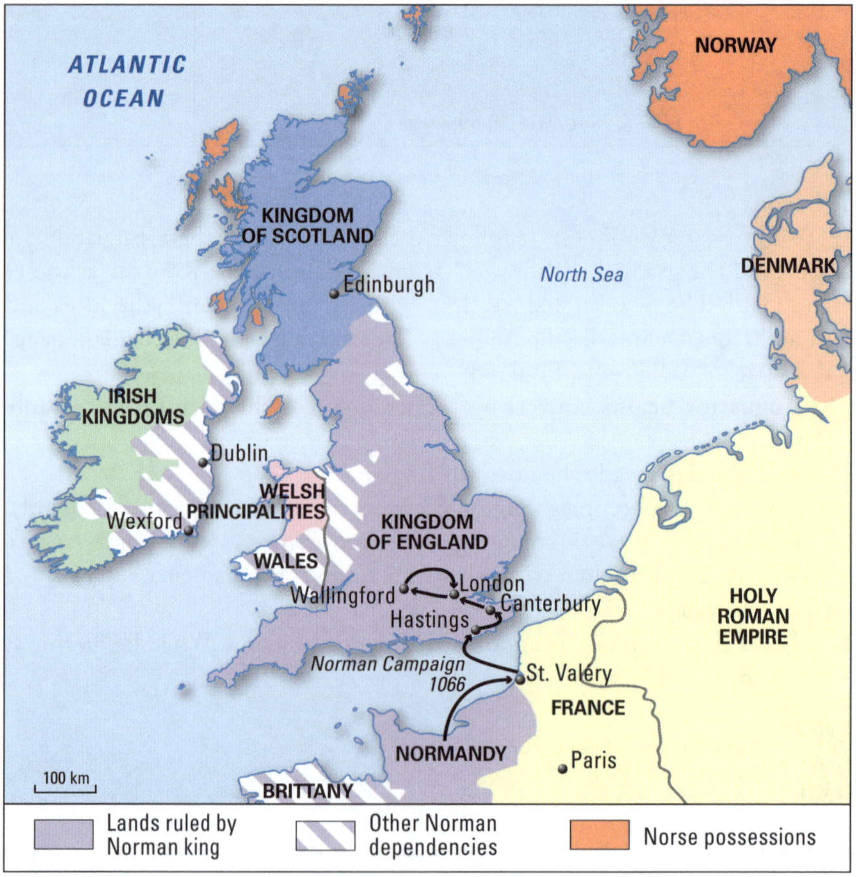

1170: Thomas Becket, Archbishop of Canterbury, criticises the king's rights over the church and is murdered.
1189: Richard "The Lionheart"* succeeds Henry II.
1203-04: John Lackland* loses most of the French lands.
1215: John Lackland is forced to sign the Magna Carta*.
1284: Wales becomes part of the kingdom.
1295: Edward I summons* his "Model Parliament", which a few decades later will separate into two chambers: the nobility and the clergy will form the House of Lords, whereas the House of Commons will be for representatives of towns and counties.
1305: Scottish revolt led by Robert (the) Bruce: Scotland becomes independent.

to defeat: *vaincre, battre*; **The Domesday Book:** *le Livre du Jugement*; **property:** *propriété, biens*; **a feudal hierarchical structure:** *une structure hiérarchique féodale*; **to grant:** *accorder, octroyer*; **a knight:** *un chevalier*; **to stretch:** *s'étendre*; **Common Law:** *le droit coutumier*; **customs:** *des coutumes*; **Richard "The Lionheart":** *Richard Cœur de Lion*; **John Lackland:** *Jean sans Terre*; **The Magna Carta:** *La Grande Charte*; **to summon:** *convoquer*

A Hundred and fifty years of war

1337-1453: The Hundred Years' War, a long conflict for the domination of France. England first holds large territories in France (1420: Treaty of Troyes), but France has gradually gained back its land (except for Calais) by the end of the war, in 1453.
1348: The Black Death (or plague*)
1381: The Peasants' revolt against taxation is crushed* but leads to the end of serfdom*.
1455-1485: The Wars of the Roses. They set the House of York (whose emblem is the white rose) against the House of Lancaster (the red rose), rivals for the throne of England. In 1485, Henry Tudor (a Lancaster) marries Elizabeth of York, thus bringing unity again to England.
1476: William Caxton establishes the first press in England printing books in English.

the plague: *la peste*; **to crush:** *réprimer*; **serfdom:** *le servage*

The Tudors and the Stuarts

(The Tudors)
liennathan.fr/s893dc

(Stuart England)
liennathan.fr/79ffr7

1534: Act of Supremacy: King Henry VIII breaks with Rome in order to divorce his first wife (Catherine of Aragon) and marry Anne Boleyn, his mistress: he declares himself "Supreme Head of the English Church and Clergy". This is the starting point of the Reformation. Protestantism replaces the Catholic religion (the official religion before), the monasteries are closed and their land taken.
1558-1603: Reign of Elizabeth I. Anglicanism (a via media between Catholicism and Protestantism) becomes the established religion. Although Catholicism is still banned*, there is relative stability after a period of religious extremism (Edward VI's

persecutions of the Catholics, then Mary I's persecutions of the Protestants.) Only Scotland remains outside the Anglican compromise, the radical John Knox being the originator of the Scottish Presbyterian church (election of priests, belief in predestination), whose puritan members were to oppose the Anglican church and the absolute power of the monarch. These dissidents were persecuted and many fled* abroad. Elizabeth's reign is a long one marked by the fear of an invasion to put a Catholic sovereign onto the throne.

In 1587, Mary Stuart (Queen of Scots) is executed for treason* (accused of plotting to put a Catholic sovereign on the throne), and in 1588 the Spanish Armada, ships sent to invade Britain by the Catholic king of Spain, is defeated. The reign of Elizabeth is also a period of cultural development (music, poetry, the theatre – Shakespeare) and of maritime power.

1603: James VI of Scotland becomes James I of England. He believes in the Divine Right of Kings and his reign is marked by a growing conflict with Parliament.

1605: The Gunpowder plot* is a conspiracy by a few Catholics to blow up* the Houses of Parliament while the king and the whole government are there. The plot is given away* and the conspirators executed. The discovery of the plot is still celebrated today on Guy Fawkes Day (November 5th) when bonfires* are lit and effigies of Guy Fawkes, seen as the leader of the plot, are burnt.

1611: Publication of the Authorized Version of the Bible (or King James's Bible.)

banned: *interdit*; **to flee (fled, fled):** *s'enfuir*; **treason:** *la trahison*; **the Gunpowder Plot:** *la Conspiration des poudres*; **to blow up:** *faire sauter*; **to give away:** *trahir, révéler*; **bonfires:** *des feux de joie*

Two revolutions

1625-1649: Charles I succeeds James I. He increasingly tries to rule without Parliament, but in 1628 has to sign the Petition of Right (no taxes can be raised without the consent of Parliament).

1629-1640: Charles I tries to govern the country without Parliament.

1642-1648: The Civil War pits the supporters of Parliament (Puritans or Roundheads, led by Oliver Cromwell, and helped by the Scots) against the supporters of King Charles I (Cavaliers). The latter are finally defeated.

1649: Charles I is executed and the monarchy is abolished.

1653-1658: The Commonwealth (a republic) is established, led by Cromwell, who has the title of Lord Protector of England, Scotland and Ireland, then by his son. England is governed under strict puritanical rules.

1660: After Cromwell's son steps down*, General Monck negotiates the return of Charles II (who is in exile in France) as king. He increasingly tries to rule without Parliament, which is too hostile to royal power.

1665: The Great Plague* in London

1666: The Great Fire of London destroys a large part of the city.

1679: Habeas Corpus Act (no imprisonment without trial)

1685: James II, a convert to Catholicism, succeeds to the throne.

1688: The Glorious Revolution: the crown is taken from the Catholic James II (for fear his Catholic son should inherit it) and given to William III. The principle of Constitutional monarchy is established with the Bill of Rights* and the Act of Settlement:
1689: The Bill of Rights establishes a parliamentary democracy by curbing* the power of the monarch.
1701: The Act of Settlement makes it impossible for a Catholic king to accede to the throne.
1707: Act of Union uniting England and Scotland.

to step down: *se retirer, abdiquer*; **the Great Plague:** *la Grande Peste*; **The Bill of Rights:** *la Déclaration des Droits*; **to curb:** *restreindre*

The eighteenth century

1714: Beginning of the Hanoverian Dynasty*. Since Queen Anne, the last Stuart monarch, has no descendants, George I, belonging to the dynasty of the Electors of Hanover and a descendant of James I, comes to the throne. He is succeeded by his son, George II, and by the latter's grandson, George III. The principles of constitutional monarchy mean that the executive is in the hands of the king and his Cabinet, whose powers are restrained by Parliament, itself also responsible for making laws. Two main parties appear at the beginning of the century: the Tories (more conservative and closer to the former Stuarts) and the Whigs (more liberal and defending the Bill of Rights).
1745: Jacobite rebellion defeated (the Jacobites were the supporters of James II's descendants).
1756-1763: Seven Years' War with France
1764: Invention of the Spinning Jenny*. The first factories are built in the 1770s. The industrial revolution begins to change the face of the country. The invention of the steam engine* by Watt in 1785 leads to the rapid development of railways. Canals are built. All this is made possible thanks to the use of coal as fuel.

(The industrial revolution)
liennathan.fr/5cq5d5

1776: The American colonies become independent.
1801: Act of Union, creating the United Kingdom of Great Britain and Ireland.
1805: Lord Nelson defeats the combined fleets of France and Spain at Trafalgar.
1815: The British army (under the Duke of Wellington) defeats Napoleon at Waterloo.
1829: Catholics obtain freedom of worship.
1832: The first Reform Act extends the right to vote to the middle class.

the Hanoverian Dynasty: *la Dynastie de Hanovre*; **the Spinning Jenny:** *la machine à filer le coton*; **the steam engine:** *la machine à vapeur*; **freedom of worship:** *la liberté religieuse*

▪ The Victorian age

1837-1901: Reign of Queen Victoria. It is marked by the expansion of the empire and by Puritanism (strictness and austerity in social and religious matters).
1838-48: The Chartists present petitions to Parliament, asking for universal male suffrage, vote by secret ballot*, equal constituencies* and the abolition of the need to own land to become an M.P. Their demands are rejected by Parliament and the movement dies down after 1850.
1851: The Great Exhibition* shows displays from countries all over the world, but is mainly a presentation of the latest technological achievements of British engineering.

The Victorians

Queen Victoria's reign lasted sixty-four years, and the expression "Victorian age" has become synonymous with:
– A deep religious sense: the Church of England, Evangelical Christians, non-conformist chapels as well as the Catholic church were extremely active. But this belief was also challenged* by Darwin's theory of evolution: His *Origin of Species* was published in 1859.
– Morality and middle-class respectability. It was often accompanied by philistinism, narrow-mindedness, prudishness and sentimentality.
– A belief in progress, in the possibilities of science and technology (reflected in the Great Exhibition)
– The division of Britain into "two nations", to use Disraeli's expression for the rich and the poor, which led to class conflict, social unrest, and a deep-felt need for social reform, exemplified* by the Chartist movement and a series of laws to improve the horrendous living and working conditions in large cities.

(The Victorian age)
liennathan.fr/ib8p34

1854-56: Crimean War
1859: Darwin's *Origin of Species* about natural selection and the survival of the fittest*.
1868: Creation of the Trades Union Congress*
1870: Education Act (primary education becomes free for all).
1872: Ballot Act (voting becomes secret)
1876: Queen Victoria becomes Empress of India.
1899-1902: Boer War (in South Africa).
1900: Creation of the Labour Party.

The British Empire

By the mid 19th century, Britain had a huge empire, on which "the sun never set". It brought enormous wealth (with, for instance, cotton and tea imported from India, wood from Canada, wool from Australia... – all of them contributing to the development of industry in the 19th century), but also a sense of pride and high hopes, the complacent* feeling that Britain was making the world a better place and bringing civilisation and culture to less developed countries (though it also led to greed and self-interest.) The idea is developed in many of Ruyard Kipling's poems, for instance in the first stanza of 'The White Man's Burden':

Take up the White Man's burden*–
Send forth the best ye* breed*–
Go bind* your sons to exile
To serve your captives' need;
To wait* in heavy harness*,
On fluttered* folk and wild–
Your new-caught, sullen* peoples,
Half-devil and half-child.

(Although written about the American conquest of the Philippines, the poem can be seen as a justification of imperialism, the white man's duty being to colonize other nations in order to improve their condition. The poem has proved highly controversial.)

secret ballot: *le scrutin secret*; **a constituency:** *une circonscription électorale*; **the Great Exhibition:** *la Grande Exposition*; **to challenge:** *mettre en question*; **to exemplify:** *illustrer*; **the survival of the fittest:** *la lutte pour la vie*; **the Trades Union Congress:** *la fédération des syndicats britanniques*; **complacent:** *satisfait de soi*; **a burden:** *un fardeau*; **ye:** *vous (archaïque)*; **to breed:** *élever*; **to bind:** *lier, contraindre*; **to wait... on:** *servir*; **in harness:** *attelés à la tâche*; **fluttered:** *agités, troublés*; **sullen:** *maussades, renfrognés*

The twentieth century

1911: Parliament Act (The Lords lose their power of veto.)
1914: Britain enters World War I.
1916: Easter Rising in Dublin.
1919: Women obtain the right to vote, after much campaigning on the part of the suffragettes.
1921: Ireland is divided into two.
1926: General strike*, the result of a period of industrial crisis and unemployment.
1928: Representation of the People Act: the vote is given to all men and women of 21 and above, partly as a consequence of the suffragettes' fight.
1929: Beginning of the Great Depression: bankruptcies* and unemployment
1936: Edward VIII becomes king, but abdicates the same year to marry an American divorcee.

1939: Britain declares war on Germany. Led by Winston Churchill, Britain shows courage and determination in the war against Nazi Germany.
1940: The Battle of Britain (air battles, Germany bombing strategic positions in Britain to prepare for an invasion); the Blitz (air raids on London). The war effort (rationing*, women working in industry) helps to create a spirit of solidarity.

The spirit of the Blitz

The word blitz comes from the German word *blitzkrieg* (lightning war) to describe a massive attack. During the 1940 blitz, 18,000 tons of bombs fell upon London, causing extensive destruction and fires. Some people fled, while others stayed, spending the nights in Underground stations or living in rest centres. The expression 'Spirit of the Blitz' describes the courage and endurance of the people during that time as well as the feeling of togetherness* and even of exhilaration* which often accompanied their refusal to give in.

I have nothing to offer but blood, toil, tears and sweat.

Winston Churchill, May 1940.

a general strike: *une grève générale*; **bankruptcy:** *la faillite*: **rationing:** *le rationnement*; **togetherness:** *l'entraide*; **exhileration:** *l'exaltation*

1942: Beveridge Report
1944: D-Day (Allied forces land in France)
The Butler Act makes school free and compulsory* from 5 to 15.
1945: VE-Day: end of World War II. The Labour government creates the Welfare State*, which institutes the National Health Service*, welfare payments*, unemployment benefits*, education for all.

(1945 to present: BBC time-line)
liennathan.fr/rt975x

1947-1949: Many former colonies (such as India, Pakistan, Kenya) reach independence.
1949: The UK becomes a member of NATO*.
1951-64: Conservative governments (Churchill, Eden, Macmillan, Home)
1956: Britain and France invade Egypt to regain the Suez canal, but have to pull out*.
1964-70: Labour government (Wilson): the death penalty is abolished, the Abortion* Act legalizes the termination of pregnancy, the Sexual Offences Act decriminalizes homosexuality and the Divorce Act liberalizes the divorce laws.
1969: Beginning of "The Troubles" in Northern Ireland.

1973: Britain and Ireland enter the Common Market.
1979: During the "winter of discontent", many strikes* paralyse Britain and eventually bring down James Callaghan's Labour government.
1979-1990: The first woman Prime Minister, Margaret Thatcher (nicknamed "The Iron Lady"), introduces liberal policies.
1982: Falklands War, a conflict between Argentina and Britain after the Argentinians invaded the Falkland Islands. The war is short and won by Britain.
1984: A national miners' strike* (to protest against the closure of coal pits) lasts a year and is defeated.

Thatcherism

Thatcherism is the name given to Margaret Thatcher's policies. They consist in:
– Monetarism
– Privatizations of nationalized industries (called selling the "family jewels")
– Free enterprise and a reduction of the role of the State and of public spending (many state institutions were encouraged to develop a market economy and competition)
– Curbing* the power of trade-unions*(prohibiting closed shops* and secondary strikes*, obliging unions to ballot their members before calling a strike, preventing unions from penalizing members who refuse to go on strike.)
– Strict law and order policies*
– Forceful* foreign policy abroad (The Falklands war)
Her attempt to impose one and the same local government tax (called 'poll tax'*) on individuals (and no longer households), whatever their earnings, led to protests, demonstrations, and eventually to her resignation. However, John Major, another Conservative Prime Minister, was elected in 1990.

"I came to office with one deliberate intent: to change Britain from a dependent to a self-reliant society – from a give-it-to-me, to a do-it-yourself nation. A get-up-and-go, instead of a sit-back-and-wait-for-it Britain."

Speech to the Small Business Bureau Conference (8 February, 1984)

1994: The Channel Tunnel links Britain and France.
1997: After Labour's landslide victory*, Tony Blair becomes Prime Minister. Breaking with the traditional Labour doctrines, Tony Blair calls his party New Labour. It is often described as a "Third Way*" between left and right, between social democracy and neo-liberalism: it is based on pragmatism and defends family values and social justice within a competitive market. Hong Kong returns to Chinese rule.

Blairism

Blairism is the name given to Tony Blair's policies. They consist in:
– The modernization of the Labour party: the old Labour idea of the common ownership of the means of production (Clause Four of the Labour Party's Constitution) was replaced by the idea that everyone had a right to "power, wealth and opportunity": old Labour's close financial ties* with the trade unions were also reduced (though unions still brought in half of the party's money).
– Constitutional reforms:
• A reform of the House of Lords, which now has fewer hereditary peers*.
• Devolution* with the creation of a Welsh Assembly (1998) and of a Scottish Parliament (1998).
• The adoption of the European Convention on Human Rights (2000)
– Increased spending on education
– The alliance between liberal (market-based*) economic policies and social reform (for instance the introduction of a minimum wage*, a Welfare to Work policy, improving the NHS). Tony Blair's policies brought unemployment down and increased consumer spending.
– Giving Britain a major role in world politics (the peace process in Ireland, the war in Iraq).

1999: Beginning of the reform of the House of Lords: hereditary peers will no longer be able to sit in the House of Lords, which will consist mainly of appointed members. A Scottish Parliament and a Welsh Assembly are created, giving more direct decision-making power to the people of these regions.
2001: After the 9/11 attacks, Britain supports the United States' war on terrorism.

The special relationship

The expression was first used by Churchill, who said that in the new world order after Yalta, "the fraternal association of the English-speaking peoples... a special relationship between the British Commonwealth and the United States" represented the only safe solution. The words describe the close links between the UK and the USA in terms of culture, shared goals and national interests. The Marshall Plan, NATO, the Korean war, the Cuban crisis and the installation of cruise missiles* in Britain in the 1980s are so many examples of close cooperation between the two countries.
Britain's special relationship with the USA has been particularly strong when there was a close personal relationship and/or shared political views between the heads of state (Winston Churchill and Franklin D. Roosevelt, Margaret

Thatcher and Ronald Reagan, John Major and George Bush senior, Tony Blair and Bill Clinton).
The special relationship was recently illustrated by Britain's involvement* in the war in Iraq after 9/11, an involvement for which Tony Blair was much criticized and seen, even within his own party, as subservient*, and sometimes called George Bush's "poodle"*. While Brexit should provide a rare opportunity to strengthen Britain's alliance with the United States, Mr Trump's presidency tended to strain it, with the two countries at odds over tax, technology and trade.

2002: Queen Elizabeth II's Golden Jubilee.
2003-2004: Britain sends troops to Iraq.
2005: Tony Blair is re-elected for a third term. Terrorist attacks cause huge explosions in London, killing 52 people.
Britain's unconditional support for the United States begins to be questioned as troops fight and die in Iraq and as violence there keeps increasing. Civil partnerships give same-sex couples legal rights.
2007: Tony Blair stands down* as Prime minister and is replaced by Gordon Brown.
2008: The Church of England votes to allow the ordination of women bishops.
A global 'credit crunch' leads to a stock market fall. The government takes a series of measures to help Britain's ailing banks.
2009: MPs' expenses scandal. Britain withdraws most troops from Iraq.
2010: Conservatives and Liberal Democrats form a coalition government led by David Cameron. They decide on large public spending cuts.
2011: Prince William marries Kate Middleton in a ceremony watched by millions.
It is revealed that the *News of the World* hacked the phones of several public figures.
2012: Diamond Jubilee of Queen Elizabeth II.
2014: First gay marriages held in England and Wales.
A referendum is held in Scotland on independence from the UK. To the question 'Should Scotland be an independent country?', 55.3% answer No.
2016: A referendum promised by David Cameron is held to decide whether the UK should leave or remain in the European Union. Leave wins by 51.9%. England and Wales voted for Brexit while Scotland and Northern Ireland voted Remain. David Cameron consequently resigns and is replaced by Theresa May without a leadership contest.
2017: The two-year process of leaving the EU is triggered* in March. There is still much uncertainty about the terms of UK's leaving the EU: Will Brexit be soft (with the UK remaining in the single market and accepting the free movement of people) or hard (with the UK refusing the free movement of people and as a result losing the single market)? Can Britain remain a global financial centre after Brexit? What will happen to the land border between the UK and Ireland? What will happen to the EU

citizens living in the UK and to the UK citizens living in Europe? Could Brexit revive Scotland's desire for independence?
Several terrorist attacks take place in Manchester and London.
Theresa May calls a general election hoping for a strong mandate to negotiate Brexit. The Tories lose their majority but form a government thanks to a deal with the Democratic Unionist Party of Northern Ireland.
2016-2019: Theresa May negotiates a Brexit withdrawal agreement with the EU, but with no overall majority in Parliament, it is rejected three times. She resigns.
2019: The general election which follows Theresa May's resignation gives a large majority to the Conservatives. Boris Johnson, a pro-Brexit campaigner, wins the Conservative leadership contest. He later unlawfully decides to prorogue* Parliament to limit opposition to Brexit. The ensuing crisis leads to another general election, which once again gives a large majority to the Conservatives. Under Jeremy Corbyn the Labour Party is accused of poor leadership (lack of clarity over Brexit) and anti-Semitism among party activists.
Boris Johnson pledges to 'get Brexit done' and not extend talks beyond December 2020.
Abortion and gay marriage become legal in Northern Ireland.
2019-2021: Growing pro-democracy protests, demonstrations, and violence in Hong Kong, originally against a proposed extradition law that would send suspects of a crime to mainland China for trial. Dissidents are alarmed about the erosion of political freedoms and the draconian national security law imposed from Beijing. This triggers the worst crisis in Hong Kong since its handover to China in 1997.
2020: Emergency measures (including, border screening* and quarantine, lockdowns*, curfews*, working from home, masks, social-distancing measures, the closing of schools and non-essential shops) are taken to fight the Covid-19 pandemic, which first appeared in China's Hubei province but quickly spread all over the world. By the end of the year a second wave of the disease leads to a soaring* of daily infections.
The Anglo-Swedish pharmaceutical and biotechnology company AstraZeneca develops and licenses a vaccine for Covid-19.
Because of the pandemic the number of people claiming unemployment benefit rises by 69%. Shopping moves online. Aviation, tourism and catering* are hardest hit in spite of huge government bailouts*. Britain guarantees 80% of wages to workers who have been furloughed*.
In response to China's draconian new national-security bill on Hong Kong, Britain will make it easier for Hong Kongers born before 1997 to settle in Britain.
A post-Brexit trade agreement is approved.
2021: Brexit becomes official on January 31, but conditions and trade deals will be negotiated during a transition period ending on December 31st. The main problem remains the Northern Ireland border 'backstop* 'to avoid a hard border with Ireland'.

Since Northern Ireland remains part of the EU's single market (in order to avoid checks on the border with Ireland), goods arriving there from Britain have to undergo EU checks. They will take place in the Irish Sea, something unionists refuse as they would feel cut off from the rest of the UK. In April, this leads to renewed tension and violence on the streets of Belfast and other cities.
New variants of Covid-19 spread around the world. By the end of January, the death toll from Covid passes 100,000 in the UK. An extensive vaccination programme is launched and starts drastically reducing the number of deaths. On July 19th ('Freedom Day'), all restrictions are lifted even though the number of contaminations is still high.
In its defence and foreign policy review, Britain decides to increase its nuclear stockpile for the first time since the cold war.
September: The UK, US and Australia sign a historic security pact in the Indo-Pacific (AUKUS), in an effort to counter China's influence there. Australia abandons a contract with France for conventional submarines in favour of a nuclear submarine program with the US. For the UK this is line with 'Global Britain', the UK's post-Brexit foreign policy ambitions : the country now intends to have a global outlook beyond Europe.

prorogue: *proroger*; **border screening:** *contrôle des frontières*; **lockdown:** *confinement*; **curfew:** *couvre-feu*; **soaring:** *envolée*; **catering:** *restauration*; **bailout:** *aide, renflouement*; **furlough:** *chômage technique*; **backstop:** *safeguard, garantie*; **compulsory:** *obligatoire*; **the Welfare State:** *l'État-providence*; **the National Health Service:** *la Sécurité sociale*; **welfare payments:** *des prestations sociales*; **unemployment benefits:** *les allocations de chômage*; **NATO:** *OTAN*; **to pull out:** *se retirer*; **abortion:** *l'avortement*; **a strike:** *une grève*; **the Falklands War:** *la guerre des Malouines*; **a miners' strike:** *une grève des mineurs*; **to curb:** *réduire*; **a trade union:** *un syndicat*; **the closed shop system:** *système où seuls des ouvriers appartenant à un certain syndicat sont embauchés*; **law and order policies:** *des mesures d'ordre public*; **forceful:** *énergique*; **the poll tax:** *un impôt local prélevé par habitant*; **a landslide victory:** *une victoire écrasante*; **the Third Way:** *la Troisième Voie*; **ties:** *des liens*; **a peer:** *un pair*; **devolution:** *la décentralisation*; **market-based economic policies:** *l'économie de marché*; **the minimum wage:** *le salaire minimum*; **involvement:** *la participation*; **a cruise missile:** *un missile de croisière*; **subservient:** *servile, obséquieux*; **a poodle:** *un caniche*; **to stand down:** *démissionner*; **to trigger:** *déclencher*

(BBC site devoted to the history of Britain)
liennathan.fr/9djp44

(An archive of politically significant audio material (e.g. political speeches))
liennathan.fr/8y3a2q

4 TWELVE DATES WHICH SHAPED BRITAIN'S CONSTITUTIONAL MONARCHY

The United Kingdom is a constitutional monarchy* (or parliamentary monarchy), which means that the powers of the sovereign are limited by those of Parliament.
Britain has no single document which amounts to a written constitution. Instead,

a number of successive statutes* and acts* provide what can be called an **unwritten constitution***. It is more flexible and pragmatic than a written constitution since it can be changed by an act of parliament and evolve almost organically with the times.

a constitutional monarchy: *une monarchie constitutionnelle*; **statutes:** *des lois écrites*; **acts:** *des lois votées par le Parlement*; **an unwritten constitution:** *une constitution non codifiée*; **to evolve:** *évoluer, changer*

■ 1215: Magna Carta*

This was a charter presented in 1215 by a delegation of Barons in order to establish the respective rights and duties of the King, the Church and the Barons. It
– guaranteed the freedom of the church
– curtailed* the powers of the king (who could not impose taxes without the agreement of a council).
– protected individuals against arbitrary imprisonment or punishment without prior judgement*. All individuals now had a right to a "fair trial"*.
– protected individuals from the arbitrary seizing* of their land.
Faced with the imminent rebellion of his barons, King John signed the charter limiting his powers at Runnymede (a meadow near Windsor). It is considered as a first step in the resistance against royal despotism and towards individual liberty.

Magna Carta: *la Grande Charte*; **to curtail:** *limiter*; **a prior judgement:** *un jugement préalable*; **a fair trial:** *un jugement équitable*; **to seize:** *saisir*

■ 1534: The Act of Supremacy

This Act, legally passed by Parliament, made Henry VIII "supreme head of the Church of England" and set aside the authority of the Pope. It established royal supremacy over the national church. This was the starting point of the Reformation in England. It became a Protestant country and the monasteries were dissolved.

■ 1628: The Petition of Right

A Declaration limiting royal power, which the two houses of Parliament forced Charles I to accept. It demanded that:
– no taxes should be levied* without the consent of Parliament
– no one be imprisoned without trial
Following from the Magna Carta, the Petition of Right asserts* the rights of individuals. Although Charles I signed the Petition, he did not abide by* it, which led to the Civil War.

to levy taxes: *prélever des impôts*; **to assert:** *affirmer*; **to abide by:** *respecter (la loi)*

■ 1679: Habeas Corpus

As a reaction against Charles II's arbitrary detention of people, Parliament voted this act to forbid arbitrary arrests and imprisonment. Prisoners must be brought before a judge or a jury within three days of their arrest, and either charged* or freed. The Habeas Corpus Act is still in force today, although it can be suspended in times of crisis.

to charge: *inculper*

■ 1689: The Bill of Rights

It deals with the relationship between the monarch and Parliament.
– It contains the Declaration of Right accepted by William III and Mary II when they came to the throne, a document which is the basis for constitutional monarchy since it makes the arbitrary use of royal power illegal. The sovereign now must govern according to the statutes voted by Parliament; he or she cannot raise taxes unless Parliament has agreed.
– It excludes Catholics from the succession to the throne.

■ 1701: Act of Settlement

It concerns the rules of succession, once more stating that the sovereign cannot be a Catholic and that illegitimate or adopted persons cannot succeed to the throne* either.

| **to succeed to the throne:** *succéder (à la couronne)*

■ 1707: Acts of Union

The 1707 Act of Union united England and Scotland. A second Act of Union in 1800 (effective in 1801) united them to Ireland. Both Scotland and Ireland lost their respective Parliaments and sent their MPs to Westminster. All merged into the United Kingdom.
In 1921, part of Ireland obtained Home Rule* and left the United Kingdom. Although the union of England with Scotland still holds, Scotland, Northern Ireland and Wales have now gained a measure of autonomy*, with Parliaments and an assembly.

| **Home Rule:** *l'autonomie*; **a measure of autonomy:** *une certaine autonomie*

■ 1832: Reform Act

An act which contributed to democracy since it
– extended the franchise* by giving the vote to more property owners and to those paying a certain amount of rent. It gave the right to vote to much of the middle-class.
– reformed the constituencies*. Indeed, before 1832, some cities which had grown very quickly because of the industrial revolution were not even represented, while smaller towns might have several MPs. There were even "rotten boroughs*", places with no inhabitants (like Dunwich, for centuries buried under the sea), which were represented in Parliament, rich landowners nominating their members as they pleased.

| **franchise:** *le droit de vote*; **a constituency:** *une circonscription électorale*; **rotten boroughs:** *des bourgs pourris*

■ 1911: Parliament Act

The House of Lords lost its power of veto over financial legislation, and its delaying powers* were limited for other legislation.
By thus limiting the power of the House of Lords, the Act established the elected chamber, the Commons, as the supreme legislative body.

The Parliament Act also established that general elections* must take place every five years (instead of seven, as before).

| **delaying powers:** *le pouvoir de retarder une loi*; **general elections:** *des élections législatives*

■ 1928: Equal Franchise Act

After the 1832 Reform Act, a series of other acts gradually extended the franchise until 1928, when all men and women aged 21 and over could vote. In 1969, the age was lowered to 18.

■ 1972: European Communities Act

After the United Kingdom joined the EEC in 1973, European laws and the decisions of the European Court of Justice started taking precedence* over UK laws.

| **to take precedence over:** *prévaloir sur*

■ 2000: The European Convention on Human Rights

It was adopted by the United Kingdom in 2000, so that the European Court of Human Rights can overrule the decisions taken in UK courts. In spite of Brexit, the UK is still committed to the ECHR, but it will not be bound by changes to EU law. Besides these acts, courts also enforce laws deriving from custom (common law*) and from former decisions taken by courts (case law*). They constitute precedent*.

| **to overrule:** *prévaloir sur*; **common law:** *le droit coutumier*; **case law:** *les précédents judiciaires*; **to constitute precedent:** *faire juris-prudence*

(Britain's unwritten constitution)
liennathan.fr/h623dp

CONTROVERSIAL ISSUES

■ Civil liberties today

Civil liberties* (meant to protect individuals from the abuses of state power) have increasingly been threatened during the last two decades. A number of elements have contributed to this:

The war on terrorism

Can security and civil liberties be reconciled?

In the wake of* 9/11, the 2001 Terrorism Act gave the police powers to search and arrest people on mere suspicion that they might be terrorists. It also made it legal to lock up indefinitely any foreigner suspected of posing "a risk to national security" or to have trials without a jury. Besides, evidence* obtained by such

contentious* means as telephone tapping* is now permissible, sometimes with defendants not given access to that evidence. And anyone linked to a banned organisation now has to prove that (s)he is not a terrorist - something surprising in a country where the basis of the legal system is that anyone is deemed* innocent until proven guilty. It can be seen as a violation of the presumption of innocence springing from* the fear that all asylum seekers may be potential terrorists. Some see it as taking advantage of people's fears in troubled times in order to take draconian measures which restrict their liberties.
However, the government said these measures were temporary and they were replaced by the 2005 Prevention of Terrorism Act, which created "control orders", inspired by ASBOs (anti-social behaviour orders). Again in 2006, a law was passed banning the glorification of terrorism, which some see as trampling on* freedom of speech. Suspected terrorists can still be held for up to 28 days (instead of 90 days previously)without being charged*.

ID cards

Another idea bolstered by* the fear of terrorism is the possible introduction of ID cards (identity cards). The aim would be to constitute a central register with the details (including biometrics) of every resident in the country.

Advantages	Fears
– ID cards would help the fight against fraud, criminality and terrorism, and might deter* illegal immigrants. – With a unique ID number per person, it will be easier for government departments to share information. – It will not be immediately compulsory and will be phased in* gradually, which should prevent dramatic failure.	– It will be costly*. – How accurate and secure would the information they contain be? – How to make sure that the system is not open to misuse*? That it will not invade people's privacy*? → This makes the scheme highly controversial in the eyes of civil liberties champions, who see it as proof of the lengthening arm of the state.

"There is a difficult balance to strike between national security, public protection and individual rights."

David Blunkett, Home Secretary, September 2001

"Let no one be in any doubt. The rules of the game are changing."

Tony Blair, after the London bombings

Scientific developments

Another possible danger lies in genetic research. The possibility that all newborn babies might be screened* to create their DNA profiles* has raised a number of questions:

– Will it then be possible for insurers to set different premiums* depending on the person's DNA?
– Might some employers not use DNA information to discriminate between employees?
– What if the police had everyone's DNA in their database*? Would this be a good thing (making it easier to catch criminals), or could it also be potentially dangerous? And the DNA database (Britain has the world's largest DNA database) is, according to civil liberties watchdogs*, evidence of Britain turning into a "surveillance state", something also reflected by the growing number of closed-circuit television cameras.

A government with a large majority, as was the case with Tony Blair's, has free rein to pass any law that increases their power.
However, the Freedom of Information Act, which came into effect* in 2005, gave anyone in the world the right to request information held by public authorities and other non-governmental organisations, which represents a huge step towards more open government and individual liberty.

The question for me is: whose civil liberties? Of course the offender has rights; but so has the victim. If the practical effect of the law is that people live in fear because the offender is unafraid of the legal process, then, in the name of civil liberties, we are allowing the vulnerable, the decent, the people who show respect and expect it back, to have their essential liberties trampled on.

Tony Blair, 2006

civil liberties: *les libertés civiques*; **in the wake of:** *à la suite de*; **evidence:** *des preuves*; **contentious:** *contentieux, contesté*; **telephone tapping:** *le fait de brancher un téléphone sur écoute*; **to deem:** *considérer*; **to spring from:** *venir de*; **to trample on:** *bafouer*; **to charge:** *accuser*; **to bolster:** *fortifier*; **to deter:** *dissuader*; **to phase in:** *introduire (une mesure) progressivement*; **costly:** *coûteux*; **the misuse:** *l'utilisation abusive*; **to invade so's privacy:** *empiéter sur la vie privée de qqn*; **to screen:** *faire subir un test*; **a DNA profile:** *un profil ADN*; **a premium:** *une prime (d'assurance)*; **a database:** *une base de données*; **civil liberties watchdogs:** *des groupes de défense des droits civiques*; **to come into effect:** *entrer en vigueur*

5 THE MONARCHY

"Above all things our royalty is to be reverenced, and if you begin to poke about it you cannot reverence it… Its mystery is its life. We must not let in daylight upon magic."
"The Sovereign has, under a constitutional monarchy such as ours, three rights - the right to be consulted, the right to encourage, the right to warn."

Walter Bagehot, English economist, 1867

The United Kingdom is a parliamentary or constitutional monarchy*: since the 1688 Glorious Revolution, the powers of the sovereign have been limited by Parliament.

The sovereign is the Head of State*, the Head of the Church of England , the Head of the Armed Forces, and the Head of the Commonwealth.
The British monarchy is hereditary and respects the right of primogeniture*. Since 2011 sons and daughters have had equal rights of succession: a first-born daughter would have precedence* over younger brothers. The ban on the monarch being married to a Roman Catholic was also lifted.

The sovereign "reigns" but does not "rule": his or her functions are in fact limited and mainly symbolic since he or she must be politically impartial and cannot vote:
– appointing* the Prime Minister (but (s)he must be the leader of the party which won the general elections*). Only occasionally, when there is no majority in the House of Commons for instance, can the sovereign choose the future Prime Minister after consulting various politicians.
– creating new peers*, appointing senior civil servants* and granting honours* (although mostly the result of recommendations) as well as giving the Royal Pardon*. Since the sovereign is the "Fountain of Justice", the decisions taken in courts are taken in her/his name.
– dissolving Parliament (at the request of the Prime Minister) and opening Parliament* (but her/his speech is written by the Prime Minister) - the time when the sovereign delivers the formal Speech from the Throne* is the only time when (s)he is allowed to enter Parliament.
– signing the bills passed in Parliament (Royal Assent*) so that they become Acts*.
– declaring war & signing international treaties - but only ratifying what the government has decided, and not necessarily after a vote in Parliament (the Falklands war) was started without Parliament being consulted).
As Head of the Church of England, the sovereign appoints archbishops and bishops.

The monarch has a mainly symbolic function as Head of the Commonwealth and representative of the nation, creating cohesion because of her/his popularity. The sovereign is a figurehead* (Walter Bagehot called the monarch the 'dignified' branch of the constitution, as opposed to the 'efficient' one, Parliament and the government) who stands above party politics, even though he/she has regular meetings with the Prime Minister. Royal ceremonies with a great deal of pageantry* such as the State Opening of Parliament or royal visits are hugely popular. The royal family is also very active in a large number of charities.

"The greatest wisdom of a constitutional king would show itself in well-considered inaction."

Walter Bagehot

The Royal Coat of Arms, in which the lion stands for England and the unicorn for Scotland. Inside the shield*, the three lions represent England, the single lion Scotland and the harp Ireland.

a constitutional monarchy: *une monarchie constitutionnelle*; **the head of state:** *le chef d'État*; **the right of primogeniture:** *la règle de primogéniture*; **an heir:** *un héritier*; **to have precedence over:** *avoir préséance sur*; **to appoint:** *nommer*; **general elections:** *des élections législatives*; **a peer:** *un pair (du royaume)*; **senior civil servants:** *les hauts fonctionnaires*; **to grant honours:** *octroyer des distinctions honorifiques*; **the Royal Pardon:** *la grâce royale*; **to open Parliament:** *inaugurer les sessions du parlement*; **the Speech from the Throne:** *le discours du Trône*; **an act:** *une loi* ; **Royal Assent:** *l'assentiment royal*; **a figurehead:** *une figure de proue*; **pageantry:** *la pompe*; **a shield:** *un blason*

(The Monarchy)
liennathan.fr/92kjj9

(The official website of the British Monarchy)
liennathan.fr/355wxn

A Chronology of English Kings and Queens

HOUSE OF TUDOR

Henry VII Tudor = Elizabeth of York
(1485-1509)

Henry VIII (1509-1547)
- Edward VI (1547-1553)
- Mary I (1553-1558)
- Elizabeth I (1558-1603)

Margaret = James Stuart of Scotland
- James V of Scotland
  - Mary Stuart, Queen of Scotland
- Margaret
  - Henry Stuart
    - James VI

HOUSE OF STUART

James I (1603-1625)

Charles I* (1625-1649)
- Charles II (1660-1685)
- James II (1685-1688)
  - Mary II = William of Orange (1688-1694) (1688-1702)
  - Ann (1702-1714)

Elizabeth = Frederich, Elector Palatine
- Sophia = Elector of Hanover
  - George I of Hanover

HOUSE OF HANOVER (WINDSOR, after 1914)

George I of Hanover (1714-1727)
George II (1727-1760)
George III (1760-1820)
- George IV (1820-1830)
- William IV (1830-1837)
- Edward, Duke of Kent †1829
  - Victoria (1837-1901)
    - Edward VII** (1901-1910)
      - George V (Windsor) (1910-1936)
        - Edward VIII (1936)
        - George VI (1936-1952)
          - Elizabeth II (1952-)

*Commonwealth: Oliver Cromwell (1653-1658)
Richard Cromwell (1658-1659)
**Edward VII (Sax-Coburg-Gotha)

CONTROVERSIAL ISSUES

The Monarchy is often said to be in crisis these days because of the behaviour of some members of the royal family (marital scandals*, Prince Charles's divorce, then second marriage, Prince Andrew's association with Jeffrey Epstein, a convicted paedophile), because it is seen as too distant from the people, and because of its cost. The royal family is expensive, costing the taxpayers around £800,000 a year.

However, it has also proved capable of change, for instance when the Queen cut her Civil List* (£7.9m until 2011 – mainly used to pay staff, and for official ceremonies) and in 1993 decided to pay taxes on her income as a reaction to public criticism. In 1997, the death of Diana, Princess of Wales (who had been very active in defending children and landmine victims), and the outpouring of grief that followed it, highlighted people's desire for a more modern and compassionate monarchy. However, the death of the Queen Mother in 2002 and the public emotion on the occasion of her funeral or the wedding of Prince William and Catherine Middleton in 2011, viewed by tens of millions in Britain and around the world, were proof of the British people's attachment to the monarchy. In April 2016, as the queen celebrated her 90th birthday, a poll showed that she was getting increasingly popular. 76% of respondents also said a queen or king should remain as head of state.

The marriage of Prince Harry and Meghan Markle (a mixed race American divorcee) seemed to show that the monarchy could evolve in a more multicultural age, even though the couple later decided to step back from duties as 'senior royals' and become financially independent.

Because of the intrusion of the press into the private lives of the royal family, it is losing much of its former mystique.

The controversy around the monarchy focuses upon two main questions:

- **Should the monarchy be kept?**

Arguments for...	... and against
– It provides a sense of continuity between past and present. – It is a striking and clear symbol of Britain and stands for the unity of the country. – It is highly popular in Britain, where people are patriotically attached to their sovereign, and it brings in millions of tourists attracted to the pageantry, rituals and magic associated with the ceremonial of royalty.	– It is costly. – It is mostly pointless.

▪ Should the monarchy change with the country it represents?

Arguments for	... and against
There have been many suggestions that the monarchy should be modernized and become less aloof* and closer to the people. Many have called for a "bicycle monarchy", as in the Netherlands, with the royal family living more simply or marrying commoners*.	Perhaps it is better to preserve the dignity and theatricality of the monarchy. As Walter Bagehot said, "We must not let in daylight upon the magic" of royalty.

marital scandals: *des scandales matrimoniaux*; **the Civil List:** *la somme allouée à la famille royale*; **aloof:** *distant*; **a commoner:** *un roturier*

6 THE GOVERNMENT

(Fonctionnement du gouvernement)
liennathan.fr/72vr9e

The British political system

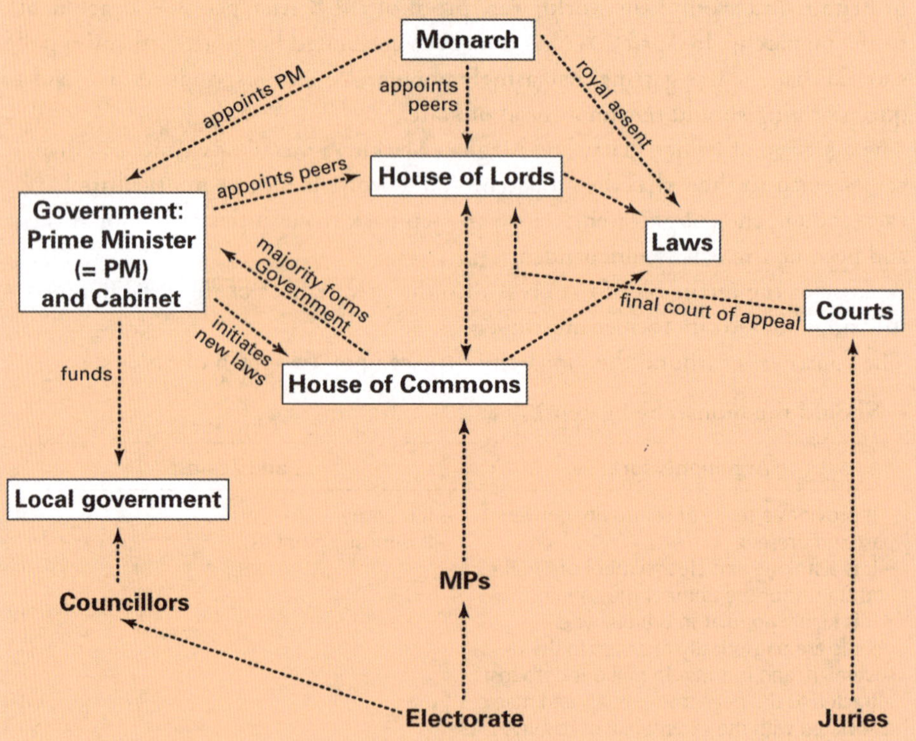

The UK ceased to be bound by EU law on 31 December 2020. However, some categories of EU law will be retained, amended or not, and become part of domestic UK law, described as "retained EU law".

THE LEGISLATIVE POWER*

England is the mother of Parliaments.

John Bright, English Liberal politician, 1865.

Parliament

It is made up of two Chambers: the House of Lords* and the House of Commons*, each providing checks* on the other. Because Parliament is situated in the London borough of Westminster, it is also sometimes called The Palace of Westminster, or simply 'Westminster'.

the legislative power: *le pouvoir législatif*; **the House of Lords:** *la Chambre des Lords*; **the House of Commons:** *la Chambre des Communes*; **to provide checks:** *limiter les pouvoirs*

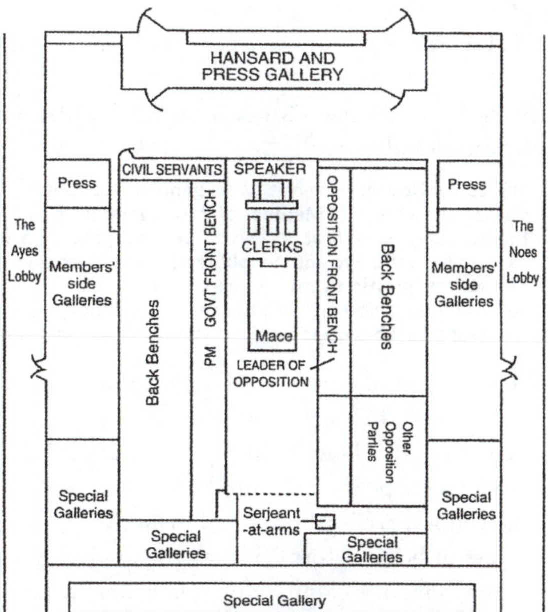

– The **House of Commons** (or Lower House*) is elected for a maximum of 5 years. After the General Elections*(see General Elections below), the leader of the party* with the largest number of votes becomes Prime Minister. MPs (Members of Parliament*) represent the interests of the voters of their constituencies*, discuss and vote on new legislation and control the executive (the ministers). A Speaker* is elected with each new parliament, to chair* all debates. He then becomes politically impartial. Each party uses Whips* to ensure party discipline and make sure that MPs are present for important votes (they may, for instance, issue "three-line whips", that is to say urgent instructions (underlined three times) to MPs, asking them to attend important debates). In order to vote, MPs leave the House of Commons through the aye or no lobbies*.

Composition of the House of Commons (2020)

Conservative: 363

Labour: 199

Scottish National Party: 45

Liberal Democrat: 12

Democratic Unionist Party: 8

Sinn Fein: 7

Independent: 6

Plaid Cymru: 3

Social Democratic & Labour Party: 2

Alba Party: 2

Alliance: 1

Green Party: 1

Speaker: 1

Total 650

The majority party and the opposition sit facing each other, the rectangular shape of the House of Commons reflecting the British two-party system.

A front-bencher* is a member ofparliament who is part of the government or of the shadow cabinet* (the cabinet formed by the main opposition party) and who sits on the front benches*.

A backbencher* is a simple member of parliament; he/she sits behind the front benches.

Once a week, MPs who belong to the opposition can question the government during Question Time*. It provides a check on the government and avoids too much secrecy.

the PM = the Prime Minister; an MP = a Member of Parliament; an MSP = a Member of the Scottish Parliament

The Lower House: *la chambre basse*; **general elections:** *des élections législatives*; **the leader of a party:** *le chef/leader d'un parti*; **a Member of Parliament:** *un député*; **a constituency:** *une circonscription électorale*; **the Speaker:** *le président des débats*; **to chair:** *présider*; **a whip:** *un député qui assure la discipline de vote dans son parti*; **the aye and no lobbies:** *les couloirs empruntés par les députés pour voter oui ou non*; **(Prime Minister's) Question Time:** *la séance de questions posées au Premier ministre*; **a frontbencher:** *un ministre ou membre du cabinet fantôme*; **the shadow cabinet:** *le cabinet fantôme*; **the front benches:** *les bancs des ministres*; **a backbencher:** *un député sans portefeuille ou fonction particulière*

– The **House of Lords** (or Upper House*) - is made up of non-elected members, called peers* or peeresses*: hereditary peers (whose heirs will inherit the title when they die: Dukes, Marquesses, Earls* & Countesses, Viscounts, Barons & Baronesses), peers appointed for life*, high judicial officers*, such as the Lord Chancellor*, archbishops* and bishops* of the Church of England. But it is in the process of being reformed, with the gradual disappearance of hereditary peers (only 92 now remain in a phase of transition) in order to create a "more representative and democratic" second chamber. Several options are being considered: only elected members or a blend of appointed and elected members. But who would elect the members? And how could elected members replicate the wide range of expertise which is now to be found in the House of Lords, with its scientists, writers, lawyers and businessmen? Besides, what would the functions of the new chamber be? These questions have yet to be answered.

The main functions of the House of Lords are now:
– to scrutinise* and revise bills* from the House of Commons, making sure that they are in keeping with* the constitution,
– to block or delay* bills (for no more than a year, but since 1909, they have had no power over finance bills) so as to give the Commons time to revise them,
– to initiate new legislation,
– to debate (discuss) current issues* in a fair and open way since this Chamber is above party politics.
– It is also a final Court of Appeal*, the last court to which a case can be referred.

The main strength of the House of Lords is therefore the fact that it provides an independent, non-political check to the House of Commons and the government. But under the so-called 'Salisbury convention', the House of Lords will not oppose the government on its manifesto commitments.

the Upper House: *la chambre haute*; **a peer:** *un pair (du royaume)*; **a peeress:** *une pairesse*; **an earl:** *un comte*; **appointed for life:** *nommés à vie*; **judicial officers:** *des magistrats*; **the Lord Chancellor:** *le ministre de la Justice / Garde des Sceaux*; **an archbishop:** *un archevêque*; **a bishop:** *un évêque*; **to scrutinise:** *examiner, étudier*; **a bill:** *un projet de loi*; **to be in keeping with:** *s'accorder avec*; **to delay:** *retarder*; **current issues:** *des questions, problèmes d'actualité*; **a Court of Appeal:** *une cour d'appel*

The passing of a bill*

The different steps in the passing of a bill before it becomes an Act of Parliament*:
– First Reading* (the text of the bill is given to all members of Parliament to read). A Green Paper* explains its aims.
– Second Reading: the bill is discussed, with arguments for and against presented. The government defends it in a White Paper.
– The bill and its implications is studied by a standing committee* of MPs
– Third Reading: the bill is once again discussed in the House of Commons, with some amendments proposed by the committee. A vote then takes place, the MPs leaving the chamber to the right (to vote yes) or left (to vote no) of the speaker.
– If approved the bill goes to the House of Lords, where the same procedure is followed.
– If the House of Lords accepts the bill, it becomes an Act of Parliament and receives "Royal Assent*".

to pass a bill: *voter un projet de loi*; **an Act of Parliament:** *une loi*; **a Reading:** *la lecture d'un projet de loi au parlement*; **a Green paper:** *un livre blanc*; **a standing committee:** *un comité permanent*; **Royal Assent:** *l'Assentiment Royal*

THE EXECUTIVE POWER

The Prime Minister

Power without principle is barren, but principle without power is futile. This is a party of government and I will lead it as party of government.

Tony Blair

The British Prime Minister* wields considerable power*. He

- presides over the Cabinet, deciding upon the agenda* and chairing the meetings*
- decides on the budget (with the Chancellor of the Exchequer)
- decides what the government's policy* will be, including foreign policy
- appoints* high officials*.

the Prime Minister: *le premier ministre*; **to wield power:** *exercer un pouvoir*; **an agenda:** *un ordre du jour*; **to chair a meeting:** *présider une réunion*; **the government's policy:** *la politique du gouvernement*; **to appoint:** *nommer*; **a high official:** *un haut fonctionnaire*

British Prime Ministers since 1945:

Clement Attlee (L) 1945-1951 • Winston Churchill (C) 1951-1955 • Anthony Eden (C) 1955-1957 • Harold Macmillan (C) 1957-1963 • Sir Alec Douglas-Home (C) 1963-1964 • Harold Wilson (L) 1964-1970 • Edward Heath (C) 1970-1974 • Harold Wilson (L) 1974-1976 • James Callaghan (L) 1976-1979 • Margaret Thatcher (C) 1979-1990 • John Major (C) 1990-1997 • Tony Blair (L) 1997-2007 • Gordon Brown (L) 2007-2010 • David Cameron (C) 2010-2016 • Theresa May (C) 2016-2019 • Boris Johnson (C) 2019-

The Cabinet

A cabinet is a combining committee – a hyphen* which joins, a buckle* which fastens, the legislative part of the state to the executive part of the state.

Walter Bagehot, 1867

The cabinet consists of the Prime Minister and of some 20 senior ministers*, chosen by the Prime Minister. They meet every week at 10 Downing Street (the residence of the Prime Minister) and decide on government policy. Members of the Cabinet will then have to support any decision taken: this is called collective responsibility*.

Here are the names of some important members of the Cabinet:
The Deputy Prime Minister*
The Chancellor of the Exchequer*
The Home Secretary*
The Lord Chancellor*
The Foreign Secretary*

Secretaries of State* are helped by several Junior Ministers*.
Thousands of non-political civil servants (metonymically referred to as Whitehall - the London area where many government buildings are to be found) work behind the scenes* for whichever government is in place. Britain's civil service* is over-centralised and often criticised for not being fully efficient.

a hyphen: *un trait d'union*; **a buckle:** *une boucle (qui sert à attacher)*; **a senior minister:** *un ministre de rang élevé*; **collective responsibility:** *la responsabilité collective*; **the Deputy Prime Minister:** *le vice-Premier ministre*; **the Lord Chancellor:** *le ministre de la Justice / le Garde des Sceaux*; **the Chancellor of the Exchequer:** *le ministre des Finances / chancelier de l'Échiquier*; **the Foreign Secretary:** *le ministre des Affaires étrangères*; **the Home Secretary:** *le ministre de l'Intérieur*; **a Secretary of State:** *un ministre*; **a Junior Minister:** *un secrétaire d'État*; **behind the scenes:** *dans les coulisses*; **the civil service:** *les fonctionnaires*

Parties

There are two main parties which alternate in government:
– The Conservative Party* (also called Tory Party), which traditionally defends right-wing liberal policies* (individualism, tax reduction*, mixed economy, private enterprise, freedom of choice in education, property ownership).
After David Cameron's election as leader of the party in 2006, "compassionate conservatism" became the motto* of the party.
– The Labour Party*, traditionally the party of the working class, linked to the trade unions*, defending public ownership* and high public spending* on social services and education. With his "third way", however, Tony Blair placed his party, which he called "New Labour", at the centre of the political spectrum*. The links between the Labour party and the trade unions were reduced, and the aim was to combine economic liberalism and social concerns.
– A third party, the Liberal Democrat Party*, which is more liberal, pro-European and in favour of constitutional reform, has recently played an important part, too. At the moment they have little chance of a majority in Parliament, although they joined a coalition government with the Conservatives after the 2010 general election.
– Other parties include Plaid Cymru (the Welsh nationalist party), the SNP (Scottish National Party), the Irish 'Democratic Unionist Party' (for other Irish parties), the extreme right-wing BNP (British National Party) and the Communist Party at the other end of the political spectrum*.

the Conservative Party: *le parti conservateur*; **right-wing liberal policies:** *une politique libérale de droite*; **tax reduction:** *l'allégement de l'impôt*; **a motto:** *une devise*; **the Labour Party:** *le parti travailliste*; **a trade union:** *un syndicat*; **public ownership:** *la nationalisation*; **public spending:** *les dépenses publiques*; **the political spectrum:** *l'éventail politique*; **the Liberal Democrat Party:** *le parti libéral démocrate*

General Elections*

General elections* to elect MPs* must take place at least every five years, but the Prime Minister can call for* new elections any time before the end of the five years. The age of voting is 18. The leader of the party which obtains a majority of seats* in the House of Commons becomes the new Prime Minister. The opposition party forms a Shadow Cabinet*. The voting system used is the simple majority system (also called First-past-the-post System*): the candidate who obtains the largest number of votes is elected. This has advantages and drawbacks.

Advantages	Drawbacks
• It makes for strong parties in power rather than weak coalitions, and thus encourages political stability.	• It is a disadvantage for small parties, which will not be represented in Parliament even though they may have had a high percentage of votes nationally. People consequently hesitate to vote for a third party which has no chance of being elected. • It is undemocratic since a party can win a majority of seats without winning a majority of votes.

This voting system partly explains why only two main parties dominate British politics, as is reflected in the adversarial architecture of the House of Commons, with two sides facing each other. Many have asked for proportional representation* to be introduced. In a 2011 referendum, British voters rejected plans to replace the first-past-the-post electoral system for the House of Commons with the alternative vote (AV) system. The change was part of the Liberal Democrats' platform, but was strongly opposed by Prime Minister Cameron, his argument being that such a system would reduce the majority and power of any government.
There can also be by-elections* if a seat becomes vacant after an MP dies or resigns.

2019 General election

	% Votes	Seats under FPTP	Seats under PR	Difference in Seats
Labour	32.2%	202	216	14
Conservatives	43.6%	365	288	-77
LibDems	11.5%	11	70	59
Brexit Party	2.0%	0	10	10
Greens	2.7%	1	12	11
SNP	3.9%	48	28	-20
Plaid	0.5%	4	4	0
Others (includes speaker)	4%	1	4	3

general elections: *les élections législatives*; **to call for:** *demander*; **an MP:** *un député* **(members of parliament); a seat:** *un siège*; **the Shadow Cabinet:** *le cabinet fantôme*; **the first-past-the-post system:** *le scrutin majoritaire à un tour*; **proportional representation:** *la représentation proportionnelle*; **a by-election:** *une élection partielle*

DEVOLUTION*

After Labour's victory in 1997, referenda were held in Scotland and Wales the same year, resulting in a measure of devolution*.

The Scottish Parliament

The 129-seat Parliament (known as Holyrood), established in 1998, can make up to 3% changes to the taxes decided on by the London Parliament, and legislates* freely in the fields* of education, health, law, transport, agriculture and local government. But it has no jurisdiction* over the constitution, foreign policy, defence and immigration, which concern the whole of the United Kingdom.
There has recently been a resurgence of Scottish nationalism and a rise of the SNP (Scottish National Party), which won an absolute majority in the 2011 parliamentary elections and promised a referendum on the independence of Scotland in September 2014. After Scotland voted 55% to 45% to reject independence, the three main UK

parties agreed, as promised if it voted no, to transfer to Scotland added powers over income tax and welfare payments. This, however, has led to the re-emergence of a constitutional issue: 'the English question'.
Scotland, Wales and Northern Ireland have their own assemblies, which decide on domestic policy, but they still send MPs to Westminster and vote on matters such as English education or health. England has no reciprocal rights and no say when it comes to Scottish, Welsh or Irish domestic policy. It is therefore seriously disadvantaged and a constitutional reform is now likely to be undertaken.
A second referendum on independence has been proposed in case pro-independence parties won an outright majority in the 2021 elections to the Scottish Parliament. With an alliance between the SNP (64 seats in 2021) and the pro-independence Greens (8 seats in 2021), there would now be a majority for a referendum , but it is a slight one and nothing has yet been decided.

The Welsh Assembly

The 60-seat assembly cannot raise taxes*, but can decide on policy concerning such areas as education, health, transport and culture.

devolution: *la décentralisation*; **to legislate:** *légiférer*; **a field:** *un domaine*; **to raise taxes:** *lever des impôts*; **to have jurisdiction:** *pouvoir légiférer*

(The official homepage of the Scottish Parliament)
liennathan.fr/2ddu86

(The official homepage of the Welsh Assembly)
liennathan.fr/d8r59b

(The official homepage of the Conservative Party)
liennathan.fr/ii4s57

(The official site of the Labour Party)
liennathan.fr/j7iq24

(The official site of the SNP)
liennathan.fr/44t7mq

CONTROVERSIAL ISSUES

Constitutional monarchy or "elective dictatorship"*?

In 1976, Lord Hailsham (a former Conservative Lord Chancellor*) said that the British government was increasingly totalitarian.
– There are no "checks and balances*" to curtail* the power of governments with a large majority.
– There are threats to civil liberties*.
– It is the government which controls Parliament rather than Parliament which controls the government.

Is the Prime Minister's power too great? Is his power now similar to that of an American President? Checks do exist (with Prime Minister's Question Time, every week in parliament, with the opposition, the media, the courts, but there is little challenge* from the government itself. The members of the Cabinet are bound by loyalty (collective responsibility*) and it is in their interest to keep the government in power. Besides, the tendency has recently been for Prime Ministers to reduce the power of the Cabinet. In 2006, for example, the Commons voted against an inquiry* into the Iraq war, which many MPs had been asking for. This led *The Guardian* to declare that "The Commons has become little more than an electoral college for the prime minister."

In his first statement as Prime Minister, Gordon Brown outlined* a number of possible constitutional reforms to help government become "a better servant of the people". In order to improve British democracy, the power of the executive would be surrendered or limited in a number of fields.

Here were some of the possibilities:
• MPs would have power to decide whether to declare war and sign international treaties (until then royal prerogatives).
• There might be a consultation on a possible Bill of Rights.
• A National Security Council would be created to "coordinate the military, policing, intelligence and diplomatic action."
• The Prime Minister would lose the right to appoint Church of England bishops, and hearings* might be held on key public appointments.

"It's possible to do more to bring government closer to the people... It can be enhanced by devolving* more power to the people."

Gordon Brown, June 2007

an elective dictatorship: *une dictature élue*; **checks and balances:** *des mécanisme d'équilibre*; **to curtail:** *réduire*; **civil liberties:** *les libertés civiques*; **a challenge:** *une remise en question*; **collective responsibility:** *la responsabilité collective*; **an inquiry:** *une enquête*; **to outline:** *esquisser, présenter les grandes lignes*; **intelligence:** *services de renseignements*; **a hearing:** *séance pendant laquelle un projet de loi est discuté*; **to devolve:** *déléguer, transmettre*

Spin*

The term is used derogatorily* in politics to describe the biased* presentation of information by a government in order to put the best possible gloss* on its policies and therefore get them accepted.

Spin may involve deception* and manipulation through such ploys* as high-flown* rhetoric, euphemisms, sound bites* (excerpts from a speech or statement chosen for their pungency* or appropriateness), the presentation of only one side

of the situation, the distortion of statistics, or even downright lies. Governments have also been known to "bury"* unpleasant news by releasing* it on a day when a far more important event will make the headlines. Spin also includes the hyping* of some initiatives, which make the news again and again.
The Labour government of Tony Blair was often accused of spin.
To avoid the fate of former Labour leader, Neil Kinnock, who had been vilified* by tabloids, Tony Blair became obsessed with the way his government was seen and nominated a "director of communications", an expert in communication also familiary called "spin doctor*".
After Britain went to war in Iraq although no weapons of mass destruction had been found, the BBC even reported that the threat from Iraq had been hyped so that fighting the war might be more acceptable. The claim was later disproved*, but it reflects people's distrust* of politicians.

The parliamentary expenses scandal

In 2009, the Daily Telegraph began to leak details of MPs' expense claims. It revealed gross misuse of 'additional costs allowances' – the money awarded to MPs with constituencies outside Greater London in order to run a 'second home'.
False accounting, fraud, tax evasion and lies were widespread among all parties, and among backbenchers and frontbenchers alike.
The scandal led to numerous resignations and de-selections as well as to the creation of an Independent Parliamentary Standards Authority to manage MPs' expenses.

The definition of "doublethink" in *1984*:
" To use conscious deception while retaining the firmness of purpose that goes with complete honesty. To tell deliberate lies while genuinely believing in them, to forget any fact that has become inconvenient".

George Orwell, *1984*

"The secret of success is sincerity. Once you can fake that, you've got it made."

Groucho Marx

"There are three kinds of lies: lies, damned lies and statistics."

Benjamin Disraeli

spin: *la présentation de l'information sous le meilleur jour possible*; **derogatorily:** *avec mépris*; **biased:** *qui n'est pas objectif*; **gloss:** *le vernis, éclat*; **deception:** *la tromperie*; **a ploy:** *un stratagème*; **high-flown:** *ampoulé, grandiloquent*; **sound bites:** *des petites phrases*; **pungency:** *mordant*; **to bury:** *enterrer*; **to release:** *publier*; **to hype:** *lancer avec grand renfort de publicité*; **to vilify:** *calomnier*; **a spin doctor:** *un conseiller en communication*; **salesmanship:** *l'art de la vente*; **to disprove:** *réfuter*; **distrust:** *la méfiance*

7 JUSTICE, LAW & ORDER

English law is based on

– Common law*, which is not written but derives from precedent, that is to say from case law* (the decisions taken by judges previously).
– Legislation: acts of Parliament (Statute law*)
– European Union law
(For instance, for some 800 years, Britain had a "double jeopardy" common-law principle according to which someone could not be tried* again for an offence he or she had been acquitted of*. But in 2003, the Criminal Justice Act reformed the law and allowed serious cases to be retried if compelling new evidence* had come to light. Thus common law has now been superseded* by an Act of Parliament.)

Two basic principles underlie criminal law*:
1. The presumption of innocence: everyone is presumed innocent until proven guilty.
2. No one can be imprisoned unless found guilty.

Courts

There are different levels of courts:

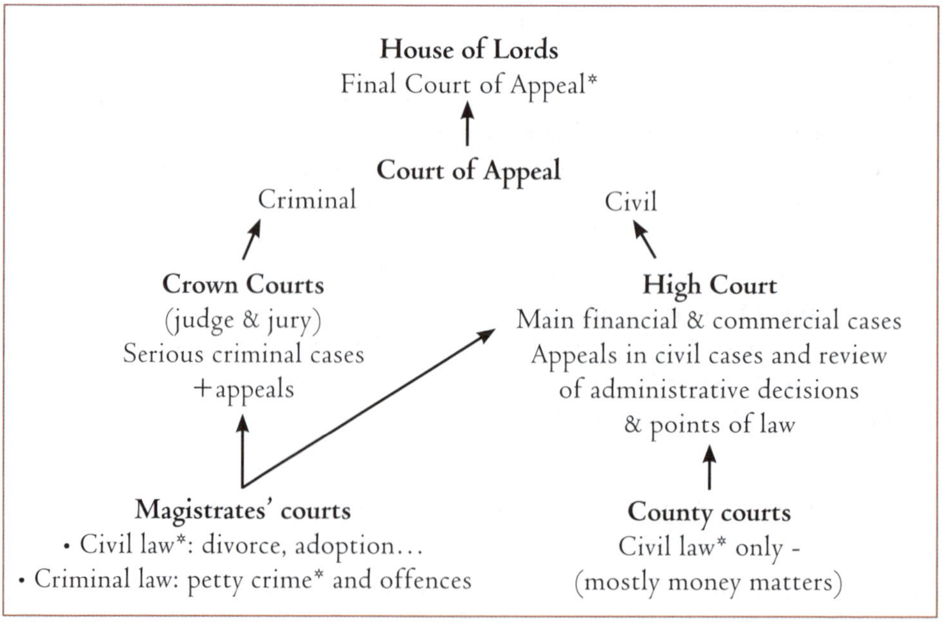

Judges and lawyers

The Lord Chancellor* is at the head of the judiciary, but is also a member of the executive (since he is part of the Cabinet) and of the legislative body (since he presides over the House of Lords).

In Magistrates' courts, the presiding judge is a lay magistrate*, also called a Justice of the Peace* (JP). JPs are not lawyers* and often have practically no legal training*. But they are distinguished members of the community who wish to help. They are not paid (except in London).
Other judges are former lawyers*.
There are different types of lawyers:
– Solicitors* are legal advisers in all kinds of family matters (e.g. divorce proceedings, the drafting* of wills*), in property sales and in criminal matters (they gather information for the barristers to use in court).
– Barristers* plead cases* in court, using the instructions and information given by the solicitors. Traditionally, they did not see the clients, who only dealt with the solicitors, but the rules are now changing.

■ A trial

The Crown Prosecution Service (headed by the Director of Public Prosecutions) decides whether a person should or should not be charged with a crime.
Anyone accused of a serious crime and pleading "not guilty"* is tried* by a jury. In England juries consist of 12 jurors* (who must be between the ages of 18 & 70 and have lived in Britain for 5 years). The two sides – the prosecution* and the barrister for the defence* – summon witnesses* and plead against or for the accused. Then the jury return a verdict* and the judge decides on the sentence*. Here are a few possible court decisions:
A fine*
Binding over*
Tagging*
Community service*
A curfew* order
A prison sentence
Capital punishment was abolished in Britain in 1965 but could then still theoretically be inflicted for treason. The European Convention on Human Rights, adopted by the United Kingdom in 2000, made the death penalty illegal.

common law: *le droit coutumier*; **case law:** *la jurisprudence*; **statute law:** *le droit écrit / la législation*; **to try so:** *juger qqn*; **to acquit:** *acquitter*; **evidence:** *des preuves*; **to supersede:** *remplacer*; **criminal law:***le droit pénal*; **presumption of innocence:** *la présomption d'innocence*; **a court of appeal:** *une cour d'appel*; **civil law:** *le droit civil*; **petty crime:** *la petite criminalité*; **the Lord Chancellor:** *le ministre de la Justice*; **a lay magistrate:** *un magistrat qui n'est pas juriste de profession*; **a justice of the peace:** *un juge de paix*; **a lawyer:** *un juriste*; **legal training:** *la formation juridique*; **a solicitor:** *un avocat, un notaire*; **to draft:** *rédiger*; **a will:** *un testament*; **a barrister:** *un avocat*; **to plead a case:** *plaider la cause de qqn*; **to plead (not) guilty:** *plaider (non) coupable*; **a juror:** *un juré*; **the prosecution:** *l'accusation*; **the defence:** *la défense*; **to summon a witness:** *citer un témoin*; **to return a verdict:** *rendre un verdict*; **the sentence:** *la peine, la sentence*; **a fine:** *une amende, la sentence*; **to bind over:** *mettre en liberté conditionnelle*; **to tag:** *mettre un bracelet électronique*; **community service:** *un travail d'intérêt général*; **a curfew:** *un couvre-feu*

(The home page of the justice and prisons department of the Home Office)
liennathan.fr/d98d5q

(The official site of the British criminal justice system)
liennathan.fr/k8uq88

Anti-social behaviour*

Growing social inequalities and the widespread use of drugs and alcohol have led to a rising tide of incivility and disorder. This can take the form of yobbishness*, hooliganism*, street violence, inner-city* gang culture, and anti-social behaviour* in general (intimidation, excessive noise, graffiti writing, drinking in the street, public loutishness*, bullying*, and more recently "happy slapping", an attack on a victim which is filmed by a third party, the film then being sent to as many friends as possible.)

Incivility is at the top of the public's list of concerns. New Labour had pledged* to be 'tough on* crime, tough on the causes of crime' and therefore tried different ways of cracking down* on anti-social behaviour:
– Through a policy of draconian laws (zero tolerance*)
– By putting more police on the streets
– By developing CCTV (closed circuit television) in order to deter criminals
– By giving the police & the courts more power

Since 2000, magistrates have had the option of issuing ASBOs (anti-social behaviour orders), prohibiting* - for at least two years - the offender* from drinking in pubs or visiting known troublemakers*, or behaving in a way likely to constitute harassment*, and cause alarm or distress. Any breaching* of the order can lead to a prison sentence. But ASBOs have been much criticized for being too easily obtained and for putting young people behind bars when no real offence has been committed.
– By allowing (since 2005) most pubs and licensed premises* to remain open later instead of closing at 11pm. This may lead to more drinking (and binge drinking* is widespread among young people), but does not send drinkers on to nightclubs, where they can find drugs after 11 pm.
– By occasionally imposing teenage curfews.

The Anti-Social Behaviour, Crime and Policing Act 2014 replaced ASBOs with criminal behaviour orders aimed at making it easier and quicker for Agencies to react. They include powers such as dispersal orders, closure of premises, Public Space Protection Orders and Criminal behaviour orders.

to pledge: *promettre*; **tough on:** *intransigeant en matière de*; **yobbishness:** *le comportement des voyous, des casseurs*; **hooliganism:** *le vandalisme*; **inner-city:** *le quartier pauvre du centre des villes*; **anti-social behaviour:** *l'incivilité*; **loutishness:** *la grossièreté*; **bullying:** *les brimades*; **to crack down on:** *prendre des mesures énergiques contre*; **zero tolerance:** *la tolérance zéro*; **to prohibit:** *interdire*; **an offender:** *un délinquant*; **a troublemaker:** *un perturbateur*; **harassment:** *le harcèlement*; **to breach:** *enfreindre*; **licensed premises:** *les lieux où la vente d'alcool est autorisée*; **binge drinking:** *beuverie*

Prisons: lock in or let out?

British prisons are criticized for being overcrowded and having almost reached full capacity.
The Blair government, who had promised to be tough on crime, recommended stiffer sentences*, believing that prison remained a strong deterrent*.
The coalition government elected in 2010 had promised to cut the prison population but in spite of plummeting crime, stiffer sentences have meant overcrowding and worsening conditions.
What are the options?
– Give more lenient sentences*? But the government wants to sound tough and insists that offenders be given heavier sentences.
– Build more prisons? This is a costly option.
– Find alternatives to prison like community sentences*, curfews*, letting prisoners out wearing electronic tags* ?
– Release* prisoners early? But many re-offend and end up locked up for even longer.
What is undeniable is that prison rarely reforms prisoners and that more effective alternatives should be found.

stiffer sentences: *des peines plus lourdes*; **a deterrent:** *une mesure qui a un effet dissuasif*; **a lenient sentence:** *une peine légère*; **a community sentence:** *un travail d'intérêt général*; **curfew:** *couvre-feu, liberté surveillée*; **an electronic tag:** *un bracelet électronique*; **to release:** *libérer*

8 POPULATION

There were over 68 million inhabitants in Britain in 2019. The tendency is for the population to become older as the birth rate* tends to decline. Life expectancy* was 80.2 years for men and 83.3 years for women in 2020. Families are also growing smaller, more atomised, with an increasing number of one-parent families*. The proportion of senior citizens* (or OAPs* - old age pensioners) is also going up.

the birth rate: *le taux de natalité*; **life expectancy:** *l'espérance de vie*; **a one-parent family:** *une famille mono-parentale*; **a senior citizen / OAP (old age pensioner):** *un retraité*

Class

The UK remains a very unequal country, with a large gap* between the rich and the poor (the haves and the have-nots*).
Class differences are still strongly marked in Britain, appearing mainly through education (excellent fee-paying independent schools* vs state education, Oxford and Cambridge), occupation, address and accent, and they explain why there is still little social mobility. As for accents, regional speech characteristics are not found in the

upper class, who speak RP* (Received Pronunciation). Localized accents and dialects become stronger and stronger as one moves down the class ladder*.
There are however signs that Britain is becoming more and more meritocratic, probably even more so than the United States. Oxford and Cambridge now do their best to attract poor students, some colleges having also created a 'foundation year' to give them additional preparation. In 2020, 68% of Oxford undergraduates came from state schools. In terms of accent, Estuary English (EE) - a mixture of RP and south-eastern and Cockney accents - is increasingly spoken by all classes and in all parts of the country.

Traditional class distinctions are:
– The aristocracy, Upper Middle and Upper Class: The Establishment* (birth, inherited money, often ownership of land, public schools then Oxford or Cambridge if possible), but also higher managerial and administrative work
– Middle Class: money coming from one's profession (e.g. teachers, solicitors, journalists)
– Lower Middle Class: secretaries, many white collar workers*, junior managerial work
– Skilled Working Class* : skilled manual workers (e.g. bus driver, some blue-collar workers*)
– Unskilled Working Class: e.g. cleaners
– Underclass*: unemployed, dependent & homeless people*, who are outside the mainstream of society and live below the poverty line*.

The children of the upper and middle classes remain the most likely to reach a position of power, in government or in business. But belonging to the upper classes no longer gives an automatic passport to power, which is nowadays mainly wielded* by business and finance. Celebrities in the worlds of sport or television also enjoy a sort of upper-class status.

You see this creature with her kerbstone* English: the English that will keep her in the gutter* to the end of her days. Well, sir, in three months I could pass that girl off as a duchess at an ambassador's garden party. I could even get her a place as lady's maid or shop assistant, which requires better English.

Professor Higgins, in George Bernard Shaw's *Pygmalion*, 1914

a gap: *un écart*; **the haves and the have nots:** *les nantis et les démunis*; **a fee-paying school:** *un établissement privé*; **RP:** *la prononciation standard*; **the class ladder:** *l'échelle des classes*; **the Establishment:** *les élites, les milieux dirigeants*; **a white-collar worker:** *un col blanc*; **the skilled working class:** *les ouvriers qualifiés*; **a blue-collar worker:** *un col bleu, un travailleur manuel*; **homeless people**; *les sans-abri*; **the underclass:** *la sous-classe*; **below the poverty line:** *sous le seuil de pauvreté*; **to wield power:** *exercer un pouvoir*; **the kerbstone:** *le rebord du trottoir*; **the gutter:** *le caniveau*

Wealth* and income*

There is a very wide gap between the highest incomes and the lowest ones. Among the latter, one finds a high proportion of:
– people from ethnic minorities (as opposed to white people)

– people from the North of England (as opposed to people from the South): one speaks of a North-South divide*.
– women as opposed to men.
– young people : the wealth of the 55-to-64-year-olds is over five times that of the 16-to-34-year-olds.

wealth: *la richesse*; **an income:** *un revenu*; **the North-South divide:** *le fossé entre le Nord et le Sud*

Ethnic minorities

The British population is far more ethnically mixed than it used to be.
The 2011 census* showed that:

86% of the population of England and Wales were of white ethnicity.
- English / Welsh / Scottish / Northern Irish / British: 80.5%
- Other White: 4.4%
- Irish: 0.9%
- Gypsy or Irish Traveller: 0.1%

7.5% of the population was Asian or Asian British.
- Indian: 2.5%
- Pakistani: 2%
- Other Asian: 1.5%
- Bangladeshi: 0.8%
- Chinese: 0.7%

3.3% of the population was Black.
- African: 1.8%
- Caribbean: 1.1%
- Other Black: 0.5%

2.2% of the population was of mixed or multiple ethnicity.
- White and Black Caribbean: 0.8%
- White and Asian: 0.6%
- Other mixed: 0.5%
- White and Black African: 0.3%

(The 2021 Census was postponed because of Covid-19 and the results will be released in stages over the next year.)
The Commission for Racial Equality investigates cases of racial discrimination, while the government encourages equal opportunities* in all areas of work.

a census: *un recensement*; **equal opportunities:** *l'égalité des chances*

(Official government site for UK statistics)
liennathan.fr/72kj5i

CONTROVERSIAL ISSUES

Immigration and multiculturalism

The arrival of many immigrants in the last two decades (increasingly from Africa rather than from Commonwealth countries as earlier) has had a visible impact on the face of the country. London, which attracts more foreigners than the rest of the country is full of ethnic restaurants, temples and mosques, giving it a truly multi-ethnic feel.
Until quite recently, Britain prided itself on* its good race relations and on being a multicultural model.

"Not a flattening process of assimilation but equal opportunities accompanied by cultural diversity in an atmosphere of mutual tolerance."

Roy Jenkins (Labour Home Secretary), 1966.

But the image of a tolerant multi-racial Britain is being eroded by
– instances of racial tension (for instance the race riots* in the north of England in 2001), partly fuelled by* tabloids such as *The Sun* which feed the prejudice* that most immigrants are cheats, parasites and criminals.
– the discovery, in 2005, that such communities had been harbouring* Islamist terrorism
– several terrorist attacks in Manchester and London in 2017
– the rising number of immigrants
– fears that British identity is now under threat. By encouraging new immigrants to keep their identities instead of merging into* a single British one, the government's policy has led to what has been called "plural monoculturalism"*, that is to say communities living next to each other without really communicating.

However, multi-culturalism has undeniably enriched British society; literature, the theatre, music, films and food - all now reflect the influence of diverse cultures.

The subject of immigration is therefore a highly contentious issue*, and one which greatly concerns most Britons.
The government has recently tried to encourage some legal immigration (that of skilled foreigners or of workers coming at the request of employers) while tightening rules* about other foreign workers and trying to clamp down on* illegal immigration*. Wealthy migrants who invest large sums in Britain can also apply for permanent residence.

to pride oneself on: *s'enorgueillir de*; **race riots:** *des émeutes raciales*; **fuelled by:** *alimenté par*; **a prejudice:** *un préjugé*; **to harbour:** *abriter*; **to merge into:** *se fondre dans*; **plural monoculturalism:** *le monoculturalisme pluriel*; **a contentious issue:** *un sujet à controverse*; **to tighten rules:** *devenir plus strict, renforcer la réglementation*; **to clamp down on:** *mettre un frein à*; **illegal immigration:** *l'immigration clandestine*

Should the number of economic migrants* be limited?
Those who think there are too many immigrants say they are "swamping"* Britain and want quotas introduced. Those who think the laws are already strict enough speak of "fortress Britain"*. What are the main arguments for and against immigration?

+	–
It provides: – cheap labour* which takes on jobs the British do not want to do – new skills – cultural diversity	It may lead to: – poverty – social tensions (by upsetting the racial balance* in the country) – pressure on public services (schools, hospitals)

As I look ahead, I am filled with foreboding. Like the Roman, I seem to see "the River Tiber foaming* with much blood".
(From a racist 1968 speech by Enoch Powell, a Conservative MP, who painted an apocalyptic picture of Britain invaded by immigrants. It was dubbed* his "rivers of blood" speech and led to his being sacked* from the government. The words refer to the prophecy in Virgil's *Aeneid*, Book 6, "I see wars, horrible wars, and the Tiber foaming with much blood.")

economic migrants: *les immigrés pour raisons économiques*; **to swamp:** *submerger*; **fortress Britain:** *la forteresse Grande-Bretagne*; **cheap labour:** *la main-d'œuvre bon marché*; **racial balance:** *l'équilibre racial*; **dubbed:** *appelé*; **to sack:** *renvoyer*; **to foam:** *écumer*

The difficulty of telling genuine asylum seekers* from bogus asylum seekers*:
• If they are genuine, there is a duty to give them shelter* (and the Geneva convention makes it illegal to discriminate against asylum seekers who arrive without any papers.) How can any government justify the prolonged detention of people who have committed no crime?
• But the number of asylum seekers has risen dramatically over the past few years, many arriving without any papers or documents to prove identity or persecution. Are the courts too lenient* when processing* their cases and allowing them to stay?
In 2013, Cameron's coalition government tried to reduce illegal immigration with curbs on student and work visas, and by obliging doctors and landlords to check the status of their patients and tenants.
In 2017 Theresa May said her government aimed at reducing net migration to below 100,000 a year. The migrant crisis in Europe and the controversy around Brexit and immigration have led many to feel that the UK has recently become less tolerant and open to other cultures and religious values.
Britain's immigration system is also now changing. Fewer immigrants come from the EU, more come from the rest of the world (particularly from China and India) and tend to be skilled.

According to the new Brexit immigration rules, prospective migrants will have to be skilled and guaranteed a £25,600 salary threshold to be admitted. This means that low-skilled migrants would be turned down, even though many low-skilled workers in Britain today (such as care-home workers) are immigrants.

a genuine asylum seeker: *un véritable demandeur d'asile*; **a bogus asylum seeker:** *un faux demandeur d'asile*; **to give shelter:** *donner asile*; **lenient:** *clément*; **to process a case:** *examiner un dossier*; **holding camps:** *des camps d'attente*

From immigrant to citizen

Many immigrants live close to each other in Britain, in communities where they can preserve their culture and traditions. Although this helps them to survive and even succeed, it can hinder* their integration into the wider community.

In 2003, the government decided that all immigrants had to pass a citizenship test*, something that the United States and Canada have had for years. The test became compulsory in 2007. It is on society, history and culture and can be prepared for by reading *Life in the UK*, a book produced by the government. Here are a few arguments for and against:

+

It gives immigrants a sense of belonging*.

–

It affects ethnic minorities more than white immigrants.

It would have been better to require immigrants to have good language skills in English.

Once accepted, the new immigrants attend a citizenship ceremony.

to hinder: *empêcher, faire obstacle à*; **a citizenship test:** *un test de citoyenneté*; **a sense of belonging:** *un sentiment d'appartenance*

Sample Citizenship Test questions

1. The present Queen has reigned since ☐ 1952 ☐ 1962 ☐ 1972 ☐ 1982

2. In the 16th and 17th centuries, who came to Britain from France to escape political persecution?

☐ hungry labourers ☐ Jews escaping violence

☐ Protestant Huguenots ☐ French Royal Family

3. Some issues may be debated in the Welsh Assembly and the Scottish Parliament, but remain under the control of the UK Government in London. They are:

☐ education, environment, police

☐ environment, education, taxation

☐ defence, foreign affairs, taxation, social security

☐ transport, defence

4. Judges are appointed by

☐ The Home Secretary
☐ The Prime Minister
☐ The Queen
☐ The Lord Chancellor

5. The Queen or the King can only, in a famous phrase,

☐ revise, warn, and observe
☐ rule, govern, and reign
☐ advise, warn and encourage
☐ encourage, observe and advise

6. What is the Kirk?

☐ the main church in Northern Ireland
☐ the other name of the Church of Scotland
☐ a protestant denomination based in Wales
☐ the name often given to Roman Catholics in Britain

7. What is the name and the date of the National Day of Wales?

☐ St George's Day, 23 April
☐ St Andrew's Day, 30 November
☐ St Francis' Day, 19 June
☐ St David's Day, 1 March

8. When did Britain join the European Economic Community?

☐ in 1968 ☐ in 1973 ☐ in 1982 ☐ in 1988

Answers: 1. a 2. c 3. c 4. d 5. d 6. b 7. d 8. b

Women

Women now have the same rights as men, but have they gained professional equality with them? Women have for years been confronted with "glass ceilings"* preventing them from reaching the top in professional careers - the law, medicine, the church - which are traditionally male preserves*. In 2021, Women only account for 6% of senior executive roles in the FTSE 100.
But things are changing. Among those entering these professions, women are now outnumbering* men. However, there is still a "gender play gap", one of the widest in Europe, not because of pay discrimination (women being paid less than men for the same job), which has been illegal in the UK since 1975, but because of recruitment problems. This is:
– because they prefer to work part-time

– because they do not want to be constantly available to work, which tends to be required whenever there is intense competition leading to high salaries. The 2020 Parliament has a record 34% of women, with marked differences between parties (a quarter of Conservative party MPs, over 50% of Labour party MPs).
The gender pay gap fell to 7.4% among full-time employees and 15.5% among all employees in 2020.

Arguments for and against parity laws*

For

Without parity laws, traditions and current stereotypes only reinforce the gender gap*.

Against

Can it mean that women are selected not because of their capabilities, but simply because they are women?

a glass ceiling: *un plafond de verre*; **male preserves:** *des domaines / professions réservés aux hommes*; **to outnumber:** *surpasser en nombre*; **the gender gap:** *la différence de traitement entre hommes et femmes*; **parity laws:** *les lois sur la parité*

Social mobility

A 2012 OECD report on social mobility showed that Britain has some of the lowest social mobility in the developed world, which means that people's earnings tend to reflect their parents'. Parental influence remains as important as the quality of the school you attend, something which has not improved since the 1970s, making Britain even less of a classless society.
Perhaps the main reason for this is that the best education opportunities tend to go to the richest and to the middle-class as parents' class/income is correlated with educational attainment. Achievement is not balanced fairly: for the poorest fifth in society, 46% have mothers with no qualifications at all; for the richest, it's only 3%.
Inheritance is another reason why UK society is not as upwardly mobile as it could be since with money it is easier for students to get an educational edge. This is particularly true as, contrary to many other countries, the UK taxes the estates of donors rather than the recipients of inheritance or gifts. Indeed, under the 'seven-year rule', assets given during someone's life-time are tax-free if the donor lives at least seven years after making the gift.

Should monuments to controversial historical figures remain?

In 2020, a wave of 'statue-toppling' swept across the United States and Britain. Inspired by the Black Lives Matter movement, such acts were aimed at monuments commemorating those who defended and benefited from slavery. In June

2020, the statue of Edward Colston, a 17th century Bristol slave trader was pulled down during a demonstration, then thrown into the harbour from Pero's bridge (Pero was an enslaved man who lived in Bristol). The statue had originally been erected because Colston was a philanthropist who devoted much of his wealth to support Bristol schools and charities.
In a similar way Oriel College in Oxford voted to take down the statue of Cecil Rhodes on the front of one of its buildings. A 'Rhodes Must Fall' campaign had begun in South Africa, in view of Rhodes' imperialist and racist legacy.
It is interesting to note that in 2021 the statue of Colson, now retrieved from the water, is part of a display in the M Shed Bristol museum, where it lies supine with its graffiti and red paint. Visitors are asked to complete a survey about what happened and what should happen next.

Here are some of the arguments for and against the toppling of monuments:

FOR	AGAINST
– A statue or monument bestows legitimacy and honour : a controversial figure should not have their legacy memorialised. – It is normal to keep reconsidering the past and the way we present it. – Former colonial powers should be critical of their past mistakes. – Historical memory is too often selective. Colston was revered by schoolchildren in Bristol as a philanthropist, without any mention ever being made of his being a slaver.	– We cannot erase those parts of history we do not like. They are essential to an unders-tand-ing of the present. – A statue to a past figure does not legiti-mate his or her views. It helps us confront our past and reflect on the moral issues raised.

9 RELIGION

Because there is a national, established church, religion is omnipresent in public life, from prayers in Parliament, to schools, where the day begins with a prayer, although it now tends to be ecumenical so as to take into account the variety of beliefs* represented.
There is however a marked decline in weekly church attendance, which in 2016 fell below 1 million for the first time. In 2015, the proportion of Britons who said they had no religion (49%) overtook that saying they were Christian (43%). While some religions like Islam are growing, and many inner city churches are thriving, hundreds of deconsecrated churches are being transformed into homes, restaurants or nursery schools.

The Church of England (or Anglican Church) is the established* church in England. In Scotland, the established Church is the Church of Scotland. The sovereign is Head of both the Church of England and the Church of Scotland and appoints the most senior clergy* of the Church of England, on the recommendation of the Prime Minister (twenty-six Church of England bishops* sit in the House of Lords). The fact that the church is a state church means that there are prayers* in Parliament, at state ceremonies and at school. Twenty-six archbishops and bishops (Lords Spiritual) are members of the House of Lords.

There are no established churches in Wales and Ireland.

church attendance: *la fréquentation des églises*; **a census:** *un recensement*; **a belief:** *une croyance*; **the established church:** *la religion officielle d'État*; **a bishop:** *un évêque*; **the senior clergy:** *le haut clergé*; **a prayer:** *une prière*

The Anglican Church

Its principles are defined in the Thirty-nine Articles, adopted in 1571, during the reign of Queen Elizabeth I. From then on, both Catholics and staunch Protestants were either frowned upon or persecuted, the former only gaining the right to participate fully in public life in 1829 (Catholic Emancipation Act), many of the latter, the Puritans, fleeing to America in the early 17th century. The Church of England is thus a **compromise** between the Protestant and the Catholic Churches.

– As in the Catholic Church, it is hierarchical*, ruled by bishops*, and above them by two archbishops*, the archbishop of York and the archbishop of Canterbury, the latter being "Primate of all England*".

– Its doctrines, however, are closer to those of the Protestant Churches: they emphasize the importance of the Bible, and reject the Immaculate Conception* and the cult of the Saints. Man will be judged by God, and possibly saved*, so that it is his own life, his reading of the Bible and his personal experience of religion that matter, not confession or the intercession of the church hierarchy. Anglican priests can marry and, since 1981, a number of female priests have been ordained*.

The liturgy of the Church of England is based on The Book of Common Prayer. There are several tendencies within the Anglican Church:

– High Church is closer to the Catholic Church, and stresses the importance of rituals, sacraments* and ceremonies.

– Low Church is closer to the Protestant Churches: it emphasizes the importance of the Bible and prefers simple services*, few ornaments and practical humanitarian action.

– Broad Church believes in tolerance and liberalism.

It hath been the wisdom* of the Church of England, ever since the first compiling of her Publick Liturgy, to keep the mean* between the two extremes, of too much stiffness* in refusing, and of too much easiness in admitting any variation from it.

The Book of Common Prayer, 1662

The Anglican Church has recently taken quite liberal stances*, condemning government policies such as Mrs Thatcher's or the war in Iraq. In 1985, it allowed the ordination of women as Anglican priests, and in 2014 voted to give final approval to legislation allowing women to become bishops.
Two problems have recently sparked a great deal of controversy within the Anglican Church: should it allow gay* priests and same-sex marriages*?

hierarchical: *hiérarchique*; **a bishop:** *un évêque*; **an archbishop:** *un archevêque*; **the Primate of all England:** *le Primat d'Angleterre*; **the Immaculate Conception:** *l'Immaculée Conception*; **to save:** *sauver*; **to ordain:** *ordonner (un prêtre)*; **a sacrament:** *un sacrement*; **a service:** *un office*; **wisdom:** *la sagesse*; **a mean:** *un moyen terme*; **stiffness:** *la raideur*; **a stance:** *une position*; **a gay priest:** *un prêtre homosexuel*; **same-sex marriage:** *le mariage entre personnes du même sexe*.

The Church of Scotland is Presbyterian. It is ruled* democratically by elected assemblies, and there is no church hierarchy. The teachings of the Bible are at the centre of Presbyterians' worship.

A multi-faith* society

But Britain is also a multi-faith* society, with many other Christian Churches:

Protestant churches	Other denominations*	Catholic Church
– United Reformed Church (Presbyterians and Congregationalists) – Baptist Church – Methodist Church	– Quakers – Unitarians – Seventh-Day Adventists – Pentecostal Church – The Salvation Army – Jehovah's Witnesses – Christian Scientists	– Catholic Church

Britain has also many Muslims*, Hindus, Sikhs and Buddhists, most of whom came to Britain with the most recent waves of immigration.

multi-faith: *multi-confessionnelle*; **to rule:** *diriger*; **denomination:** *confession*; **a Muslim:** *un musulman*

Religion In Britain – Census shows 71.7% identify as Christians

	2001	2011
Christian	71.7	59.3
No religion	14.4	25.1
Muslim	3	4.8
Hindu	1.1	1.5
Sikh	0.6	0.8
Jewish	0.5	0.5
Other religions	0.6	0.8

(The official National Statistics guide to UK geography)
liennathan.fr/72kj5i

(The official site of the Church of Scotland)
liennathan.fr/q76hy6

CONTROVERSIAL ISSUES

■ Should the Anglican Church be disestablished*?

To reflect the multi-culturalism of the nation, Prince Charles has repeatedly said that if he became king, he would wish to become "Defender of Faith*" (that is to say of all faiths) rather than "Defender of the Faith" (the Christian faith only), the title British monarchs have inherited since Henry VIII. But how can a sovereign defend all faiths, when there are fundamental differences between them? Should the Anglican church then be disestablished?

Arguments for	Arguments against
– The links between Church and State prevent the Church from being as critical of the government as it could be. – Having an established church is unfair* to all the other faiths in the country. – The Anglican Church no longer reflects the religious diversity of the country.	– Because of its links to the state, the Church of England is constantly involved in secular matters* – The Church of England is still capable of criticism of the government. – It is very active in creating bridges between the different faiths. – It is a good thing to maintain a Christian influence over public life.

to disestablish: *séparer l'Église de l'État*; **Defender of Faith:** *défenseur de toute foi*; **unfair:** *injuste*; **secular matters:** *des questions d'ordre séculier*

■ Muslims* in Britain: the politics of identity

For years, Britain prided itself on* its liberal policies, often following with incomprehension the French row* over the wearing of headscarves*. In 1989, Ayatolah Khomeini's fatwa against Salman Rushdie for writing *The Satanic Verses* opened the debate about Muslim fundamentalism in Britain. After the terrorist attacks on the USA in September 2001 and those in London in July 2005, Britain was shocked to discover that some of the terrorists were British-born Muslims. A growing number of British Muslims are indeed said to be plotting* against their country. Might the liberal policies towards Muslims have encouraged terrorism to develop in the country?
The terrorist attacks badly damaged community relations as many people started distrusting* Muslims, believing that they were all fundamentalists and terrorists.

Many Muslims felt targeted by the police. And increasingly, the British government is recognizing that a government has a right to ask a minority community to integrate*. How can one reconcile tolerance of another culture or religion and the need for integration within the mainstream community*?
Muslims are indeed often criticized for tending to remain together, often in inner-city areas*, without trying to fit into British society. It is this cultural separateness which is the most alarming aspect of British multiculturalism. In 2006, Jack Straw, then Leader of the House of Commons, took a stand* against full-face veils*, which he said emphasized separateness and made communication difficult. This opened a debate on religion and race and on the danger for a community of isolating and separating itself from others. This is one of the reasons why, for instance, the government is trying to bring Muslim schools into the state sector, where it believes pupils are less likely to become radicalised.
The controversy broke out again in 2014 when Ofsted found "a culture of fear and intimidation" in some Birmingham schools, where hard-line Muslims were said to impose their views. Many say that toleration has indeed its limits. Is it possible to tolerate those who, in certain schools or mosques, teach a literal interpretation of Islam and for instance advocate keeping wives in purdah (secluded from the sight of men)? It recommended instead that all schools should "promote British values".

Arguments in favour of banning* the *burqa* and *niqab*:	Arguments for:
– Since most women wear them because men ask them to, it reflects the oppression of Muslim women by men. – It constitutes a refusal to integrate into British society. – One's religion should not be openly displayed* in a largely secular society. – In certain places like schools, they can be disturbing for pupils.	– Some women choose to wear the veil for fashion or cultural reasons. – Banning the veil might be a form of racial discrimination. – If Britain is not tolerant of Muslim practices, how can it ask Muslims to be tolerant? – A ban might encourage more women to wear the veil.

If we are to build a plural* society on the foundation of what unites us, we must face up to what divides. But the questions of core freedoms* and primary loyalties can't be ducked*. No society, no matter how tolerant, can expect to thrive* if its citizens don't prize what their citizenship means – if, when asked what they stand for as Frenchmen, as Indians, as Britons, they cannot give clear replies.

Salman Rushdie

There is more that holds us together than divides us. I believe there are some cultural aspects we should share – speaking English and having a sense of British history

and traditions for example. And all of this needs to be grounded* in a set of non-negotiable values. They belong to us all. They are found in Islam as much as in Christian, Sikh, Hindu, Jewish and other traditions:
+ respect for the law
+ freedom of speech
+ equality of opportunity
+ respect for others and responsibility towards others.

Ruth Kelly, Secretary of State for education, 2006

Muslims: *les musulmans*; **to pride oneself on:** *s'enorgueillir de*; **a row:** *une querelle*; **a headscarf:** *un foulard*; **to plot:** *comploter*; **to distrust:** *se méfier de*; **to integrate:** *s'intégrer*; **the mainstream community:** *la communauté dominante*; **inner-city areas:** *les quartiers pauvres du centre des villes*; **to take a stand:** *prendre position*; **the full-face veil:** *le niqab*; **to ban:** *interdire*; **to display:** *afficher*; **plural:** *pluriel, diversifié*; **core freedoms:** *les libertés fondamentales*; **to duck:** *éviter*; **to thrive:** *prospérer*; **to ground:** *fonder*

10 EDUCATION

Education is compulsory* in England until the age of 16.

Schools

Types of schools according to age of pupils		
State-funded		
Preschool	Nursery School / Kindergarten	3 → 5
Primary schools	Primary school	5 → 11
	Infant school	5 → 7
	Junior school	7 → 11
Secondary schools	• Standard secondary school	11 → 18
	• Middle school	9 → 12/14
	• Senior comprehensive school	12/14 → 18
	• Secondary school	11 → 16
	• Sixth-form college	16 → 18
	• City Academies	11 → 18
Independent		
	Preparatory school	
	Boys	7 → 13
	Girls	7 → 10
	Public school	10/13 → 18

Types of schools according to studies	
Comprehensive schools	Open to pupils of all abilities. A wide range of subjects taught.
Grammar schools	Academic studies

Secondary modern schools	Less academic studies
Independent schools	Often very academic
Technical/Vocational Colleges	Vocational education*
City Academies	Outside the control of local authorities but state funded. Created to replace failing schools and open to pupils of all abilities.

Classes in secondary schools

Age	Form	Year
11	First form	6
12	Second form	7
13	Third form	8
14	Fourth form	9
15	Fifth form	10
16	Lower Sixth form	11
17	Upper Sixth form	12

State schools

– Comprehensive schools are co-educational* and open to pupils of all abilities, who are often streamed* depending on their level.
– Grammar schools are often more academically-oriented.
State schools are free*. They have to follow a National Curriculum*, with compulsory and optional subjects.

Independent schools are private and often have very good academic records*. They include public schools, which are expensive, selective, mainly taking their pupils from the upper middle-class – but grants* are given to very bright children whose parents could not afford* the tuition fees*. Some pupils are boarders*, the others day pupils. Most independent schools are single-sex.
Independent schools do not have to adhere to the National Curriculum. Pupils there are taught academic subjects but also given a more general education (good manners, fair play, speaking in public...).
Preparatory schools prepare pupils for an entrance exam (the Common Entrance Examination) to enter public schools at the age of 13.

> The "sacred nine", the nine best-known public schools, are: Eton, Harrow, Rugby, Winchester, Westminster, Charterhouse, Shrewsbury, Merchant Taylor's, St Paul's.

Traditionally, British schools lay the stress on* sports, team spirit*, loyalty and the development of character as much as on intellectual abilities.
Morning assemblies (when the whole school meet for prayers and information concerning the day ahead), the playing of sports, and school uniforms encourage a community spirit.

Pupils later often wear their "old school tie" (a tie in the colours of their public school or university) to show their pride in their "alma mater" (the school or university they attended), and become part of an "old boy network*" of pupils or students who attended* the same public school or university and who later keep in touch and help one another professionally.
In 1988, a National Curriculum was introduced: 30% to 40% of the time is devoted to three compulsory* core subjects*: English, maths and sciences. Students choose among other disciplines for the rest of their studies. Tests are administered at different ages to assess how well pupils are doing.

compulsory: *obligatoire*; **vocational education:** *enseignement professionnel*; **co-educational:** *mixte*; **streamed:** *répartis par niveaux*; **free:** *gratuit*; **the National Curriculum:** *le programme obligatoire*; **academic records:** *les résultats scolaires*; **a grant:** *une bourse*; **to afford:** *pouvoir payer*; **tuition fees:** *les frais de scolarité*; **a boarder:** *un interne*; **to lay the stress on:** *insister sur*; **team spirit:** *l'esprit d'équipe*; **the old boy network:** *le réseau d'anciens élèves*; **to attend a school:** *être élève dans une école*; **a core subject:** *une discipline de base*

Examinations

– GCSEs : you take* your GCSEs (General Certificate of Secondary Education) at 16 (at the end of year 10), taking exams individually in different subjects. Students usually take from 5 to 10 subjects, which are graded* from 1 to 9, 9 being the highest mark.
– GCE A-Levels (General Certificate of Education, Advanced levels) are taken at 18, at the end of secondary education. They are prepared for in two years. In the first year, students study 3 to 5 subjects to obtain AS Level qualifications; in the second year, the subjects are reduced to about three at A2 Level. A-Levels are graded from A* down to E. The results are important to get into the university of your choice, which might, for instance, require 3 Bs.
Many students who apply* to go to university delay* their studies for a year in order to take a gap year* to travel or work to pay for their studies.

to take an exam: *passer un examen*; **to grade:** *noter*; **to apply:** *poser sa candidature*; **to delay:** *retarder*; **a gap year:** *une année de congé*

Higher education

Universities are independent and select their students according to their A-level results. Students apply to several universities and are either rejected or accepted conditionally, depending on their A-Level grades.
There are four types of universities:
– The old universities: Oxford, Cambridge (England), St Andrews, Glasgow, Aberdeen, Edinburgh (Scotland). They are prestigious and considered as poles of excellence.
– The redbrick universities (late 19th century, and mostly built in brick): e.g. Leeds
– The new universities (built after WWII): e.g. the University of Sussex at Brighton
– The former polytechnics* (specialized in professional and technical education), which became universities in 1992
The Open University mainly provides correspondence courses for adults.

There are also Colleges of Further Education, which mainly provide vocational training*.
Most students choose to go to universities away from their homes, and live on the campus. Teaching consists of lectures* (for large groups of students), seminars* and tutorials* (when students meet in very small groups and read their essays to their tutors). Tuition fees are high (up to £9,250 a year for full-time study in 2021) and many students have to borrow* money in order to pay for their studies and lodgings. But student grants* are also given to students from poorer backgrounds.
The pandemic much affected universities. What with their teaching online, the collapse of international travel and social-distancing measures, many international students (who provide some 20% of the income of many of the best universities) deferred or gave up coming to the UK. Indeed, as an example, a UK undergraduate student starting at UCL in 2021 will pay £9,250 a year in tuition fees, while overseas undergraduates, including EU students since Brexit, will pay £31,200 for the same studies.

Diplomas:
Undergraduate studies*:
– BA*= Bachelor of Arts
– BSc*= Bachelor of Science
Bachelor degrees are ranked from I (First) to II.1, II.2, III, and Pass.

Postgraduate studies*:
– MA*= Master of Arts – MSc= Master of Science – PhD*= Doctor of Philosophy

There is great flexibility on the British labour market*, where people tend to be recruited at a certain level of studies, with less regard than in France to the discipline they specialized in.

As more and more students want a university education, there is increased competition between applicants as well as between universities. As a result, many universities are acting like businesses in a market-driven economy. Modern, spruced up campuses help attract more students. Many universities now also have campuses abroad, particularly in growing economies and in Asia. British universities provide a curriculum, part of the teaching staff, and support in return for a high fee. Students thus get a prestigious qualification at a much lower cost, close to their homes, and without the problems of a visa application. Manchester, for instance, has campuses in Singapore and Hong Kong, UCL* in Qatar, and Westminster in Uzbekistan.

polytechnics: *équivalent des IUT*; **vocational training:** *la formation professionnelle*; **a lecture:** *une conférence, un cours magistral*; **a seminar:** *une séance de travail en très petits groupes*; **a tutorial:** *équivalent d'une colle*; **tuition fees:** *les frais de scolarité*; **to borrow:** *emprunter*; **a grant:** *une bourse*; **undergraduate studies:** *études pour obtenir une licence*; **a BA:** *l'équivalent de la licence littéraire*; **a BSc:** *l'équivalent de la licence scientifique*; **postgraduate studies:** *troisième cycle universitaire*; **an MA:** *l'équivalent du mastère*; **a PhD:** *un doctorat*; **the labour market:** *le marché du travail*; **UCL:** *University College London*

(The site of British universities)
liennathan.fr/dk9b34

Which schools for Britain's future?

The tendency has recently been to:
– Encourage schools which specialize in certain fields (e.g. music, sciences, religious schools) and have strong individual aims and ethos*.
– Develop schools which are independently run and become self-governing*, with foundation status, which will give them more freedom to choose admissions, staff* and syllabus*, and run their budgets.
– Create City Academies, to replace failing schools*. The latter are demolished and replaced by state-of-the-art* buildings. The new schools are funded* partly by government, partly by businesses or by a sponsor such as a charity*, religious group or university which will also have a say in the running of the school.
– Close failing schools and expand popular ones or help run the failing ones.
The tendency towards self-governing, specialist schools, and academies first appear-ed as New Labour policies, but has since been endorsed by the Conservatives. The aim is now to give schools more autonomy, free them from local authority control, allow parents to launch new ones, and encourage performance-based pay for teachers.

The resulting debate
These ideas have been received with a mixture of interest and wariness*, and raise a number of questions.
Could the new 'specialist schools' lead to backdoor* academic selection? Or if they cannot select pupils by ability, will they not choose children from well-off families since they are more likely to ensure* better results for the school?

How to decide which schools children go to?
– Selection according to academic ability? This is a possibility not favoured by Labour.
– Selection by catchment areas*? That favours the rich, who can buy houses near the best schools.
– Selection according to parents' choice? But can it work if some schools are better than others?

the ethos: *l'esprit*; **self-governing:** *autonome*; **the staff:** *le personnel*; **a syllabus:** *un programme*; **failing schools:** *les plus mauvaises écoles, celles qui sont en situation d'échec*; **state-of-the-art:** *ultra moderne, dernier cri*; **to fund:** *financer*; **a charity:** *une fondation ou œuvre de bienfaisance*; **wariness:** *la réserve, la circonspection*; **backdoor selection:** *une sélection déguisée*; **to ensure:** *garantir*; **the catchment area:** *le secteur de recrutement scolaire*

The future of A-levels

The improvement in GCSE and A-level results has led to accusations of grade inflation, more and more students getting excellent A-levels grades. Is there a dumbing-down* of exams? Are A-levels becoming too easy? Or are students better prepared? How can the brightest be differentiated from weaker students? But the criticism against the exam is a broader one, as many complain that specializing in three subjects only at age 16 is far too restrictive. Many schools have chosen to prepare their students for the International Baccalaureate (IB), for which students have to study six subjects, among which maths, science and one foreign language.

a dumbing down: *une baisse du niveau*

For or against tuition fees*?

From 2012, and in spite of Lib-Dem opposition, universities were allowed to charge students up to £9,000 a year for tuition (up to £9,250 in 2021 for UK students, but much higher for international undergraduates). Tuition remains free in Scotland.
This is highly controversial as it may not help social mobility.

ARGUMENTS FOR	ARGUMENTS AGAINST
– The government's view is that graduates* earn more than non-graduates, and will be able to pay the loan back. "The fair way to reform the system is to say to students that if you go to university, you will earn more money, so you will have to make a contribution – the idea of rights and duties going together is at the foundation of a modern civic society." Tony Blair, from an interview in *Time*, Oct. 27 1997.	– Will students from poorer homes be put off* by the fear of large debts? – If universities can decide on the fees they ask for, will that not transform higher education into a market? Or is it already a market? Many universities already favour foreign students because they bring in more money.

top up fees: *frais de scolarité universitaire supplémentaires*; **to fill the coffers:** *remplir les coffres*; **cash-strapped:** *à court d'argent*; **a graduate:** *un diplômé de l'université*; **to put off:** *dissuader, décourager*

Is education too elitist?

British education is still determined by class, most of the elite having been educated at top private fee-paying schools.
Conscious that many parents are faced with the choice between poor state schools and independent schools whose fees they cannot afford, several companies plan

to open chains of low-cost, for-profit schools. But can they succeed where state schools have failed? And the government is talking of using a lottery system whenever demand exceeds the places available in a given school.
Although Oxford and Cambridge try to be more meritocratic in their recruitment policies*, they remain elitist and linked to power. To counter the fact that the process of selection tends to favour students from fee-paying schools, universities are being encouraged to take on more state-school pupils. But many rejected private-school pupils with excellent grades now feel discriminated against*.

the recruitment policy: *la politique d'admission*; **to be discriminated against:** *être victime de discrimination*

11 THE WELFARE STATE

Born of the need to rebuild post World War II Britain and of the generous ideas of the Beveridge Report (1942), the Welfare State* was created in order to provide a wide-ranging* system of social security in order to fight the five "giants" Beveridge talked of: Want*, Disease*, Ignorance, Squalor* and Idleness*. People would pay a contribution taken from their salaries and would be entitled* to benefits* and grants* in case of sickness, invalidity or death, to help raise children and for pensions. It would also provide free consultations with GPs* and hospital care. The National Insurance Act was passed in 1945. The population would be protected 'from the cradle to the grave'*.

"Social insurance fully developed may provide income* security; it is an attack upon Want. But Want is one only of five giants on the road of reconstruction and in some ways the easiest to attack. The others are Disease, Ignorance, Squalor and Idleness."

William Beveridge

How fares* the Welfare State over 70 years after Beveridge's report? Two main issues have been a major concern.

the welfare state: *l'État providence*; **wide-ranging:** *de grande envergure*; **want:** *la nécessité*; **disease:** *la maladie*; **squalor:** *des conditions de vie sordides*; **idleness:** *l'oisiveté*; **to be entitled to:** *avoir droit à*; **benefits:** *des allocations*; **a grant:** *une aide*; **a GP, a general practitioner:** *médecin généraliste*; **from the cradle to the grave:** *du berceau jusqu'à la tombe*; **income:** *le revenu*; **how fares:** *comment se port*

The NHS

Created in 1948 to provide free medical treatment for all, the NHS* has since been the victim of its popularity. It remains free for all, except for a flat-rate* prescription charge* for whatever medicines are prescribed (which many are exempt from paying). Patients are free to consult a GP, who if need be will refer them to a consultant*. But problems have accumulated over the years because of:

– the longer life expectancy* and an ageing* population
– the cost of advanced medical technology

– people's constantly increasing expectations*
– the growing number of one-parent families*

Under Mrs Thatcher, a market economy was introduced into the NHS, with hospitals and community services becoming NHS trusts, that is to say self-governing providers* which competed against each other for referrals* by GPs, the purchasers*, since the more patients they treated, the more funds* they got. GPs became fundholders*, with specific budgets. In 1991, a Patient's Charter* was introduced listing patients' rights and the standards they can expect.
Labour abandoned such a competitive approach and created foundation hospitals, semi-independent hospitals which have more freedom to run their affairs and are allocated money according to their activities, to how busy they are – something which can be called "payments by results". Primary-care trusts (PCTS), larger organisations made up of several GPs, dentists, and ophthalmologists, are the purchasers* of care for their patients from the hospitals. The old principle of the NHS as health provider is being replaced by one in which the NHS purchases medical treatment from public or private providers*, treatment remaining free for the patient. The Conservatives' 2012 Health and Social Care Act put more decisions about the purchase of care in the hands of GPs.

In the meantime, in spite of record spending on the NHS, many problems remain:
– long waiting lists* to see a hospital consultant, then to have an operation
– rocketing* deficits
– staff shortages*
– with lack of funds for district nursing and social care, many hospital beds are occupied by people who should not be there.
– the dwindling number of GPs as the job has become less attractive.
– the spread of Covid-19, which overstretched the NHS, particularly in terms of intensive care.
It is now possible for patients who need certain operations (cataract or hip replacement* for example) to go to have their operations in private hospitals or abroad, paid for by the NHS. Another controversial solution would be to raise money with a social-insurance scheme or an inheritance levy.
There is also a private sector which is totally separate and available through private health insurance.

the NHS: the National Health Service, *service national de santé*; **flat-rate:** *forfaitaire*; **the prescription charge:** *la somme à payer pour obtenir les médicaments inscrits sur l'ordonnance*; **a consultant:** *un spécialiste*; **life expectancy:** *l'espérance de vie*; **ageing:** *vieillissant*; **an expectation:** *une attente*; **a one-parent family:** *une famille monoparentale*; **a referral:** *le fait d'envoyer un malade à un hôpital ou à un spécialiste*; **a provider:** *un fournisseur*; **a purchaser:** *un acheteur*; **funds:** *des fonds*; **a fundholder GP:** *un médecin généraliste qui gère son propre budget*; **the Patient's Charter:** *la Charte du patient*; **a waiting list:** *une liste d'attente*; **to rocket:** *monter en flèche*; **staff shortage:** *le manque de personnel*; **a hip replacement:** *une prothèse de hanche*

(The official site of the NHS)
liennathan.fr/xhv247

▪ BENEFITS* vs WORK

A large number of benefits provide social help, for example:
– The Jobseeker's Allowance* is paid to the unemployed provided they look for work.
– Working Families tax credit* helps low-income families.
– Maternity pay, Sick pay and Child benefit are paid irrespective of income.
There is also a whole range of grants, loans and fuel payments* to help those in financial difficulties.

Can the cycle of welfare dependency be broken?
During the Thatcher years, the very principle of the Welfare State was partly challenged by the idea that people were responsible for their own lives and should therefore deserve welfare*. This is to be linked with the Protestant work ethic*, which celebrates work and prosperity.

New Labour introduced its New Deal – a number of reforms to reduce the Welfare deficit and welfare dependency, such as
– means-testing* for certain benefits (rather than giving the same flat-rate to everyone),
– tax credits* to make it more interesting for low-income families to work than to receive unemployment benefits*.
– a "Welfare to Work"* policy to encourage unemployed and disabled people to seek a job rather than remain on unemployment benefits and be dependent on the state. Through advice and counselling, people are encouraged to work, offered subsidized* jobs, or given the chance of acquiring further training* or education.

The belief is thus that systematic benefits can only be a disincentive to work* and that some types of welfare erode personal responsibility and community spirit. Instead, people should be encouraged to improve their skills and desire to work.
These measures seem to have worked, since Britain has one of the lowest unemployment rates* in Europe (4.8 % in 2021). But if it is easier to find work in Britain than in France, it is also easier to lose it. There is a great deal of job insecurity and fear of redundancy*. Work, which is not limited to a 35-hour week, also tends to be more intensive. In 2018, the Conservative government simplified the welfare system and introduced Universal Credit, which merges and replaces six existing benefits: Child Tax Credit, Housing Benefit, Income Support, income-based Jobseeker's Allowance (JSA) income-related Employment and Support Allowance (ESA) and Working Tax Credit.

Our fellow citizens working every hour of every day to put food on the table ask this: why should my taxes go to people who could work but don't? Or to those who live in homes that hardworking people could never afford? Or to people who have no right to be here in the first place?
I say this to the British people: you have every right to be angry about a system that is unfair and unjust – and that's why we are sorting it out.
We've capped* welfare. We've capped housing benefit. We've insisted on new rules so that if you reject work, you lose benefits.

David Cameron, Conservative Party Conference, 2013

Jobseeker's Allowance: *allocation chômage dépendante de la recherche d'un emploi*; **fuel payment:** *indemnité de chauffage*; **benefits:** *allocations, prestations*; **tax credits:** *les crédits d'impôt*; **to deserve welfare:** *mériter l'assistance publique*; **the Protestant work ethic:** *l'éthique protestante du travail*; **means-testing:** *faire dépendre les allocations des ressources*; **unemployment benefits:** *les allocations de chômage*; **welfare to work:** *le fait de passer des allocations au travail*; **subsidized:** *subventionné*; **training:** *la formation*; **a disincentive to work:** *quelque chose qui n'incite pas à travailler*; **the unemployment rate:** *le taux de chômage*; **redundancy:** *les licenciements pour raisons économiques*; **to cap:** *limiter*

CONTROVERSIAL ISSUES

The Nanny state*

The expression is pejorative and describes a state which, like a nanny*, overprotects the individual with a series of excessive interventionist measures, for instance to prevent people from leading unhealthy lifestyles. It is also described as meddling*. Although the expression is used for any country, it is the British government which has recently been most often accused of "nannyism".

Examples of such regulation:
- laws concerning the legal smoking or drinking age (above the age of majority)
- censorship*
- forbidding smoking in public places
- high taxes or controls on junk food*. In September 2006, for example, the British government sent schools and parents leaflets with strict guidelines as to what a child's packed lunch should contain.
- felling* horse chestnuts* along city streets to prevent people from slipping on the fallen conkers*.
- forbidding the smacking* of children (even by parents), and more generally teaching parents family values.

So what can be said for or against such regulations?

+	–
– The state has a duty to control people's harmful behaviour. – This harmful behaviour (for instance taking drugs or too much alcohol) leads to diseases which cost the taxpayer* a great deal. – People in lower socio-economic groups might not follow mere advice and need regulations to counter* the effects of disadvantage. For example, it is easier for affluent* families to buy fresh food, and go to health clubs, and they are more likely to be aware of health issues.	– It is dangerous and degrading to let the government interfere and control all aspects of our lives. – People should have the freedom to make their own choices. – Such help is patronizing* and paternalistic. – Its real aim is to discourage people from suing* the state.

For the government, the problem is finding a balance between merely informing and using bans.

"Some may call it the nanny state but I call it a force for good."

Margaret Hodge (Labour MP), 2004

We need to find the right balance, rejecting both the nanny state and the Pontius Pilate state which washes its hands of its citizens' health.

John Reid, Feb. 2004

the nanny state: *l'État assistance, l'État-nounou*; **a nanny:** *une nurse, une nounou*; **to meddle:** *s'occuper de ce qui ne vous regarde pas*; **censorship:** *la censure*; **junk food:** *une nourriture mauvaise pour la santé*; **to fell a tree:** *couper un arbre*; **a horse chesnut:** *un marronnier*; **a conker:** *un marron*; **to smack:** *donner une paire de claques*; **the taxpayer:** *le contribuable*; **to counter:** *compenser*; **affluent:** *riche*; **patronizing:** *condescendant*; **to sue:** *poursuivre en justice*

12 THE MEDIA

"The people will believe what the media tell them they believe."

George Orwell

Fleet Street (the name of the street in the City where most newspapers used to be printed) is still used metonymically for the press, even though newspapers are now produced outside central London.

The British traditionally read many papers, which tend to be cheaper than in France. A distinction is made between the quality press* (the more serious newspapers) and the popular press (or gutter press*), which devotes most of its pages to sensational news*. The difference used to be one of size too, the quality press consisting of broadsheets* and the popular press of tabloid*, that is half size, sheets, hence the name 'tabloids*'; but this distinction is disappearing as most newspapers are now moving to the smaller size or to the 'Berliner' format, which is between the two. The British also read Sunday papers, thick editions with many sections* and magazines, which provide a survey of the week's news among other things.

Often attacked for intruding on people's privacy* and looking for sleaze*, the press has adopted a code of practice (developed by the Press Complaints Commission) in order to try and self-regulate*. But it remains, on the whole, very lowbrow* (partly the result of the circulation* wars between papers and the need to keep readers by pandering to* their tastes) but also very powerful. For instance, on the day of the 1992 general election, the pro-Conservative *Sun*, showed Neil Kinnock (the Labour candidate) with his head inside a light bulb and the words: "If Kinnock wins today will the last person to leave Britain please turn out the lights." The Tories won the election and the next day the newspaper boasted that it was "the *Sun* wot won it"*. A more recent example is that of *News of the World*, a lowbrow Sunday newspaper, with a huge circulation of between 3 and 4 million copies, which specialised in scandalous revelations about the lives of politicians and stars. In 2011, it was revealed that the newspaper, as well as others in the News International group, had been engaging in police bribery and had been hacking the phones of celebrities, politicians and members of the Royal Family. This 'phone-hacking scandal', also called 'Murdochgate' led to several resignations and condemnations, and to the closure of the newspaper in July 2011. In 2013 the press set up their own regular, IPSO (the Independent Press Standards Organisation).

But British newspapers are currently in difficulty because of low revenues (party due to price wars in order to gain readers), an advertising slump* (advertisers now preferring other media) and competition from free papers (or freebies) and online journalism*. The future does not look any brighter as fewer and fewer young people now read a newspaper, preferring to get their news from the radio, TV or the internet.

the quality press: *la presse de qualité*; **the gutter press:** *la presse à scandale*; **sensational news:** *des nouvelles à sensation*; **a broadsheet:** *un journal grand format*; **a tabloid:** *un journal populaire de petit format*; **a section:** *un supplément*; **to intrude on people's privacy:** *s'ingérer dans la vie privée des gens*; **sleaze:** *le sordide, le vulgaire, les scandales*; **to self-regulate:** *s'autoréguler*; **lowbrow:** *peu intellectuel*; **the circulation:** *le tirage*; **to pander to:** *se prêter aux exigences de*; **wot won it:** *populaire pour*; **a slump:** *une baisse*; **online journalism:** *le journalisme en ligne.*

The daily paper *Metro*, distributed free, has over one million daily readers.

A few magazines:

- *The Economist* (Independent / Liberal): political, financial and social topics.
- *The New Statesman* (Labour): political, social and cultural topics.
- *The Spectator* (Conservative): political, social and cultural topics.

PAPERS	POLITICAL LEANING	CIRCULATION 2017
Quality dailies		
The Times	Centre-Right	368,929
The Guardian	Centre-Left	132,341
The Daily Telegraph	Conservative / Centre-Right	360,345 (2019)
The Independent	Economically Liberal / Politically Centrist	(1)
The Financial Times	Economically Liberal / Politically Centrist	157,982
i	Centre-Left	217,182
Quality Sunday papers		
The Observer	Centre-Left	156,217
The Sunday Times	Centre / Centre-Right	645,108
The Sunday Telegraph	Conservative / Centre-Right	248,288
The Independent on Sunday	Centre-Left	(1)
Popular dailies		
The Daily Mail	Centre-Right	1,169,241
The Daily Express	Right-wing	296,079
The Sun	Right-wing	1,250,634

The Daily Star	Right-wing	277,237
The Daily Mirror	Left-wing	451,466
The Evening Standard (free)	Centre / Centre Right	798,168
Popular Sunday papers		
The Sun on Sunday	Right-wing	1,013,777
The Sunday People	Populist / Labour	125,216
Sunday Express	Right-wing	252,733
Sunday Mirror	Left-wing	367,244
The Mail on Sunday	Right-wing	967,043
The Daily Star Sunday	Right-wing	162,345

(1) Now only as online editions

The BBC (the British Broadcasting Corporation, affectionately nicknamed "Auntie") is a publicly-funded corporation*, which has been broadcasting* "in the public interest" since the 1920s. It has five radio stations (Radio 1, 2, 3, 4 & 5) and two main television channels (BBC1 (more popular) & BBC2 (more cultural)). BBC 3 and 4, BBC Parliament and BBC News 24 are for digital reception. The BBC also broadcasts all over the world with the BBC world service. The BBC is independent, politically impartial, and does not broadcast any advertising. It is financed by a licence fee*of £159 a year (in 2021) and managed by a board of Governors which is accountable to* Parliament. The BBC is also supervised by the independent regulator Ofcom.

In 2021, it was revealed that the BBC had used deception and false documents to secure an interview with Princess Diana. It helped undermine an institution which is already in turmoil.

Although the BBC aims at being universal ('the same music rings as sweetly in mansion as in cottage', as the BBC's first director-general, John Reith, said), the less educated are less likely to watch it. As for young people, an increasing number spend more time on YouTube or on Netflix than on live TV. And yet all households pay the same fee. There has been talk of transforming the BBC into a subscription service (like Netflix) or to develop some paid-for services, but this is still unimaginable to many.

There is also a commercial sector (financed by advertising) with ITV (Independent Television), Channels 4 and 5 , as well as satellite and cable television.

Sky TV is available with satellite dishes.

Coronation Street vs Eastenders

Both are among the most popular soap operas* on British television and they compete to get the highest ratings*. Both are social realist series.

Coronation Street has been broadcast on ITV since 1960 and follows the lives of a number of working-class people in an imaginary ordinary street of terraced houses in Manchester, with the pub as central meeting-place.

Eastenders (since 1985 on BBC) focuses on a fictional Victorian square in London. It aims at reflecting everyday life in an inner city, and is more outspoken than Coronation Street, in terms of both language and issues covered (unemployment, homosexuality, rape, drug-dealing, prostitution, racial prejudice, AIDS, etc.)

a publicly-funded corporation: *une compagnie financée par des fonds publics*; **to broadcast (broadcast, broadcast):** *diffuser*; **the licence fee:** *la redevance*; **a soap opera:** *un feuilleton télévisé*; **the ratings:** *le taux d'audience*; **accountable to:** *responsable devant*

The home page of the BBC (radio and television)
liennathan.fr/g9ev35

(The home page of *The Observer*)
liennathan.fr/r8n53d

(The home page of *The Times*)
liennathan.fr/56zf5x

(The home page of *The Economist*)
liennathan.fr/736mwv

(The home page of *The Guardian*)
liennathan.fr/2r5nc2

(The home page of *The New Statesman*)
liennathan.fr/i8ub22

(The home page of *The Independent*)
liennathan.fr/669ayq

CONTROVERSIAL ISSUES

How independent is the British press?

Because newspapers want to make a profit and wage savage price wars* against one another, their first aim is to attract readers, not to educate or really inform them. This is compounded* by the fact that the ownership of newspapers is concentrated in the hands of a few press barons* (e.g. Rupert Murdoch's News International, which owns *The Times, The Sunday Times* and *The Sun*), which leads to uniformity of point of view. Newspapers rarely challenge mainstream ideas*: instead, they encourage the popular avidity for sex (with for instance the Page Three girl*, the photograph of a topless female model which, until 2013, appeared on page 3 of *The Sun*), scandal, gossip and sensational news, also known as sleaze. Junk journalism* has now become the norm. Britain is puritanical, so that many of the sex scandals which the gutter press loves can cause the downfall of any politician, another instance of the enormous power of the press in Britain.

a price war: *une guerre des prix*; **compounded:** *aggravé*; **a press baron:** *un baron de la presse*; **mainstream ideas:** *les idées dominantes*; **the page three girl:** *la photo de pin up en page trois*; **junk journalism:** *le journalisme de mauvaise qualité*

13 BRITAIN AND EUROPE

A few dates

1957: The Treaty of Rome creates The European Economic Community (France, West Germany, Italy, The Netherlands, Belgium, Luxembourg).

1961-1967: Britain twice applies for membership of the EEC, a proposal twice vetoed by General De Gaulle.

1973: The UK joins the EEC, a decision confirmed by referendum two years later.

1986: The Single European Act creates the Single Market, that is to say free trade within EEC countries.

1990: Britain enters the EMS (European Monetary System), linking the pound with European currencies*, but has to withdraw* two years later because of the declining value of the pound.

1993: The EEC becomes the European Union. The UK ratifies the Maastricht Treaty (for closer political, economic and legal cooperation) but opts out* of the Social Chapter* (which relates to social policy) in order to avoid EU regulations on the rights of workers.

1997: Labour's landslide victory*. Tony Blair, a pro-European who had promised to put Britain "at the heart of Europe", takes a number of important decisions.

– In **1997**, Britain signs the Social Chapter (thus introducing a minimum wage in Britain).

– In **2000**, the United Kingdom adopts the European Convention on Human Rights*, which means that European law now takes precedence over British law.

– In **2005**, Britain votes in favour of enlargement which, it believes, might work against closer political integration.

2015: David Cameron promises an in/out referendum before 2017.

2016: A referendum on the UK's membership of the EU is held. Leave wins with 51.9% of the votes.

2017 (March)**:** Theresa May notifies the European Council of the UK's intention to leave the EU. The deal she negotiates with the EU will later be rejected by Parliament.

2019-2020: After three years of political instability, Boris Johnson is elected Prime Minister and succeeds in getting Parliament to accept his Brexit deal. Brexit becomes official on January 31 2020, but trade deals will be negotiated during a transition period.

There have always been strong anti-European feelings in Britain (fuelled by a Europhobic popular press), which has always preferred its loose economic and cultural links with the Commonwealth to political ties with Europe. Brexit results from years of distrust of EU policies, considered by many as responsible for most of the problems of the UK.

a currency: *une monnaie*; **to withdraw:** *se retirer*; **to opt out:** *choisir de ne pas participer à*; **the Social Chapter:** *la charte sociale, le chapitre social du traité de Maastricht*; **a landslide victory:** *une victoire écrasante*; **the European Convention on Human Rights:** *la Convention européenne des droits de l'homme*

CONTROVERSIAL ISSUES

Should European integration be strengthened?

Here are some of the major arguments advanced for and against staying in the EU in the months leading to Brexit.

LEAVE	STAY
– It will be easier for the UK to control immigration. With free labour movement within the EU, migrants have flooded Britain. Lax* border controls in other EU countries allow illegal immigrants and terrorists to enter the UK. – Leave would allow the UK to negotiate tailor-made* trade links with countries such as China or Russia. – The UK would save billions if it no longer contributed to the EU budget. – It would allow the UK to rebuild its ties with the Commonwealth and strengthen the Special Relationship with the United States. – London will remain a major financial centre. – The UK's courts would be sovereign again and its laws no longer be superseded* by those of the EU Court of Justice. – The UK's Parliament will regain its sovereignty and no longer be subservient to* the bureaucrats of Brussels. – The UK might lose its cultural identity if it remained in the EU.	– With Brexit, border controls might move from Calais to Dover. – 44% of the UK's exports are to Europe, bringing some £400 billions a year – exports would face barriers with Brexit. – Immigration is good for Britain, bringing skills and productivity. Immigrants pay more in tax than they use in public services. – In a globalising world, the UK's interests are best served if it remains in the EU and works closer with other countries rather than isolate itself. – In terms of defence, and in a world marked by terrorism and uncertainty, the UK will be safer inside the EU, with close allies. It might lose global clout* if it leaves the EU. – Many banks will re-locate on the continent. – Many jobs are linked to the EU, in the financial sector in particular. – EU regulations have improved life and protected consumers. – What will happen to the border between the Republic of Ireland and Northern Ireland in terms of both trade and the free movement of people?

lax: *négligent, relâché*; **tailor-made:** *sur mesure*; **supersede:** *remplacer*; **subservient to:** *soumis à*; **cout:** *influence, poids*

(The official site of the European Union)
liennathan.fr/8m7z4w

14 IRELAND

MAJOR DATES IN THE HISTORY OF IRELAND

▪ Conquests

432: Saint Patrick brings Christianity to Ireland, previously a Celtic country.
795: Viking invasions
12th century: the Anglo-Normans conquer Ireland. Henry II, the British king, becomes Lord of Ireland. A parliament is established in Dublin.

▪ Under English domination

1541: Henry VIII brings the reformation to Ireland and is confirmed as King of Ireland by the Irish Parliament. English Protestants are sent to Ireland and colonise it. However, the country remains essentially Catholic.
1594-1603: Irish Catholic rebellion led by the Earl of Tyrone. It is crushed*.
17th century: The best land is given to English settlers*, thus ensuring that the country remains in British hands. It is the beginning of the Plantation Policy*.

1649: Cromwell crushes* an Irish rebellion, with massacres and further confiscation of land.
1690: The Catholic James II, having lost his throne after the Glorious Revolution, tries to recover it with the help of France and Ireland. He is defeated by William of Orange at the Battle of the Boyne.
18th century: Further laws restrict the rights* of Catholics. Most of the land is owned by British landlords*, called "absentee landlords" because they live in Britain and employ poor Irish tenants* to work the land.
1795: The Orange Order* is created, with the aim of maintaining Protestant domination over Ireland.
1800: Act of Union: Great Britain and Ireland become the United Kingdom. The Irish Parliament is abolished; Ireland ceases to be a 'colony' and sends MPs to Westminster.
1829: Roman Catholic Emancipation Act: Catholics are given the same rights as Protestants. But they represent a much poorer part of the population.
1845-1849: The Great Famine (due to the failure of the potato crop) leads to the death of over a million Irishmen and to massive emigration, mainly to the United States. In the second half of the century, poverty leads to the creation of several organizations to defend tenants*' rights and nationalism.

a currency: *une monnaie*; **to withdraw:** *se retirer*; **to opt out:** *choisir de ne pas participer à*; **the Social Chapter:** *la charte sociale, le chapitre social du traité de Maastricht*; **a landslide victory:** *une victoire écrasante*; **the European Convention on Human Rights:** *la Convention européenne des droits de l'homme*

Towards independence

1873: Home Rule* League created by Parnell to try and gain self-government. Until 1916, there is rising tension between the nationalists, who want to get Home Rule, and the Protestants, who want to remain within the United Kingdom.
1916: Easter Rising*: a rebellion by Irish Republicans is put down* by the British army.
1918: The nationalist Party (Sinn Féin), led by de Valera, wins the majority of Irish seats at the election. They proclaim a Republic, with de Valera as President.
1919: Creation of the Irish Republican Army (IRA)
1921: Anglo-Irish Treaty: division of Ireland into Ulster (mainly Protestant) remaining part of the United Kingdom with its own parliament at Stormont, and the Irish Free State, a British dominion with full self-government rights.
1937: The Irish Free State becomes a sovereign state, Eire.
1947: Eire becomes the Republic of Ireland. It leaves the Commonwealth in 1949.

The Republic of Ireland has a Parliament with two chambers, the Dail (with elected members) and the Seanad (Senate). A President is directly elected for 7 years. He/she chooses the Prime Minister.

1973: Ireland joins the EEC and becomes increasingly prosperous.
1983: An amendment to the constitution is the basis for strict anti-abortion laws.
1985: Anglo-Irish agreement gives the Republic of Ireland a consultative role in the government of Northern Ireland.
1991: Ireland joins the European Union.
1997: Divorce becomes legal under certain circumstances.
2002: The euro becomes the national currency. Voters reject the government's attempt to further tighten* anti-abortion laws.
2009: Ireland votes in favour of the EU's Lisbon Treaty.
2008-10: Global financial crisis leads to recession and high unemployment. An EU/IMF bailout* means four years of spending cuts and high taxes.
2013: Abortion is allowed under limited circumstances.
2015: Same-sex marriage is approved by referendum.
2018: Abortion is legalised
2020: Sinn Fein takes the largest number of first-choice votes in the general election.

Home Rule: *l'autonomie*; **a rising:** *un soulèvement*; **to put down:** *réprimer*; **tighten:** *renforcer*; **bailout:** *aide financière, renflouement*

(Ireland timeline)
liennathan.fr/8dy2m4

Northern Ireland

1968: Beginning of «The Troubles», years of tension and riots* between the Protestant and Catholic communities in Ulster. The Protestants want to remain in the UK, the Catholics want Ulster to be reunited with the Republic of Ireland. Each community develops para-military organisations (the IRA - Irish Republican Army - for the Catholics, the UVF - Ulster Volunteer Force - for the Protestants) which commit acts of terrorism. Years of violence follow, with bombings, riots and assassinations.

Nationalists = the Catholics who want Northern Ireland reunited with the Republic of Ireland.
The word 'Republican' applies to the more intransigent Nationalists.
Unionists = the Protestants who want Northern Ireland to remain part of the United Kingdom.
The word '**Loyalists**' refers to the more hardline Unionists.
Orangemen* belong to the Orange Order (the name comes from William of Orange), an organisation created in 1795 to protect Protestantism in Northern Ireland.

1972: In the wake of 'Bloody Sunday' (when British soldiers open fire on marchers) the British government suspends the Irish parliament and applies far more repres-

sive policies. As a result the IRA launches a bombing campaign in both Ireland and England.
1985: Anglo-Irish agreement* between the British and Irish governments: it marks the beginning of closer cooperation.
1993-1994: Both the IRA and Loyalist groups declare a ceasefire.
1998: Peace agreements (Good Friday Agreement): a democratic assembly (Northern Ireland Assembly) and cross-party* cabinet are created to govern Northern Ireland.

The Good Friday Agreement (10 April 1998)

Terms :
Ireland shall not be one united country without the consent of a majority in Northern Ireland.
The people of Northern Ireland have the right to call themselves either Irish or British.
A multi party assembly will be elected to govern the community.
A north/south council will be set up to consider areas of mutual interest.
An Anglo-Irish council will be set up to consider areas of mutual interest.
All people shall have basic human rights, civil rights and equality.
Linguistic diversity is to be recognised – Irish to be taught in all schools.
Paramilitary groups are to be decommissioned within two years.
There will be a gradual reduction in the number of security forces deployed in Northern Ireland.
We must work towards having an unarmed police force.
Political prisoners are to be released providing the ceasefire is maintained.

A referendum held on 23rd May 1998 showed an overwhelming majority of the people of Ireland supporting the Good Friday Agreement.

«Northern Ireland Timeline» History on the Net © 2000-2021, Salem Media.

But the Peace Process* went through ups and downs, and the assembly was dissolved* at times as the two main sides could not agree on issues such as the decommissioning* of arms.
2007: Sinn Féin agrees to support the Northern Ireland police, which leads to the restoration of a devolved government* in Belfast, with power sharing between Protestants and Catholics.
2010: Hillsborough Castle Agreement: Britain will hand over control of the six counties' police and justice system to Northern Ireland.
2019: Abortion and gay marriage become legal.
2021: renewed tension in Belfast and other cities about the post-Brexit trading rules. The Democratic Unionist Party in particular strongly opposes the new border for goods between Northern Ireland and mainland Britain.

Main parties
UUP (Ulster (Official) Unionist Party): a Protestant party with close ties to the Conservative Party on the mainland. They want Ulster to remain part of the United Kingdom
DUP, Ulster Democratic Unionist Party: a more hardline Loyalist party led by the Reverend Ian Paisley.
SDLP (Social Democratic and Labour Party): A nationalist party in favour of achieving unity with the Republic of Ireland through constitutional means.
Sinn Féin: A nationalist party (the name means "we ourselves"), which fought for a united Ireland at the beginning of the XXth century. Linked with the IRA, it used to advocate* violent action, but has recently turned to political and constitutional forms of action.

a riot: *une émeute*; **Orangemen:** *Orangistes*; **an agreement:** *une entente, des accords*; **closer cooperation:** *une coopération plus étroite*; **cross-party:** *ayant des membres de tous les partis*; **the Peace Process:** *le processus de paix*; **to dissolve:** *dissoudre*; **to decommission:** *retirer de la circulation*; **a devolved government:** *un gouvernement indépendant*; **bailout:** *aide financière, renflouement*; **to advocate:** *recommander, être partisan de*

(The official site of the Northern Ireland Assembly)
liennathan.fr/58cvn6

15 BRITISH AND IRISH LITERATURE: MAJOR TRENDS AND WRITERS

MEDIEVAL LITERATURE (UNTIL 1509)

▪ English medieval literature was influenced by the continent after the Norman Conquest, and Celtic legends and Northern sagas (e.g. *Beowulf*) gave way to **romances*** (chivalry*, courtly love*, honour and courage). Among the best examples are *Sir Gawain and the Green Knight* (1375-1400) and *Le Morte d'Arthur* (about King Arthur and the Knights of the Round Table*.)

▪ An English form of theatre appeared with
– **Mystery plays*** (short plays inspired by the Bible)
– **Miracle plays*** (based on the lives of the saints)
– **Morality plays*** (in which the characters are allegories of vices and virtues).
e.g. *Everyman*
But the best-known medieval writer is **Geoffrey Chaucer**, with his *Canterbury Tales* (1386-1400), a series of tales told by pilgrims* on their way to Canterbury. The pilgrims represent the diversity of society (a miller, a monk, a widow, a prioress…) and their stories reflect the changing values of the time.

a romance: *un roman de chevalerie*; **chivalry:** *la chevalerie*; **courtly love:** *l'amour courtois*; **the Knights of the Round Table:** *les chevaliers de la Table ronde*; **a mystery play:** *un mystère*; **a miracle play:** *un miracle*; **a morality play:** *une moralité*; **a pilgrim:** *un pèlerin*

THE RENAISSANCE (1509-1660)

The heyday of drama*

The theatre became hugely popular in the second half of the 16th century. Plays were mainly performed outside, in a court or inn, and attended by people from all classes. Thrust stages* made for a closer contact between actors and audience. Women's parts* were performed by young men, which led to a great deal of sexual ambiguity.

– Revenge tragedies* presented complex intrigues and bloody deeds* of revenge: for instance **Sackville** and **Norton**'s *Gorboduc* (1561) or **Webster**'s *The White Devil* (1611).

– **Christopher Marlowe**'s plays show hubristic* heroes searching for power and glory. e.g. *The Tragical History of Doctor Faustus* (1588)

– **Ben Jonson**'s plays are satires of the vices and follies* of his time (avarice, hypocrisy): e.g. *Volpone* (1606)

– **William Shakespeare**'s plays are far more complex and subtle. There are four main types:

• **History plays**, about the lives of 14th and 15th century English kings, with a didactic aim*: to glorify the past of England, show the virtues of a good king and the need for authority to avoid civil war. e.g. *Richard II* (1595), *Richard III* (1593), *Henry V* (1599).

• **Comedies:** Some early comedies are based on misunderstanding*, mistaken identity and farce. e.g. *The Comedy of Errors* (1594), *The Merry Wives of Windsor* (1598). Shakespeare's later comedies are romantic comedies, also based on disguise and mistaken identity, but with a more serious reflection upon love. e.g. *As You Like It* (1600), *Twelfth Night* (1601), *A Midsummer Night's Dream* (1595).

• **Tragedies:** Shakespeare's great tragedies describe flawed* heroes who are the victims of their own ambition (*Macbeth*, 1606), jealousy (*Othello*, 1604), blindness (*King Lear*, 1606), and indecisiveness* (*Hamlet*, 1601). The initial error leads to a series of human and cosmic catastrophes and to the hero's torment and death.

• **Romances:** Shakespeare's last plays are less sombre and are based on forgiveness* for past wrongs and the reunion of parents and children. e.g. *Pericles* (1607), *The Winter's Tale* (1609), *The Tempest* (1611).

Poetry

The most popular form of poetry in the second half of the 16th century was the **sonnet**, adapted from Petrarch. They sung the joys and pains of platonic love* or developed *the carpe diem* theme. e.g. the sonnets of **Sidney** and **Spenser**.

Shakespeare's *Sonnets* (1609) are far more personal and original, some addressed to a young man, others to a lady.

In the first half of the 17th century, the group of **Metaphysical poets**, whose main representative is **John Donne**, wrote intellectual poems, both sensual and religious, based on reasoning and striking unexpected metaphors, called conceits.

But the end of the Renaissance is dominated by the figure of **John Milton**, a staunch* Puritan, whose main work, *Paradise Lost*, is a long epic* about Satan's rebellion and the fall of man.

the heyday of drama: *l'âge d'or du théâtre*; **a thrust stage:** *une scène qui avance au milieu du public*; **women's parts:** *les rôles féminins*; **a revenge tragedy:** *une tragédie de la vengeance*; **a bloody deed:** *un acte sanglant*; **hubristic:** *à l'orgueil démesuré*; **folly:** *la sottise*; **a didactic aim:** *un but didactique*; **misunderstanding:** *la méprise*; **flawed:** *imparfait*; **indecisiveness:** *l'irrésolution*; **forgiveness:** *le pardon*; **platonic love:** *l'amour platonique*; **staunch:** *loyal, sincère*; **an epic:** *une épopée*

THE RESTORATION AND THE EARLY 18TH CENTURY (1660-1740)

Restoration theatre

The theatres, which had been closed during the Commonwealth, reopened during the Restoration and drama became a favourite court entertainment. There were **heroic plays*** about love and honour (those of **Dryden**, for example), **tragedies** showing a respect for the three unities of classical drama (**Dryden**'s *All For Love*, 1678), and **comedies of manners***.

The latter (e.g. **Congreve**'s *The Way of the World*, 1700; **Farquhar**'s *The Beaux' Stratagem*, 1707; and later in the 18th century, **Goldsmith**'s *She Stoops to Conquer*, 1773 and **Sheridan**'s *The School for Scandal*, 1777) make use of wit* and humour to satirize* the manners of their time.

The age of reason

A reaction against the religious and political divisions of the early 17th century set in* during the Restoration, and until the mid 18th century, literature was dominated by the need for balance*, dignity, rationality and tolerance. All forms of excess were condemned through satire (in the poetry of **Dryden** and **Pope**), and dark irony (for instance in **Swift**'s *Gulliver's Travels*, 1726).

a heroic play: *une tragédie héroïque*; **a comedy of manners:** *une comédie de mœurs*; **wit:** *l'esprit*; **to satirize:** *faire la satire de*; **to set in:** *survenir, s'installer*; **balance:** *l'équilibre*

THE SECOND HALF OF THE 18TH CENTURY (1740-1790)

The rise of the novel

Although **Aphra Behn** had already written tales and a philosophical novel (*Oroonoko*, 1688), as well as plays in the late 17th century, it is mainly the rise of the middle-class* in the 18th century which led to the birth of a new genre, the novel, depicting the society of the time while aiming at both entertaining* and reforming the readers. Defoe's novels deal with the attempt to survive in difficult circumstances (*Robinson Crusoe*, 1719). **Richardson**'s novels are **epistolary*** and portray* exemplary, virtuous heroines who are the victims of libertines (*Clarissa*, 1747-48). **Fielding**'s novels are **picaresque**: as the hero travels, he moves from innocence to experience as he meets with hypocrisy and greed*, but also genuine instances of charity and love. As for **Sterne**'s works (*Tristram Shandy*, 1760-67), they are sentimental and **metafictional works*** which already parody the conventions of the novel.

■ **Towards sensibility**

The second half of the 18th century is marked by a spirit of sensibility present in
– poetry: melancholy and gloomy settings* in the poetry of **Gray** and **Collins**; picturesque* nature in the poems of **Thomson** and **Cowper**.
– the novel: set amid wild nature, **Gothic novels*** explore the workings* of fear within the sensitive minds of innocent heroines who are the victims of wicked relatives and locked up in terrifying castles and abbeys (**Mrs Radcliffe**, *The Mysteries of Udolpho*, 1794; **Mary Shelley**'s *Frankenstein*, 1818, about the creation of a supernatural monster by a scientist).

the middle-class: *la bourgeoisie*; **to entertain:** *divertir*; **epistolary:** *épistolaire*; **to portray:** *peindre*; **greed:** *la cupidité*; **a metafictional work:** *une œuvre de métafiction*; **a gloomy setting:** *un cadre lugubre*; **picturesque:** *pittoresque*; **a Gothic novel:** *un roman gothique*; **the workings:** *le mécanisme*

THE ROMANTIC AGE (1780-1837)

■ A **pre-romantic** poet: **William Blake**. A rebel against all social, political and religious constraints*, William Blake was a visionary and prophetic poet. (*Songs of Innocence*, 1789; *Songs of Experience*, 1794).

■ The **first generation** of Romantic poets. **Wordsworth**'s poetry celebrates the importance of nature to reach transcendental insight* (*The Prelude*, 1805). **Coleridge**'s poetry focuses more on the strange and the supernatural, on the way poetic imagination can transform reality (*The Rime of the Ancient Mariner*, 1798).

■ The **second generation** of Romantic poets. Although by nature a neo-classicist who made use of satire and wit, **Byron** created melancholy, restless* and wandering* heroes who embodied* the Romantic rebels (*Childe Harold's Pilgrimage*, 1812). An idealist and a rebel, **Shelley** rejected all conventions and institutions in his highly lyrical poetry (*Prometheus Unbound*, 1820). The poetry of **Keats** tries to reconcile the world of transience* and death and the eternal world of beauty and art (*Odes*, 1820).

■ **The novel**

Although written in the first two decades of the 19th century, **Jane Austen**'s **novels of manners** partake* more of the spirit of the 18th century with their detached,

ironic portrayal of the gentry* and their emphasis on control and morality (*Pride and Prejudice*, 1813, *Emma*, 1816).
Walter Scott's **historical romances** are set in the past of Scotland during periods of transition when the heroes have to make a choice between idealism and the changing social order (*Waverley*, 1814).

a constraint: *une contrainte*; **insight:** *la vision, la compréhension*; **restless:** *qui ne tient pas en place*; **wandering:** *errant*; **to embody:** *incarner*; **transience:** *l'éphémère*; **to partake of:** *tenir de*; **the gentry:** *la petite noblesse*

THE VICTORIAN AGE (1837-1901)

The contradictions of the age (religious interrogations and philistinism, philanthropy and complacency*) are reflected in both poetry and the novel.

- The **poetry** of **Tennyson** and **Arnold** conveys the loneliness and anxiety of man in a changing universe. **Browning** makes use of **dramatic monologues** which allow us to hear the voices of troubled and complex minds.

- **The Victorian novel**

The Victorians loved reading. Many novels were published serially* in magazines, the readers discovering the new instalment* each month. They enjoyed a good plot, and a lot of sentiment, as well as mystery and suspense.
This is to be found in
– The tales of violent, passionate love written by **the Brontë sisters** (Charlotte Brontë, *Jane Eyre*, 1847; Emily Brontë, *Wuthering Heights*, 1847).
– **Charles Dickens**'s novels, which use both pathos* and humour to condemn the social evils of his time and reform society (*Oliver Twist*, 1838; *Great Expectations*, 1861).
– **Thackeray**'s novels of manners reflect his disillusionment about human nature and condemn the selfishness, vanity and corruption of the upper classes (*Vanity Fair*, 1848).
– **George Eliot**'s novels are concerned with the moral and spiritual development of heroines and the way their character is shaped by their environment (rural and provincial life in her novels) (*The Mill on the Floss*, 1860).
– The realistic novels of such novelists as **Mrs Gaskell** (*North and South*, 1855) deal with the social problems of the time, the poor working conditions, utilitarianism* or the abyss* which separates the rich from the poor.

At the end of the century, increased anxiety and scepticism and a reaction against the complacency of the earlier generation led to different trends*:
– **Aestheticism*** and the art for art's sake movement* (**Wilde**'s *The Picture of Dorian Gray*, 1891). Oscar Wilde also wrote witty **comedies of manners** which criticize conventional Victorian morality and values (*The Importance of Being Earnest*, 1895).

– **Exoticism** and **novels of adventure**: **Kipling**'s portrayal of Indian life and of imperialism in his novels (*Kim*, 1901), stories and poetry; **Stevenson**'s works (*Dr Jekyll and Mr Hyde*, 1886, a Gothic tale about a dual* personality).
– **Nonsense literature**: The British love of eccentricity and the flexibility of the English language, which lends itself* to puns and wordplay*, are reflected in this type of literature. (**Lewis Carroll**, *Alice's Adventures in Wonderland*, 1865).
– The dark **naturalism** of **Hardy**'s novels, whose characters are the victims of their economic and social environment and mere puppets* in the hands of an ironic and indifferent fate* (*Tess of the D'Urbervilles*, 1891).

complacency: *la suffisance*; **serially:** *en feuilleton*; **an instalment:** *un épisode*; **pathos:** *le pathétique*; **utilitarianism:** *l'utilitarisme*; **an abyss:** *un fossé, un gouffre*; **a trend:** *une tendance, un mouvement*; **aestheticism:** *l'esthétisme*; **the art for art's sake movement:** *le mouvement de l'art pour l'art*; **dual:** *double*; **to lend itself to:** *se prêter à*; **a pun, wordplay:** *un jeu de mots*; **a puppet:** *une marionnette*; **fate:** *la fatalité*

THE EARLY 20TH CENTURY (1901-1945)

The shock and horror of the Great War, the depression of the thirties, the rise of Nazi Germany and the gradual loss of the Empire provided a background of gloom and anxiety which was reflected in literature. Thanks to Freud's works, the emphasis was increasingly laid* on the inner life*.

Poetic voices

– The **War Poets** denounced the absurdity and meaninglessness of the conflict (**Wilfred Owen, Siegfried Sassoon, Edward Thomas**).
– **W.B. Yeats** is the poet of the **Irish Renaissance**. He used symbolism and Irish folklore in his early poetry, then became more direct in his defence of Irish nationalism.
– **T.S. Eliot** is a **modernist** poet who used collage, multiple voices, clear images and a network* of allusions to convey* the chaos, fragmentation and loss of faith* of modern society (*The Waste Land*, 1922).
– The **Thirties poets**: the poetry of **W.H. Auden, Louis MacNeice** and **Stephen Spender** is concerned with the social and political problems of the time: social changes, the Spanish Civil War, the rise of Fascism.
– The Welsh poet **Dylan Thomas** celebrates the natural world and the cycles of life and death in lyrical, dense and inventive poetry.

The novel

– **Conrad**'s novels are mostly set in exotic countries and explore the inner tensions and moral courage of lonely characters in the face of extreme danger. His novels are modernist, too, in their experimentation with multiple points of view and time dislocations (*Lord Jim*, 1900).
– **E.M. Forster**, a member of the **Bloomsbury Group**, rejected conventions and taboos to celebrate friendship and loyalty (*A Passage to India*, 1924).

– **D.H. Lawrence**'s characters are torn between* nature and culture, between instincts and social and moral conventions. Only by freeing himself sexually and emotionally can man find his wholeness again (*Women in Love*, 1920).
– **Virginia Woolf** (*To the Lighthouse*, 1927) and **James Joyce** (*Ulysses*, 1922) tried to convey **stream of consciousness***, the flow of thoughts, impressions and feelings which occurs at pre-speech* level.
– **Graham Greene**'s heroes often transgress but are tormented beings whose knowledge of good and evil eventually leads them to salvation* (*The Power and the Glory*, 1940).
– The **dystopias*** of **Huxley** (*Brave New World*, 1932) and **Orwell** (*1984*, 1948) convey the fear of totalitarianism.

▪ The Theatre

– The **Irish Renaissance**, a movement linked to the fight for independence: **Synge** (*The Playboy of the Western World*, 1907), **O'Casey** (*Juno and the Paycock*, 1924).
– **George Bernard Shaw**'s plays are didactic, criticizing conventional Victorian values and exploring social concerns with wit and originality in his **problem plays**.

> **to lay the emphasis on:** *mettre l'accent sur*; **the inner life:** *la vie intérieure*; **a network:** *un réseau*; **to convey:** *transmettre*; **the loss of faith:** *la perte de la foi*; **torn between:** *tiraillé entre*; **stream of consciousness:** *le flux de la conscience*; **pre-speech:** *avant la parole*; **salvation:** *le salut*; **a dystopia:** *une dystopie*

AFTER WORLD WAR II (1945-2005)

▪ Poetry

– Reacting against the politically committed* poetry of the thirties, **John Betjeman** and **Philip Larkin** wrote more detached, ironic and terse* verse combining criticism and compassion.
– **Ted Hughes**' s poetry explores the beauty and violence of the natural world.
– **Seamus Heaney**, an Irish poet, celebrates the Irish land and the links between memory, the past and the present "Troubles" in northern Ireland.
– The poetry of **Geoffrey Hill** (1932-2016) is about human suffering and man's relation to both history and landscape (*Mercian Hymns*, 1971).

▪ Fiction

– Social and political concerns appear in the works of the so-called **Angry Young Men*** (**Kingsley Amis**, **John Braine**, **Alan Sillitoe**: *The Loneliness of the Long-Distance Runner*, 1959), who criticize the class system of post-war Britain. The **campus novels*** of **David Lodge** and **Malcolm Bradbury** satirize the academic world.
– Experimentation with point of view and technique is to be found in the novels of Samuel Beckett and in **Lawrence Durrell**'s *Alexandria Quartet*, four novels presenting the same events from four different points of view. **John Fowles** plays with the

conventions of the novel, using pastiche, parody and multiple endings (*The French Lieutenant's Woman*, 1969).
– **William Golding** is a moralist, who explores the darkness, savagery and irrationality in the heart of man (*Lord of the Flies*, 1954).
The symbolic novels of **Iris Murdoch** focus on philosophical and intellectual questions (*The Sandcastle*, 1957). Also a moralist, **Anthony Burgess** is concerned with good and evil, free will* and determinism (*A Clockwork Orange*, 1962).
– The novels of **Doris Lessing** (1919-2013) show idealistic and committed heroines who try to free themselves from the constraints of society (*The Golden Notebook*, 1962).
– The novels of **Graham Swift** explore the past – both personal and collective – and the relationship between different generations (*Waterland*, 1984).
Kazuo Ishiguro's characters are lonely and rigid characters, obsessed by duty, but full of illusions and regrets (*The Remains of the Day*, 1989).
– **Magic Realism** (an alliance of realism, fantasy and the supernatural) is to be found in the works of **Salman Rushdie** (*Midnight's Children*, 1981, a tale about modern India) and **Angela Carter** (*The Bloody Chamber*, 1979, a rewriting of some of Perrault's tales).
– The dark, violent side of modern society is reflected in the novels of **Martin Amis** (*London Fields*, 1989), while those of Ian McEwan explore cruelty, violence and tragedy (*Atonement*, 2001).
– **Jonathan Coe** writes scathing satires on the society of his time (*What a Carve Up!*, 1994, about the Thatcher years).
– Several writers with a multicultural background have written about their experience between two cultures : **Hanif Kureishi** (*The Buddha of Suburbia*, 1990), **Monica Ali** (Brick Lane, 2003), **Zadie Smith** (*On Beauty*, 2005), **Bernardine Evaristo** (*Girl, Woman, Other*, 2018).

▪ The Theatre

– The Angry Young Men and their working class realism, also called **kitchen sink drama** (**John Osborne, John Arden, Arnold Wesker**).
– The **theatre of the absurd*** (failures, marginal characters in a hostile or meaningless world): **Samuel Beckett** (*Waiting for Godot*, 1953), **Harold Pinter** (*The Dumb Waiter*, 1960).
– The **philosophical farces** of **Tom Stoppard** analyse moral, intellectual and artistic issues through wit and comedy (*Rosencrantz and Guildenstern are Dead*, 1966).
– The **theatre of cruelty***: the Marxist plays of **Edward Bond** explore violence in modern society (*Saved*, 1965).
– The plays of Brian Friel (*Translations*, 1980), who wrote about the people of County Donegal and the divisions of Ireland.

committed: *engagé*; **terse:** *concis*; **Angry Young Men:** *jeunes gens en colère*; **a campus novel:** *un roman universitaire*; **free will:** *le libre arbitre*; **kitchen sink drama:** *le théâtre réaliste sur la misère des gens ordinaires*; **the theatre of the absurd:** *le théâtre de l'absurde*; **the theatre of cruelty:** *le théâtre de la cruauté*

16 BRITISH PAINTING: MAJOR MOVEMENTS AND ARTISTS

THE ELIZABETHAN AGE

In the late 16th century, the art of miniature flourished* in England and was used mainly to portray Queen Elizabeth I, some courtiers*, and some types or humours* such as melancholy. They made extensive use of symbolism.
The best-known miniature painters of the time were **Nicholas Hilliard** and **Isaac Oliver**.

| **to flourish:** *se développer*; **a courtier:** *un courtisan*; **a humour:** *une humeur*

THE 17TH CENTURY

Painting became very popular at court and many foreign painters settled in London, bringing large-scale* portraits into fashion.
Van Dyck in particular painted refined and elegant portraits of Charles I and his family and of Cavalier* followers*.
After the Restoration, **Sir Peter Lely** carried over the genre with fashionable court portraits.

| **large-scale:** *grand format*; **a Cavalier:** *un royaliste, partisan de Charles Ier*; **a follower:** *un partisan*

THE 18TH CENTURY

Although allegorical and mythological Baroque paintings were fashionable in the early 18th century, a more British type of painting began to achieve recognition*.

■ **Conversation pieces*** appeared around 1720. A conversation-piece is a picture representing a whole group (a family or friends), in informal poses and usually against a background showing their estate*. Such paintings were social statements* and therefore very popular with the gentry* and the rising middle-class*.

■ **Hogarth's satires of society**
Although **Hogarth** also painted conversation pieces, he is best remembered for paintings forming series, with a clear moral message. Thus series like 'The Harlot*'s Progress' or 'Marriage à la Mode' are warnings against the temptations and corruption of city life and the dangers of a marriage of convenience*. Hogarth produced engravings* of his paintings, thus helping to make painting a more popular art.

■ **Portrait painting**
Sir Joshua Reynolds was a successful portrait painter, who gave both solidity and liveliness to his subjects. **Thomas Gainsborough**'s portraits are more delicate, natural and

informal, announcing the rise of sentimentalism in the second half of the 18th century. His portraits are also often given a pastoral background so that figures and landscapes seem integrated.

to achieve recognition: *être reconnu*; **a conversation piece:** *un tableau de genre*; **an estate:** *une propriété, un domaine*; **a social statement:** *une affirmation de son statut social*; **the gentry:** *la petite noblesse*; **the middle-class:** *la bourgeoisie*; **a harlot:** *une prostituée*; **a marriage of convenience:** *un mariage de convenance*; **an engraving:** *une gravure*

THE ROMANTIC AGE

At the end of the 18th century and in the early 19th century, romanticism was reflected in a new interest in the picturesque* and the sublime.

Imaginative and dramatic paintings

In keeping with* the Gothic movement in literature, **Henry Fuseli** painted sensational subjects (depicting terror or cruelty) often inspired by literature.
The poet **William Blake** was also a painter and engraver, whose illuminated books and watercolours* illustrate his visionary views with great intensity and urgency.

Landscape painting

Paintings of picturesque nature (hills, mountains, waterfalls) became increasingly popular in the second half of the 18th century. As the century came to a close, the picturesque gave way to the sublime - harsh and wild Alpine scenes, for instance - as the ideal landscape to cause emotion and terror. The name of **John Constable** is associated with paintings of the Stour Valley in Suffolk, with its farms and meadows. Concentrating on sky, light and atmosphere, Constable tried to convey a sense of movement within nature and of seasonal change. **Joseph Mallord Turner** too was interested in rendering the nuances of light but he preferred the more sublime scenery of lakes, sea and mountains, to which he lent vaporous* luminosity or dynamic movement.

the picturesque: *le pittoresque*; **in keeping with:** *en rapport avec*; **a watercolour:** *une aquarelle*; **vaporous:** *vaporeux*

THE VICTORIAN AGE

Turner kept painting until 1851 and remained highly influential. Two other tendencies characterize Victorian painting.

Genre painting*

Genre painting, that is to say the portrayal of scenes from everyday life, was very popular in the 19th century. The Victorians were sentimental and particularly appreciated scenes with family, children and animals, but they were also very interested in historical scenes.

▪ The Pre-Raphaelites

The Pre-Raphaelite Brotherhood was a group of painters who wanted to recapture the simplicity and purity of art before Raphael, when it was in close contact with nature. They wanted to inspire and elevate people's minds by depicting* religious, moral and noble themes, and many of their paintings were inspired by literature and the Bible. Working at a time when the Chartist movement was at its height*, they also often dealt with social themes. They represented nature faithfully, sometimes with photographic precision, and made use of pure colours.
The main founders* and followers* were: **Dante Gabriel Rossetti**, **Edward Burne-Jones**, **William Holman Hunt**, **John Everett Millais** and **Ford Madox Brown**. **William Morris**, another Pre-Raphaelite, also created his own firm to design furniture and fabrics*, which led to the Arts and Crafts movement.

genre painting: *la peinture de genre, de mœurs*; **to depict:** *dépeindre*; **at its height:** *à son apogée*; **a founder:** *un fondateur*; **a follower:** *un disciple*; **a fabric:** *un tissu*

THE MODERN AGE: BEFORE WORLD WAR II

Several movements appeared in British painting in the first half of the 20th century, reflecting the currents of the time.

▪ The Camden Town Group

These painters (mainly **Walter Sickert**, **Augustus John** and **Spencer Gore**) were influenced by neo- and post-impressionism.

▪ The Bloomsbury Group

A number of painters (**Duncan Grant**, **Vanessa Bell**, **Roger Fry**) were part of the Bloomsbury group, around Virginia Woolf. Their works show the influence of Fauvism.

▪ Vorticism

The paintings of **Wyndham Lewis** depict the urban and industrial society of his time, in a style reminiscent of futurism.

▪ Abstraction

The movement is best reflected in the works of **Ben Nicholson**.

▪ Surrealism

Its main British representatives are **Paul Nash** and **Graham Sutherland**.

Outside any main trend, some highly original artists emerged.
– **Stanley Spencer**'s paintings of his native Berkshire village and of the war, reflect his mystical experience.
– As for **Francis Bacon**, he is perhaps the best-known 20th century British painter.

His favourite subjects are violent, distorted human bodies which seem fragmented or paralytic. Such expressionism conveys Bacon's vision of horror and despair.

THE MODERN AGE: AFTER WORLD WAR II

- **Pop Art**

David Hockney is best-known for his cool, precise and luminous paintings of interiors and swimming-pools, and for his strikingly economical portraits.
R.B. Kitaj's works are mainly large panoramas full of allusions to literature and visual art rather than popular culture.

- **Op Art**

Bridget Riley plays with geometric shapes and colours to create optical illusions.

- **Reflecting the angst* of modern life**

Lucien Freud specializes in paintings of the body with a merciless* depiction of human flesh. **Frank Auerbach** paints urban landscapes and portraits with thick layers* of paint creating an impression of violent movement.

- The influence of **Indian painting** can be felt in the works of **Howard Hodgkin**, with their vibrant colours and small scale*. Most of them are half-abstract and represent intensely remembered memories.

- **The modern age: Postmodernism**

In both art and literature postmodernists refuse the idea of any authoritative meaning and find various ways of undermining it such as the use of pastiche, parody, absurdity and the blurring of genres and traditional categories.

- In the 1990s, a number of artists like Damien Hirst created **Britart**, unconventional art which is meant to shock people, with, for instance, the use of dead animals.

angst: *l'angoisse existentielle*; **merciless:** *impitoyable*; **a layer:** *une couche*; **small scale:** *petit format*

17 THE BRITISH CINEMA

The British cinema has had a chequered history* in the face of constant competition from America but over the years has succeeded in forging its own identity and confirming a tradition of social realism. The most successful genres besides social realism have been comedy and period films*.
Here are the most important periods and movements:

to have a chequered history: *connaître des hauts et des bas*; **a period film:** *une adaptation d'œuvre littéraire en costumes d'époque*

THE 1930s

After a slump* in the 1920s, partly due to competition from Hollywood, protective measures were introduced in 1927 (a quota of British films had to be shown in cinemas) leading to a boom in the 1930s. This was when Alfred Hitchcock emerged as a leading director* and master of suspense and intrigue, with films such as *The Man Who Knew Too Much* (1934), *The 39 Steps* (1935), and *The Lady Vanishes* (1938), before he left for Hollywood. It was also during this decade that **The Documentary Film Movement** appeared. The best-known of these realist films is John Grierson's *Drifters* (1929) and *Night Mail* (1936). They mark the starting point of the realist tradition in Britain.

| **a slump:** *une crise*; **a director:** *un réalisateur*

WORLD WAR II AND THE 1940s

With inadequate financing, the British film industry focused on fewer films, mainly exploring the documentary technique and portraying the country at war, as with *In Which We Serve* (1942). Shakespeare adaptations, like Laurence Olivier's *Henry V* (1944) and *Hamlet* (1948), were also highly popular, as well as David Lean's *Brief Encounter* (1945) and his adaptations from Dickens (*Oliver Twist* (1948)).
In the late 1940s, the desire for entertainment after the sombre war years led to the "**Ealing Comedies**"* such as *Whisky Galore* (1948) or *Kind Hearts and Coronets* (1949), uniting realism and humour verging on* the absurd.
In the 1950s, the Hammer Horror studios began producing hugely popular films: *Dracula* (1958), *The Curse of Frankenstein* (1956).

| **an Ealing Comedy:** *une comédie tournée dans les studios d'Ealing*; **to verge on:** *friser, être au bord de*

BRITISH NEW WAVE OR "KITCHEN SINK REALISM"

Heralded* by the movement called "**Free Cinema**" (films portraying ordinary working-class people with sympathy and poetry), **British New Wave*** films focused on bold* social issues – sexuality, abortion, working class revolt – also mirrored in the works of the "Angry Young Men" in literature: *Room at the Top* (1959), *Look Back in Anger* (1959), *Saturday Night and Sunday Morning* (1960), *A Taste of Honey* (1961).

| **to herald:** *annoncer*; **British New Wave:** *la Nouvelle Vague du cinéma britannique*; **bold:** *audacieux*

THE 1960s

The 60s were a period of highly successful large-scale productions like David Lean's epic films* (*The Bridge on the River Kwai* (1957), *Lawrence of Arabia* (1962), *Doctor Zhivago* (1965), the James Bond movies, and spy films*.

| **an epic film:** *un film à grand spectacle*; **a spy film:** *un film d'espionnage*

THE 1970s AND 1980s

It was a period of recession and decline, although a few successful films where produced, like *The Go-Between* (1971), Stanley Kubrick's *A Clockwork Orange* (1971) and the humorous Monty Python films. Big budget films like *Chariots of Fire* (1981), *Gandhi* (1983), *Educating Rita* (1983), *A Passage to India* (1984) were also very popular. Produced with a small budget but highly original, Peter Greenaway's *The Draughtsman's Contract* is a complex mystery based on signs and codes.

THE 1990s

In the late 1980s and the 90s, there was a revival of film-making, which renewed the tradition of **social realism**, of committed films reflecting the social problems of Britain – poverty, racism, prejudice, unemployment. Many of them were overtly critical of Margaret Thatcher's policies, as in the films of Stephen Frears (*My Beautiful Launderette* (1985)), but the tradition has been carried on and is still successful. The social criticism is often treated with subtlety and humour: Mike Leigh (*Naked* (1993), *Secrets and Lies* (1995), *Vera Drake* (2004)), Ken Loach (*I, Daniel Blake* (2016)), Peter Cattaneo (*The Full Monty* (1998)), Stephen Daldry (*Billy Elliot* (2000)).
Very successful too were **romantic comedies** like *Four Weddings and a Funeral* (1994) or *Notting Hill* (1999), as well as successful **costume dramas** and **period films** – mostly adaptations of Shakespeare or of popular novels: Kenneth Branagh's *Henry V* (1998), James Ivory's *The Remains of the Day* (1994), Joe Wright's *Pride and Prejudice* (2005).

18 A FEW KEYWORDS

A

Archers, The; A very popular radio serial*, which has been running since 1951 and relates the life of a family of farmers in the imaginary village of Ambridge.
Aristocracy: Here are the main ranks and orders:

	Title	Wife	Hereditary or not
Peers	Duke	Duchess	+
	Marquess	Marchioness	+
	Earl/Countess	Countess	+
	Viscount	Viscountess	+
	Baron/Baroness	Baroness	+ or –

	Baronet (Sir...)	Lady...	+
	Knight (Sir.../Dame...)	Lady...	–
	Orders of chilvalry: Order of the Garter* Order of the Thistle* Order of the Bath* Order of the British Empire		–

Most honorary titles and awards are announced twice a year, on the Official Birthday of the Queen in June and on New Year's Day.

Ascot: A racecourse near Windsor, famous for Royal Ascot, a summer meeting attended by royalty and famous for its display* of fashion.

Ashes (the): An imaginary prize awarded to the country which wins a series of international cricket matches.

Auld Lang Syne: *see Hogmanay*

Authorized Version: The version of the Bible ordered by King James I and published in 1611. The poetry of its language has had a deep influence upon English literature.

a radio serial: *un feuilleton radiophonique*; **the Order of the Garter:** *l'Ordre de la Jarretière*; **the Order of the Thistle:** *l'Ordre du Chardon*; **the Order of the Bath:** *l'Ordre du Bain*; **a display:** *une parade, un étalage*

B

Bank holidays: The official public holidays. In England, they are: Christmas Day, Boxing Day (December 26th), New Year's Day, Good Friday*, Easter Monday*, May Day (the first Monday in May), late spring bank holiday (the last Monday in May), August bank holiday (the last Monday in August). If a bank holiday falls on a Saturday or a Sunday, the holiday is on the following Monday.
In Scotland, Easter Monday is not a bank holiday but January 2nd is.

Beer is the most popular alcoholic drink in Britain. Lager (often imported from the continent) is drunk cold, but the English tend to prefer ale, "warm beer" usually served around 12 degrees Celsius. Bitter is dark ale, with a strong flavour of hops*; stout is very strong dark ale (like Guinness).

Bingo*: a very popular game, mainly played by women in huge bingo halls.

Blimp (Colonel): Originally a cartoon character, he now stands for narrow-mindedness and the refusal of change.

Bloomsday: Bloomsday marks the day (16 June 1904) when the action of James Joyce's *Ulysses* takes place. It is celebrated in Dublin but also by lovers of Joyce all over the world.

Boat Race, the: A yearly race on the River Thames between the rowing teams* of the Universities of Oxford and Cambridge.

Booker Prize (Man): A prize awarded each year for the best British, Irish or Commonwealth novel.

Britannia: the personification of Britain, a woman with a helmet*, trident and shield*.

British Library: Britain's national library, and a copyright library (to which publishers must send a copy of every book they publish).

Bull, John: a personification of the typical Englishman: a plain, fat, kindly Englishman resembling a bulldog.

Good Friday: *le Vendredi saint*; **Easter Monday:** *le lundi de Pâques*; **hops:** *le houblon*; **bingo:** *le loto*; **a rowing team:** *une équipe d'aviron*; **a helmet:** *un casque*; **a shield:** *un bouclier*

C

Canary Wharf: The new district east of the City, on the banks of the Thames. It is, with the City, the centre of financial dealings for Britain, with banks, insurers and law firms.

Channel Islands, The: Jersey and Guernsey are not part of the United Kingdom and have their own government. But they are Crown dependencies, with a Lieutenant-Governor representing the sovereign.

Charities: Charities are voluntary, independent organizations which are active in the fields of poverty, education, religion, human rights, the care of animals, etc. Perhaps as a result of Victorian philanthropy, there is a strong tradition of supporting charities in Britain, with many volunteers and people buying in charity shops.

City, The: The financial district in London, where the Bank of England, the Stock Exchange* and many insurance companies can be found. It is also called the Square Mile.

Cockney: a Cockney is a working-class person from the east end of London; the word also refers to the way they speak (a Cockney accent).

Cool Britannia: A pun on Rule Britannia, the unofficial National Anthem, it refers to London as the capital of fashion, the arts and the media. (from the word "cool*").

Costa Book Awards: Formally Whitbread Awards, they are a set of literary prizes awarded every year for best novel, best first novel, best children's book, best poetry, best biography and best collection of short stories.

Cricket: A typically English game, played between two teams of eleven on a grass pitch*, with a wicket* at each end. The wickets consist of cross pieces of wood (bails) resting on three vertical stumps*. In one of the teams, a bowler* tries to hit the bails defended by the opposite team's batsman*, or to cause the batsman to hit the ball back in such a way that it can be caught before it touches the ground. The bowler's team is called the fielders; the batsmen's the batsmen. The latter's aim is to score runs, that is to say to run as many times as possible between the wickets (22 metres apart) before the ball is retrieved and returned. One of the best-known pitches is Lord's in North London. The game is very popular in Britain, where there are matches between counties, as well as all over the Commonwealth with test matches between Britain and Commonwealth countries. A match can last from one afternoon to three or even five days!

the Stock Exchange: *la Bourse*; **cool:** *super, génial*; **a pitch:** *un terrain*; **a wicket:** *un guichet*; **a stump:** *un piquet*; **a bowler:** *quelqu'un qui lance la balle*; **a batsman:** *un batteur*

D

Downing Street: the street in London where the Prime Minister and the Chancellor of the Exchequer live, at numbers 10 and 11 respectively. The words 'Downing Street' are often used metonymically for the Prime Minister (e.g. Downing Street confirmed today that...).

E

Edinburgh Festival, the: A festival of drama and music held every August in Edinburgh. It is also well-known for the Fringe*, that is to say all the unofficial plays, concerts and comedy shows performed during those weeks. There are many budding* performers who start their careers at the Edinburgh Festival.

Entente Cordiale: The Franco-British agreement signed in 1904.

Establishment: The word refers to the ruling class: the Queen and her family, the aristocracy, the Cabinet and the members of Parliament as well as the leading figures in the world of finance and diplomacy, and in the church.

fringe: *marginal*; **budding:** *en herbe*

F

Field sports: Hunting, fishing and shooting are called field sports, or blood sports since they involve the killing of animals. *See Hunting*

Footsie: The FTSE, or Financial Times Share* Index, which is published daily and gives the share value of the 100 largest British companies and gives an idea of how well the British share markets are doing.

a share: *une action (en bourse)*

G

Gaelic: The word refers to two Celtic languages still spoken in the West of Scotland and in Northern Ireland.

G8: Group of Eight, A group of eight of the richest countries in the world (Canada, France, Germany, Italy, Japan, Russia, the UK, the US). They meet regularly to discuss economic policies.

Gentleman's club: An old British institution, a Gentleman's club is a private and expensive club with a bar, a restaurant, a library and sometimes bedrooms, where people can relax, work and meet other members. Gentlemen's clubs are mostly for members of the Establishment, and many have members who are interested in specific fields (politics, literature...). Most clubs are still for male members only and new applicants are carefully vetted*.

Glastonbury: A town in Somerset, famous for a festival of rock music held there every summer.

Glyndebourne: The place near Brighton where an opera festival takes place every summer.

GMT: Greenwich Mean Time: the time at the 0° longitude meridian which passes through the Royal Observatory at Greenwich.

Guy Fawkes Night: On November 5, people celebrate the discovery of the Gunpowder Plot (a conspiracy to blow up the House of Lords and all the government to put a Catholic sovereign on the throne) by burning effigies of Guy Fawkes, the leader of the plot. There are bonfires* and fireworks* traditionally bought with money children have collected by asking for a "penny for the guy". It is also called "Bonfire Night".

to vet: *étudier le dossier de quelqu'un pour décider si on l'admet*; **a bonfire:** *un feu de joie*; **fireworks:** *un feud'artifice*

H

Hogmanay: the Scottish word for New Year's Eve, which is widely celebrated in Scotland. Auld Lang Syne is sung at midnight.

Should auld acquaintance be forgot,*
And never brought to mind*?
Should auld acquaintance be forgot,
And days of auld lang syne*?

Hunting: Fox-hunting*, a sport where the animal is pursued on horseback and killed by hounds*, was an old, popular sport among the aristocracy and landowners*. It was banned in 2005.

Should auld acquaintance be forgot: Should old acquaintances (friends) be forgotten; **to bring to mind:** *rappeler*; **auld lang syne:** old long ago; fox hunting: *la chasse au renard*; **a hound:** *un chien de meute*; **a landowner:** *propriétaire terrien*

J

Jingoism: extreme nationalism, often linked with anti-Europeanism.

L

Land of Hope and Glory: A highly patriotic song sung on the last night of the Proms. The music is by Elgar.

Lion and the unicorn, the: these two animals appear on the royal arms of Britain. The lion stands for England, the unicorn for Scotland.

M

Meals and food: The main traditional British meals are:
– Early morning tea: tea drunk before breakfast, often in bed
– Breakfast: a full English breakfast can include porridge, bacon and eggs, sausages, black pudding*, mushrooms, baked beans, tomatoes, sometimes even kippers* or haddock, not forgetting toast and marmalade.
– Elevenses: coffee or tea with biscuits around 11 a.m.
– Lunch: a sandwich or a meal
– Afternoon tea: tea, cakes and pastries; cream tea (= tea, and buttered scones with jam and cream)

– Dinner: a full meal, usually including "meat and two veg*"

– In the north of England and Scotland, High Tea sometimes replaces the evening meal. It is taken early (around six p.m.) and consists of a cooked dish or of sandwiches, followed by cakes, and the whole accompanied by tea.

British food is increasingly being influenced by a large variety of international ethnic food.

'Me' generation: A derogatory* term referring to the 1970s and 1980s, when many young people were seen as exclusively concerned with money and their own selves.

MI5: The former name (though it is still used) of the British Security Service, which deals with terrorism.

MI6: The former name (though still used) of the Secret Intelligence Service, which gathers information about foreign countries.

black pudding: *du boudin noir*; **a kipper:** *un hareng fumé*; **meat and two veg:** *une viande et deux légumes*; **derogatory:** *péjoratif*

N

National Lottery: Created in 1994, the National Lottery is hugely popular. It gives money to charities and cultural projects.

National Trust: an independent organisation to protect and preserve historic sites (castles, country houses, gardens...).

Non-U: Abbreviation of "non upper-class". The term is used for an accent (or behaviour) which is not distingué.

O

Orange Prize: A British literary prize given every year to a work of fiction written in English by a woman from any country in the world.

Oxbridge: A portmanteau word* referring to the universities of Oxford and Cambridge.

a portmanteau word: *un mot-valise*

P

PC (Political Correctness). A good example for Britain is the Birmingham city council's suggestion that they should rename the Christmas holiday "winterval" so as to include all religions.

Poet Laureate: The official royal poet. He or she is appointed for life and writes verse for official occasions.

Poppy Day: Remembrance Day, in November, when people wear poppies* in their lapels* (reminiscent of the fields of northern France) in memory of those who died in the two World Wars.

Proms, the: Short for "promenade concerts", they are a series of concerts given every summer at the Albert Hall, in London. A large part of the audience has no seats and stands or sits on the floor. The Last Night of the Proms is very popular, well-known songs are performed, and the audience joins in.

Pubs: Most pubs have a public bar, where darts* and bar billiards are played, and a more refined lounge or saloon bar.

| **a poppy:** *un coquelicot*; **the lapel:** *le revers de veste*; **darts:** *le jeu de fléchettes*

R

R.P.: Received Pronunciation: the standard way of pronouncing English for middle-class speakers in the South of England.

Remembrance Sunday: The Sunday closest to November 11, when people remember those who were killed in World Wars I and II as well as in other conflicts. It is traditional for people to wear a red paper poppy, reminiscent of the poppies in the fields of France and Belgium. This is why Remembrance Sunday is also called Poppy Day.

S

St David's Day: The national day of Wales, on 1 March, but not a holiday.

St George's Day: The national day of England, on 23 April, but not a holiday.

St Patrick's Day: The national day of Ireland, on 17 March.

T

Third sector: Neither the public sector nor the private sector, the third sector refers to all kinds of non-profit-making professional organizations, charities and community-based associations, which the government would like to encourage.

Town and gown: The expression describes the contrast - and sometimes tension - which is found in many university towns, and particularly in Oxford and Cambridge, between town (the permanent residents who work there as in any ordinary town) and gown (the students and staff of the university).

TUC, the: The Trades Union Congress, the association to which over 70 unions* are affiliated. The power of the unions was curbed* by Margaret Thatcher's Conservative government in the 1980s. Today, the trade-unions still have loose links with the Labour Party.

Treasury: The government department in charge of financial affairs and headed by the Chancellor of the Exchequer.

| **a union:** *un syndicat*; **to curb:** *refréner*

W

White man's burden: An expression first used by Kipling and referring to colonialism, which was then seen by some as the duty of white people, who had to spread culture and civilization throughout the world.

Y

Yob: Back slang* for boy: a young person who behaves in a violent and offensive way.

| **back slang:** *l'équivalent du verlan*

II The Commonwealth

1 THE COMMONWEALTH

From the Empire…

From the 16th to the 19th century British colonies kept expanding all over the world. They often provided raw materials* for Britain's industry. The American colonies seceded* in 1776, and Canada became a dominion in 1867 (while still dependent on the British Crown, a dominion had a certain amount of autonomy). At the beginning of the 20th century, more and more colonies asked for their independence. Several countries gained theirs early in the century (Australia, New Zealand, South Africa). Others, mainly from Africa, Asia and the Caribbean, gained it in the years that followed World War II. Most of them chose to join the Commonwealth.

raw materials: *des matières premières*; **to secede:** *faire sécession*

(British empire: 20th century Timeline)
liennathan.fr/532fmi

…to the Commonwealth

In 1931, the Statute of Westminster defined the Commonwealth as a free association of independent states which had formerly been part of the British Empire. All of them (republics, countries, like Canada, in which the Queen is Head of State, sultanates, etc) recognize the British sovereign as Head of the Commonwealth, providing a symbolic link between the states. There is no Commonwealth constitution but there are shared principles* for peace, equality, prosperity and democracy. There are regular meetings of heads of government to discuss Commonwealth questions and international affairs. Commonwealth Games are held every four years.

The association is mainly a cultural, educational, sporting and economic one which tries to eradicate* disease, poverty and racial prejudice. It reflects Britain's success in helping its former colonies to effect a smooth transition* towards independence while keeping close ties with them – an achievement Britain is rightly proud of. This has been helped along by the fact that Commonwealth states have in common their use of the English language.

Britain's ties with Commonwealth states are also tangible through the diversity of its population, ethnic clothes and restaurants.

shared principles: *des principes partagés*; **to eradicate:** *supprimer*; **a smooth transition:** *une transition en douceur*

Some fundamental principles of the Commonwealth, as set out in the 1991 Harare Declaration:

– we believe that international peace and order, global economic development and the rule of international law are essential to the security and prosperity of mankind;
– we believe in the liberty of the individual under the law, in equal rights for all citizens regardless of gender, race, colour, creed* or political belief, and in the individual's inalienable right to participate by means of free and democratic political processes in framing* the society in which he or she lives;
– we recognise racial prejudice and intolerance as a dangerous sickness and a threat to healthy development, and racial discrimination as an unmitigated evil;
– we oppose all forms of racial oppression, and we are committed to* the principles of human dignity and equality;
– we recognise the importance and urgency of economic and social development to satisfy the basic needs and aspirations of the vast majority of the peoples of the world, and seek the progressive removal of the wide disparities in living standards amongst our members.

a creed: *une croyance*; **to frame:** *construire*; **to be committed to:** *s'engager à poursuivre (une politique, des principes)*

■ The Commonwealth today

It is made up of 54 countries.

(The official site of the Commonwealth)
liennathan.fr/5fng56

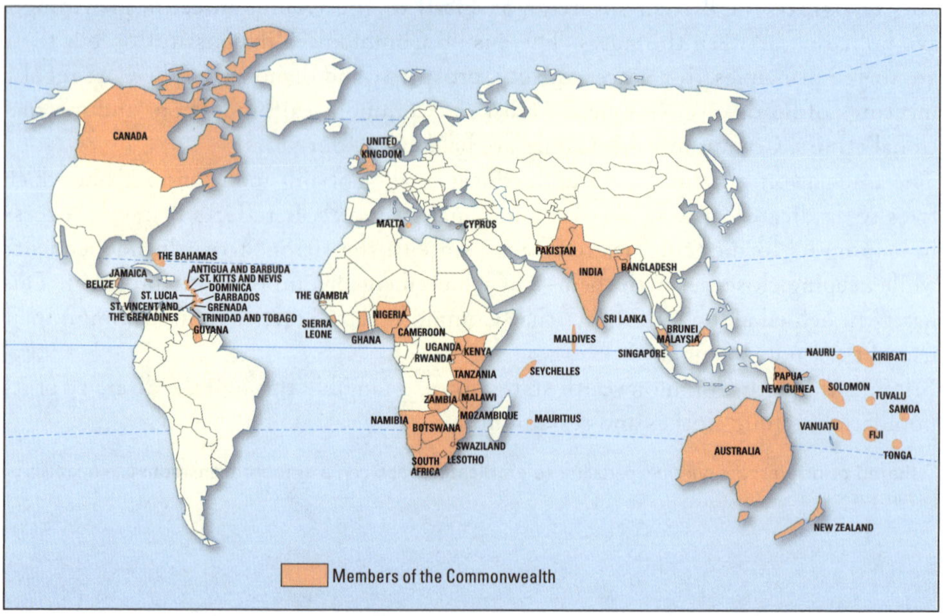

2 AUSTRALIA

(The official site of the Australian government)
liennathan.fr/399pss

Capital: Canberra

History

1770: Cook reaches the east coast of Australia and takes possession of Sydney for Britain. The land is inhabited by Aboriginals.
1787: Britain starts using Australia as a penal colony*.
19th century: Important voluntary immigration from Britain. Convicts* stop being sent to Australia around 1840.
1851: The Gold Rush brings waves of immigrants.
1901: Australia becomes independent.
1927: Canberra becomes the capital.
1967: The Aboriginal Australians are given full citizenship.
Since WWII, there has been much immigration, particularly from Southeast Asia. One problem is that of the status of the Aboriginal people, long segregated, and still living in greater poverty.
2001: In a referendum Australia decides to remain a constitutional monarchy.

2008: Prime Minister Rudd apologises to the Stolen Generations (Aboriginal and Torres Strait Islander children forcibly removed from their families between 1910 and 1970, because of a policy of assimilation.
2021 : Australia ends a $37bn deal signed with France, which was to build 12 conventional submarines. Instead, the US will give Australia the technology to build nuclear-powered submarines. The am is to counter China's influence in the South China Sea.

a penal colony: *une colonie pour bagnards*; **a convict:** *un bagnard*

■ **Type of government:** a parliamentary democracy, with a Prime Minister, as in Britain. But it recognizes the English sovereign as head of State. However, there is an increasingly strong movement in favour of transforming Australia into a republic.

■ **Population:** Australia's population is estimated at 25,839,984 in mid-2021.
There were an estimated 798,365 Aboriginal and Torres Strait Islander people in Australia in 2016 (3.3%of the population). The aboriginals who occupied the land before the English settled there were gradually driven away, losing their land and cultural traditions in the process and falling prey to many of the diseases brought by the new settlers. This drastically reduced their numbers. Many aboriginals also resisted the white colonist, which led to massacres until the early 20th century. Living on poor land in the north and the interior of Australia, aboriginals were increasingly recruited to work on sheep and cattle farms. Some indigenous Australians were granted citizenship after serving in World War II, but it was only in 1965 that they were all given the right to vote and in 1967 that they were included in the census*. In 1975, the Aboriginal Land Rights Act was passed: it granted the aboriginals the right to some traditional land. In 1998, a National Sorry Day was created to admit the wrong done to the indigenous Australians. In 2017 indigenous leaders turned down a proposal to be recognised in the country's constitution, preferring instead to push for reprentation in parliament.
Until the 1960s, Australia had an immigration policy which excluded non-Europeans, effectively keeping Australia white. Australia started admitting highly qualified non-Europeans in 1966, and went on relaxing its immigration policy so that it is now a multi-cultural society. In 2001, however, the government's very strict crackdown on* illegal immigrants, who were kept in camps, led to protests from human-rights activists.

of mixed descent: *métis*; **a census:** *un recensement*; **to crack down on:** *prendre des mesures énergiques contre*

■ **A few major writers:**
Judith Wright (poetry about the beauty and the past of the land)
Patrick White (novels about lonely beings isolated by their vision or eccentricity and faced with a hostile environment: *Voss*, 1957)

David Malouf (novels about the search for one's identity and the relationship between the past and the present from the point of view of exiles and outsiders*: *Remembering Babylon*, 1993)
Robert Drewe (novels about corruption and criminal minds, satires of Australian society: *Our Sunshine*, 1991)
Peter Carey (novels in the tradition of magic realism, that is to say combining realism and fantasy: *Illywacker*, 1985; *Oscar and Lucinda*, 1988).
Tim Winton (novels imbued with a sense of place: *Cloudstreet*, 1991).

an outsider: *un étranger*

3 NEW ZEALAND

(The official site of the New Zealand government)
liennathan.fr/63jyg5

Capital: Wellington

History

1769: Cook reaches New Zealand and claims it for Britain. The land is inhabited by Maoris.
British convicts* are sent there.
1840: Treaty of Waitangi: New Zealand becomes a British colony and the Maori chiefs recognize the British sovereignty over the island. Many conflicts with the aboriginal Maoris occur until the end of the century.
1907: New Zealand becomes a dominion
1947: New Zealand becomes independent within the Commonwealth.
2011-1015: several earthquakes cause major damage.

2019: Gun laws tightened after a far-right gun man kills 50 worshippers in two mosques.

a convict: *un bagnard*

■ **Type of government:** Constitutional monarchy, with the British sovereign as Head of State.

■ **Official languages:** English and Maori

■ **A few major writers:**
Katherine Mansfield (short stories about sensitive beings faced with selfishness and indifference; experimentation with narrative technique: *The Garden Party and other Stories*, 1922)
Janet Frame (novels and stories which focus on lonely beings isolated by their insanity or failure to communicate, *Short Stories*).

4 CANADA

(The official site of the government of Canada)
liennathan.fr/4sa39f

Capital: Ottawa

History

1534: Jacques Cartier establishes a French settlement* near the St Lawrence. At the end of the century, the country is inhabited by Eskimos, Indians, and a few white settlers and traders.
17th century: Beginning of the French colonization, chiefly along the St Lawrence River. Quebec and Montreal are established. But there is British colonization as well, with the Hudson Bay Company, trading in fish and fur, which leads to rivalry and conflict between the two countries.
1763: Treaty of Paris: France sells Quebec to the British.
1846: The boundary* between The United States and Canada is established along the 49th parallel, all the way to the Pacific coast.
1867: British North America Act: the British colonies become a dominion. It consists of Quebec, Ontario, Nova Scotia and New Brunswick.
1869: Britain cedes the Hudson Bay Company territories to Canada. They will form the remaining Canadian provinces.
1939: WWII: Canadian forces are active in Europe.
1947: Discovery of oil in Alberta.
1949: Newfoundland becomes a province; Canada joins NATO.
1949-1969: First Nations peoples gradually win the right to vote in provincial elections.
1960: First Nations peoples gain the right to vote in federal elections; a Canadian Bill of Rights guarantees civil rights and freedoms to all Canadians.
1982: Constitution Act: Canada can change its constitution without approval from Britain. It contains its Charter of Rights and Freedoms.
1989: Free Trade Agreement between Canada and the US.
1995: A referendum in Quebec rejects independence by a margin of 1%. But in 2006, Parliament agrees that the Quebecois be considered a "nation" within Canada.
1999: The Territory of Nuvanut is created in northern Canada, the first with a majority indigenous population.
2011: Canada withdraws from the Kyoto Protocol on reducing emissions of greenhouse gasses.
2017: The government will pay compensation to indigenous people taken from their families decades ago as children to be brought up by white middle-class families.

a settlement: *une colonie*; **a trader:** *un marchand*; **fur:** *la fourrure*; **a boundary:** *une frontière*

Language: Canada is bilingual, English and French being the official languages.

Type of government: Parliamentary monarchy, with the British sovereign as Head of State.

Although, theoretically, it is the Governor General (representing the British sovereign) who has executive power, it is in fact the Prime Minister who takes all decisions. He/She is the leader of the party which has the majority of votes.
Parliament consists of two houses: the House of Commons and the Senate.

- **A few major writers:**

Margaret Laurence (Her novels describe the lonely lives of women who try to escape the stifling* conventions of provincial life: *The Diviners*, 1974)
Mordecai Richler (His novels are savage and humorous satires of Canada's multicultural society: *The Apprenticeship of Duddy Kravitz*, 1959)
Alice Munro (Her short stories explore the relationships between people in small Ontario communities; the stories are often linked, showing how some of the characters evolve from one story to another, *Short Stories*),
Margaret Atwood (Poetry, novels and short stories, which often centre upon women who refuse to be victimized socially or sexually and try to liberate themselves: *The Handmaid's Tale*, 1985).
Carol Shields (realistic, domestic novels about women's search for fulfilment, *The Stone Diaries*, 1993).
Michael Ondaatje (novels about transculturalism, displacement and alienation, *The English Patient*, 1992).
Carol Shields (realistic, domestic novels about women's search for fulfilment, *The Stone Diaries*, 1993).
Michael Ondaatje (novels about transculturalism, displacement and alienation, *The English Patient*, 1992).

| **stifling:** *étouffant*

5 SOUTH AFRICA

(The official site of the South African government)
liennathan.fr/49gx8r

Three capitals: Pretoria (executive); Cape Town (legislative); Bloemfontein (judicial)
11 official languages

- **History**

1650-1700: The country is settled by the Dutch, the French Huguenots and the Germans.
1881: First Boer War, won by the Boers (Dutch settlers).
1899-1902: Second Boer War, between Britain & the Afrikaners (Afrikaners = descendants of the Dutch colonists), won by Britain.
1910: South African Act: The different states become the Union of South Africa, which enters the Commonwealth.
1914: Creation of the National Party, for the political domination of the Afrikaners, who were in favour of separating the black and white communities.

1948: The National Party is elected.
1961: The Union of South Africa becomes a republic and leaves the Commonwealth. An apartheid policy is introduced. The white population is seen as superior to the Blacks, the Coloureds (= half-castes), and the Asians, and is separated from them. Under this "white rule", all public places (including schools, government buildings, public transport...) are segregated. Black people live in townships within "homelands". Opposition parties, like the ANC (African National Congress), are banned* and their leaders imprisoned.
1976: Riots* against apartheid in the black township of Soweto.
1989: De Klerk becomes president. Mandela (imprisoned for his role in the ANC) is released from prison and apartheid laws are abolished.
1993: Nelson Mandela and President De Klerk are awarded the Nobel Peace Prize.
1994: Nelson Mandela becomes President, the first black president in the history of South Africa. Commonwealth membership restored and sanctions lifted.
1996: New democratic constitution
1999: Thabo Mbeki becomes President. Programs of redistribution and a policy of Affirmative Action are established to help with the huge remaining disparities between the economic situations of the Whites and the Blacks. However, huge differences still remain between the two communities. The country is also plagued* by the AIDS epidemic, poverty (40% of the population live below the poverty line), violence and unemployment.

2009: Parliament elects Jacob Zuma as president after corruption cases against him are dropped. He resigns in 2018 over new corruption charges.
2013: Nelson Mandela dies.
2021: Riots break out after former president Jacob Zuma refuses to appear before a commission investigating corruption during his presidency.
In spite of recurrent strikes, violence and cases of corruption, South Africa is now a prosperous country with a steadily growing economy. The country which used to be an international outcast* is now a democracy which has become politically influential and often mediates* conflicts in other African territories.

During my lifetime I have dedicated myself to this struggle of the African people. I have fought against white domination, and I have fought against black domination. I have cherished the ideal of a democratic and free society in which all persons live together in harmony and with equal opportunities. It is an ideal which I hope to live for and to achieve. But if needs be, it is an ideal for which I am prepared to die.

Nelson Mandela – April 20, 1964

to ban: *interdire*; **a riot:** *une émeute*; **to plague:** *ravager*; **Affirmative Action:** *la discrimination positive*; **an outcast:** *un paria, un proscrit*; **to mediate:** *servir de médiateur*

- **Population**

79.2% Blacks; 8.8% Whites; 8.9 % Coloureds; 2.5% Asians

- **Type of government:** Republic

- **A few major novelists:**

Alan Paton (Compassionate novels denouncing apartheid: *Cry, the Beloved Country*, 1948)
Nadine Gordimer (Novels and short stories which explore the effects of apartheid with lucidity and without sentimentality: *My Son's Story*, 1990)
André Brink (Novels about characters who rebel against the apartheid regime, *A Dry White Season*, 1979)
J.M. Coetzee (Although Coetzee's novels deal with oppression and imperialism, they are set in imaginary countries and make use of allegory, stream of consciousness and metafictional strategies: *Life and Times of Michael K*, 1983)

6 INDIA

(The official site of the government of India)
liennathan.fr/3n89eb

Capital: New Delhi

History

15th-16th centuries: East India Companies start trading* with India.
1763: Treaty of Paris: British supremacy is declared over India.
1876: Queen Victoria becomes Empress of India.
1919: Gandhi starts non-violent anti-British resistance. He advocates* civil disobedience* (boycotts, refusal to pay taxes, refusal to vote) to gain Indian independence.
1947: India gains independence. It is partitioned* between India (mostly Hindus) and Pakistan (mostly Muslims).
1948: Gandhi is assassinated. Nehru becomes Prime Minister. War with Pakistan over Kashmir.

1971: Eastern Pakistan wins its independence from Western Pakistan and becomes Bangladesh.
1984: Sikh militants press for self-rule. Prime Minister Indira Gandhi is assassinated. Her son Rajiv becomes prime minister. Gas leak in Bhopal kills thousands.
1987-1992: India sends peacekeeping troops to Sri Lanka; recurrent violence (Muslim separatist groups in Kashmir; Hindu-Muslim conflicts); Rajiv Gandhi is assassinated in 1991.
1998: India carries out nuclear tests.
2000: Population reaches 1 billion.
2002: Over 1,000 pilgrims die in a Hindu-Muslim bloodshed.
2006: India signs a nuclear agreement with the US.
2008: India launches its first unmanned mission to the moon.
2008: Almost 200 die in an attack by a Pakistan-based jihadist group in Mumbai.
2014: China invests massively in India.
2018: Gay sex is decriminalised.
2020-2021: There are over 25 million cases of Covid-19. Unemployment and health-care costs have pushed many into extreme poverty.

Since independence India has been plagued by ethnic and religious conflicts (between Hindus and Muslims, in Sri Lanka, between Pakistan, China and India over the control of Kashmir.)

Over the past decade, India's economy has grown rapidly, especially in the service industries*, IT* in particular. Many services such as accounting* or customer hotlines are being outsourced* from the United States and Europe to India, most of whose new college graduates speak English and work for low salaries.

to trade: *faire du commerce*; **to advocate:** *recommander*; **civil disobedience:** *la résistance passive*; **to partition:** *diviser*; **service industries:** *le secteur tertiaire*; **IT = information technology:** *l'informatique*; **accounting:** *la comptabilité*; **to outsource:** *délocaliser*

▪ **Type of government:** Republic

▪ **Population:** Over 1.3 billion inhabitants

▪ **Castes:** Because of the influence of Hinduism, society is divided into hereditary castes. There are five main ones: the Brahmins (scholars and priests, the highest caste), the Kshatriyas (kings and warriors), the Vaishyas (traders and artisans), the Shudras (farmers and servants) and Dalits (Untouchables, the lowest caste, sometimes considered too low to be part of the caste system). Castes determine your way of life, your habits and rituals, whom you associate with.

▪ **Religion:** Hinduism (79.80%); Islam (14.23%); Christianity (2.30%), Buddhism, Sikhism (2.40%).

- **Official languages:** Hindi and English + 14 other national languages. English also allows the different communities to communicate.

- **A few major novelists:**

R.K. Narayan (His novels and stories show sensitive individuals caught between their aspirations and the weight of traditions in a changing country: *The Guide*, 1958)
Anita Desai (Her novels and short stories describe alienated beings – often women – who strive to achieve fulfilment* and recognition: *Clear Light of Day*, 1980.)
Vikram Seth (Poetry and novels which offer a realistic portrait of India (*A Suitable Boy*, 1993) but also a satire of America in the verse novel *The Golden Gate*, 1986.)
Hari Kunzru (In *The Impressionist*, 2002, Kunzru exposes* the effects of colonialism on individual lives, focusing on those who live on the margins of society.)
Arundhati Roy's novel *The God of Small Things*, 1997, is a moving tale of love and separation, of the rivalries and social prejudices within a family.
Rohinton Mistry writes about displacement and isolation (*A Fine Balance*, 1995).
Salman Rushdie portrays the politics, culture and violence of his country (he was born in Bombay, his family emigrated to Pakistan, he has lived in the USA since the *fatwa* passed on him for alleged blasphemy after the publication of *The Satanic Verses*, 1988). His novels (*Midnight's Children*, 1981) merge realism, fantasy and the supernatural while drawing on Indian mythology and Hindi storytelling.

fulfilment: *contentement*; **to expose:** *dénoncer*

7 NIGERIA

(The official website of the government of Nigeria)
liennathan.fr/w26ny5

Capital: Abuja

- **History**

1885: Nigeria becomes a British protectorate.
1960: Nigeria gains its independence and remains in the Commonwealth.
1967: Three states secede as the Republic of Biafra, leading to a three-year civil war.
1975-1999: Military rule, several coups to seize power.
2003: First legislative elections since the end of military rule. The following years are marked by several clashes between Christians and Muslims.
2009-2014: The Boko Haram Islamist movement launches a campaign of violence.

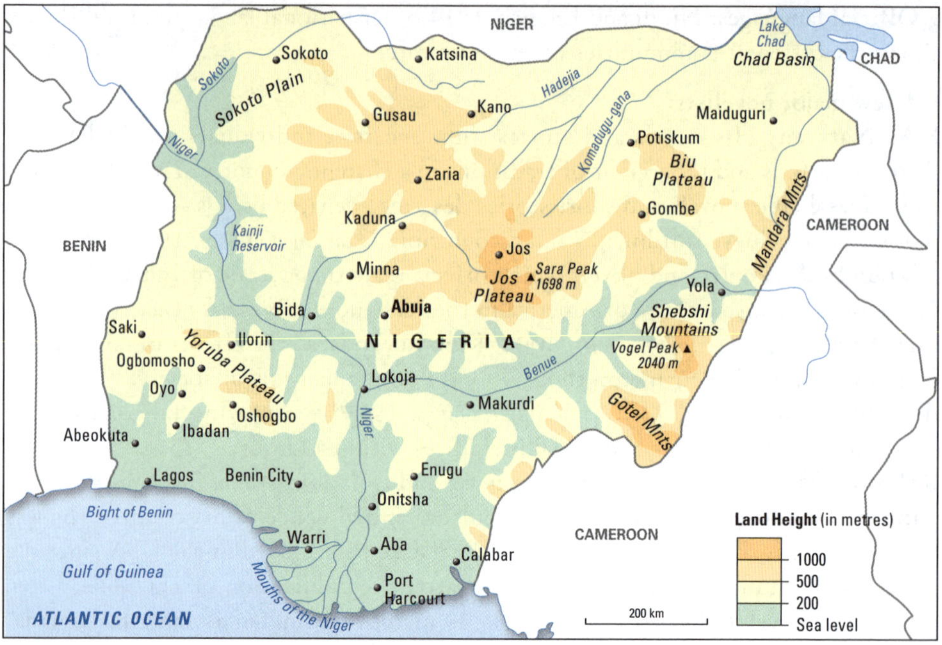

- **Type of government:** Republic

- **A few major writers:**

Chinua Achebe (His novels examine the conflicts between the traditional Igbo values and those of the Western world introduced through colonization: *Things Fall Apart*, 1958.)
Ben Okri 's novels make use of a kind of magic realism (social realism combined with African folklore and fantasy) to describe the poverty and corruption of his country (*The Famished Road*, 1991).
Wole Soyinka (His early plays are witty and inventive, and use traditional Yoruban elements such as mythology or dance (*The Lion and the Jewel*, 1963); his later plays are harsher criticisms of tyranny and corruption.) He was awarded the Nobel Prize for Literature in 1986.
Chimamanda Ngozi Adichie (a feminist and political militant, *Americanah*, 2013).

8 THE CARIBBEAN

(An introduction to the Caribbean, empire and slavery)
liennathan.fr/et88p8

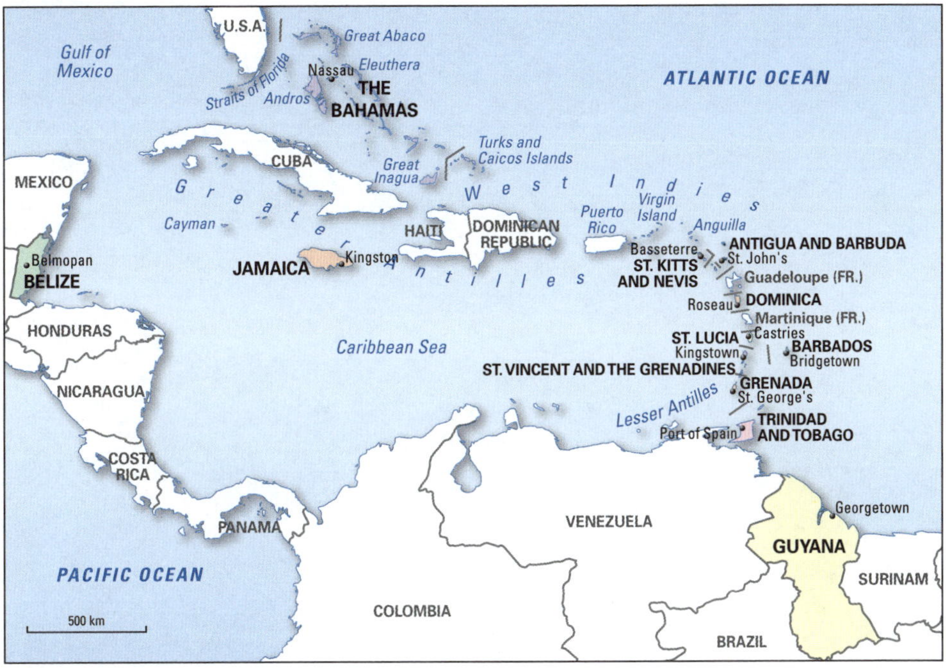

Caribbean countries within the Commonwealth

Antigua & Barbuda	Guyana
The Bahamas	Jamaica
Barbados	St Kitts and Nevis
Belize	St Lucia
Dominica	St Vincent and the Grenadines
Grenada	Trinidad & Tobago

A few major writers:

Jean Rhys (Many of her novels portray lonely, uprooted women. In *Wide Sargasso Sea*, 1966, for example, she imagines the past history of Rochester's mad wife, who is locked in the attic in Charlotte Brontë's *Jane Eyre*.)

V.S. Naipaul's novels paint a dark portrait of third-world countries, criticizing the ruinous effects of colonization: *A House for Mr Biswas*, 1961).

Derek Walcott's plays and poetry celebrate the cultural diversity of the West Indies while denouncing some of the losses caused by colonization.

III The United States

1 PATRIOTISM

Ask not what your country can do for you, but what you can do for your country.
John F. Kennedy

■ **50 states**
The United States is made up of 50 states, the federal capital being Washington D.C. (District of Columbia).

The American **flag** is called The Stars and Stripes or the Star-Spangled Banner*, or Old Glory. It has
– 13 stripes* for the 13 colonies which fought for their independence;
– 50 stars for the 50 present states.
→ (Pledge of Allegiance)
A symbol of unity, the American flag is displayed on official occasions (on July 4th for example) but many Americans like to fly the flag* outside their homes as a token* of their patriotism. On several occasions flag-burning came very close to being prohibited by Congress.

The **eagle** is the national emblem of the United States.
– It appears with the motto *e pluribus unum* (one out of many)
– the eagle holds both arrows (war) and an olive branch (peace).

The **national hymn** is The Star-Spangled Banner, which was inspired by America's resistance to the British attack on Fort McHenry during the 1812 war with Britain. This is the first stanza. The last line is a refrain in the following stanzas.

Francis Scott Key
September 20, 1814

Oh, say can you see, by the dawn's early light,
What so proudly we hailed* at the twilight's last gleaming*?
Whose broad stripes and bright stars, through the perilous fight,
O'er the ramparts we watched, were so gallantly streaming*?
And the rockets' red glare, the bombs bursting in air,
Gave proof through the night that our flag was still there.
O say, does that star-spangled banner yet wave
O'er the land of the free and the home of the brave?

the Star-Spangled Banner: *la bannière étoilée*; **a stripe:** *une rayure*; **to fly the flag:** *pavoiser*; **a token:** *un gage, un témoignage*; **to hail:** *saluer*; **gleaming:** *la lueur*; **to stream:** *flotter au vent*

(a site devoted to the flag of the United States)
liennathan.fr/wc7f35

2 GEOGRAPHY & ECONOMY

A FEW STATISTICS

Area: 9,834 millions km²

Population: 332, 915 073 (2021)
States with the largest population: California (39,613,493), Texas (29,730,311), Florida (21,944,577), New York (19,299,981)
States with the smallest population: Wyoming (581,075), Vermont (623,251), District of Columbia (714,153)

Population density%: It ranges from 1,207 inhabitants per square mile in the District of Columbia to 1.28 inhabitants per square mile in Alaska.

Main cities & population: (2021)
New York: 8,622,357
Los Angeles: 4,085,014
Chicago: 2,670,406
Houston: 2,378,146
Phoenix: 1,743,469
Philadelphia: 1,590,402

Life expectancy*: 77.3 years (2021)

Birth rate*: 12.001 per 1,000 (2021)

Death rate*: 8.28 per 1,000 (2021)

Fertility rate*: 1,781 children per woman (2021)

Average salary*: $53,490 per year (2021)

Unemployment rate*: 5.4 % (2021)

the population density: *la densité de population*; **life expectancy:** *l'espérance de vie*; **the birth rate:** *le taux de natalité*; **the death rate:** *le taux de mortalité*; **the fertility rate:** *le taux de fertilité*; **the average salary:** *le salaire moyen*; **the unemployment rate:** *le taux de chômage*

ENVIRONMENTAL ISSUES

The United States is a country prone to* natural disasters - droughts* leading to wildfires in the Western states (California, Arizona, New Mexico, Oregon), blizzards* in the North-East, hurricanes* in the South-West. Recently, extreme weather conditions have become increasingly common and such highly publicized events as Hurricane Katrina (which battered* and partly destroyed New Orleans in 2006) or the melting of the icecap* and dying polar bears have shocked the nation into a new concern about the protection of their environment. Although the United States is still the world's largest polluter*, being responsible for about 20% of the world's gas emissions, the political landscape is changing fast, with both Republicans and Democrats now considering more radical steps to reduce carbon emissions* and find alternative energy (ethanol, wind power, solar power...). Former Vice President Al Gore's film "An Inconvenient Truth" (2006) - a plea to halt the progress of global warming - has had enormous impact on the population. Here are some of the most critical issues:

– Air pollution: Of the 10 US cities with the worst air pollution, 7 are in California (including Lost Angeles, Fresno, Sacramento, San Francisco). Phoenix (California) and Denver (Colorado) also have badly polluted ozone.

– Water pollution: sewage, mines, pesticides and chemicals end up in rivers, lakes and oceans, with microplastics and metals often remaining after water purification. Colorado mines have polluted over 2000 kilometres of streams.

– Deforestation: rising population, lumbering and forest fires have led to deforestation, not always followed by tree-planting. This is particularly the case in the north west.

– Depletion of natural resources: farmland is gradually reduced because of urbanisation, oil and minerals may soon be mined out.

– Global warming: melting glaciers in Alaska, devastating hurricanes (particularly in the south-east, Louisiana in particular), wildfires in California are all the result of rising temperatures, with their effect on biodiversity.

– Fracking*: As early as the 1940s, hydraulic fracturing was used in the United States, and within a few decades turned the country into an exporter of oil, even overtaking Saudi Arabia as a producer of crude oil. The process is now used in over a dozen states. But although it produces cheaper and cleaner energy, helps America become energy independent, and creates hundreds of jobs, particularly in Ohio and Pennsylvania, fracking is controversial because of its negative impact on the environment. It might be the cause of small earthquakes as well as pollute the water supplies. President Trump was in favour of fracking while President Biden, who was in favour of a transition towards renewable energy, said he would not ban it except on federal land.

But awareness of these issues has led organizations, citizens and EPA (Environmental Protection Agency) to suggest solutions and incite change.

In 2007 for the first time, the issue of global climate change was mentioned in the state-of-the-union address. Many companies now accept the need to control carbon emissions and states like California have now imposed mandatory curbs* on them. Among the least controversial ideas are stricter regulations to make cars fuel-efficient* and the promotion of renewable energy*. Of course, some of the motivations are not environmental but stem from* the need to be less dependant on

oil from the Middle East, to make the US energy independent. In 2017, however, Donald Trump said that he would cease implementing* the Paris Agreement to combat climate change.
In 2016, President Obama signed the Paris agreement, a pledge to cut carbon emissions. The Trump administration withdrew from in in 2017 but President Biden re-joined the accord in 2021 and wants the US's energy to be carbon neutral by 2035.
Some international movements like Extinction Rebellion (XR) use non-violent civil disobedience action to try and halt global warming, biodiversity loss and the extinction of species.

prone to: *sujet à*; **a drought:** *une période de sécheresse*; **a blizzard:** *une tempête de neige*; **a hurricane:** *un ouragan*; **to batter:** *frapper*; **the icecap:** *la calotte glacière*; **a polluter:** *un pollueur*; **carbon emissions:** *les émissions de gaz carbonique*; **a mandatory curb:** *une réduction obligatoire*; **fuel-efficient:** *économique, qui consomme peu*; **renewable energy:** *l'énergie renouvelable*; **to stem from:** *venir de*; **to implement:** *mettre en œuvre*; **hydraulic fracturing:** *fracturation hydraulique*

(EPA)
liennathan.fr/263sfb

THE MAIN ECONOMIC AREAS OF THE US

- Large urban centres
- Atlantic coast megalopolis: many services (insurance, banking, administrative activities).
- Manufacturing Belt: old textile and manufacturing industries.
- Traditional manufacturing centres (coal industries in the Appalachians, steel and automobiles in Detroit...) in the process of adapting to new technologies.
- Sun Belt: a very active zone along the coast (industries linked to oil and natural gas in Louisiana and Texas, important harbours along the coast of the Gulf and the Pacific coast), but also agribusiness in California (huge farms relying on irrigation and high technology) and related activities such as food-processing.
- Most dynamic Sun Belt areas around large cities (LA, Houston, Seattle...).
- High tech businesses and parks (computers, bio-technology, "clean industries"...).
- Areas of mixed farming: fruit (citrus fruit along the coast from Florida to Louisiana), poultry in Arkansas and Alabama, peanuts in Georgia, soya, tobacco, corn and wheat).
- The Great plains with intensive agriculture (agribusiness): wheat, corn, soya
- Mountains, plateaux, forests: mainly ranching (cattle breeding)
- Active ports and intense maritime traffic

A MAP OF MANHATTAN

New York (also called "The Big Apple")
A map of Manhattan, the best-known borough of New York.

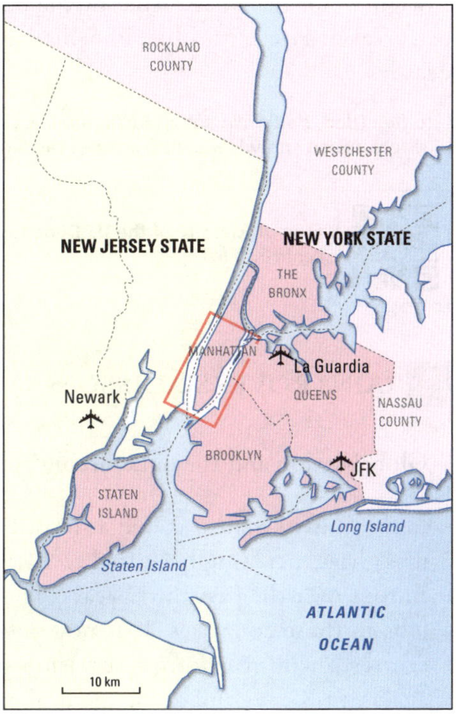

POPULATION

Several movements of population occurred in the 20th century.

– The middle classes gradually fled* city centres to move to the suburbs. As a result, suburbia* became increasingly inhabited by wealthy white people, often settling in distinct and well-defined areas depending on their income and social background. Conversely*, city centres tended to become rundown* and left to minorities and the poor. However, there has recently been a movement back towards those city centres which, like Philadelphia, Baltimore or Cleveland, have been rehabilitated.

– The massive exodus towards large Metropolitan areas in the Northeast, which resulted in urban sprawl*, has now declined as people look for better living conditions in smaller cities and more rural areas. The Sunbelt* in particular has acted as a magnet* for many, attracted by the better climate and cheaper labour. The suburban areas of large cities like Phoenix have grown particularly quickly in the last two decades.

to flee (fled, fled): *fuir*; **suburbia:** *la banlieue*; **conversely:** *inversement*; **a magnet:** *un aimant*; **rundown:** *délabré*; **urban sprawl:** *expansion urbaine*; **the Sunbelt:** *les États ensoleillés du sud et de l'ouest*

(The official site of the US Department of Labor)
liennathan.fr/78p9br

CONTROVERSIAL ISSUES

Globalisation and the outsourcing* of jobs

In the United States, as well as in Britain, manufacturing jobs (clothing, electronics) have increasingly shifted to Latin America, Asia, North Africa and Eastern Europe over the past thirty years. The reason is the low cost of labour-intensive jobs in these countries. It is now the turn of work in the service sector* (call centres for information, reservations and orders, IT*, banking, insurance, even analysing X-rays and doing medical research), and the list of skilled jobs being outsourced offshore* keeps growing every day. This is made possible by the expansion of technology in low-wage countries and by developments like broadband* which make it possible to send huge amounts of information in no time and at little cost.

As the world market is turning into a global one, countries like China and India are becoming workshops for rich countries, the former specializing in industrial goods, the latter in the service sector and call centres. China will soon be supplying half of the world's clothing markets, selling cheap clothes to large retailers* like Wal-Mart. In the United States, the result has been huge profits for businesses but a growing loss of jobs.

to outsource: *délocaliser*; **the service sector:** *le secteur tertiaire*; **IT: Information Technology:** *l'informatique*; **offshore:** *hors des frontières*; **broadband:** *l'ADSL*; **a retailer:** *un détaillant*

3 A SHORT CHRONOLOGY OF AMERICAN HISTORY

(United States time lines)
liennathan.fr/f4rq46

(United States time lines)
liennathan.fr/u5u83f

The first colonies

1492: While trying to find a sea-route to India, Christopher Columbus discovers America, then inhabited by several million native Americans.

16th century: the Spanish, French and Dutch begin exploring the coast of north America.

1607: The British Virginia Company is founded. In 1619, the first African slaves arrive to work on the tobacco plantations.

1620: Persecuted in Europe because of their religion, the Pilgrim* Fathers (English Puritans who refused to convert to Anglicanism) reach America on the *Mayflower* and found* the colony of Plymouth. Life is difficult, food scarce and the winters bitterly cold. Many die during the first months.

1629: Other Puritans found the Massachusetts Bay Colony.

1681: Pennsylvania is founded by William Penn, with the aim of welcoming people from all religions and nationalities.

1692: Salem witchcraft trials* in the Massachusetts Bay Colony.

More emigrants will settle in America over the years, forming 13 colonies in the early 18th century. Most of them are drawn to* America as a haven from* tyranny or religious persecution.

1763: Treaty of Paris, which marks the end of the French and Indian Wars (a conflict between England and France over territorial domination) and the end of French colonization.

a pilgrim: *un pèlerin*; **to found:** *fonder*; **a witchcraft trial:** *un procès pour sorcellerie*; **to be drawn to:** *être attiré par*; **a haven from:** *un refuge contre*

Towards independence

1765: First revolts of the colonies against the imposition by the British of taxes on imported produce such as sugar, coffee or wine. In order to raise money, Great Britain makes it compulsory for all newspapers and legal documents to be printed on special stamped paper* (Stamp Act).

1773: The Boston Tea Party The colonists are angered at having to pay taxes to Britain since they are not politically represented ("No Taxation without Representation" is their slogan.). When the British government try to impose a tax on tea, the colonists board* the ships in Boston harbor and throw the tea they carry into the sea.

1774: The thirteen colonies suspend trade with Britain.

1775: Blockade of Boston harbor; beginning of the war for independence, between the colonies (backed* by France) and Britain.
1776 (July 4th): Declaration of Independence. The colonies separate from Britain.
1775-1783: War of Independence: The patriots (led by George Washington) against the Loyalists (those on the side of Britain). With the Treaty of Versailles (1783), Britain recognizes the independence of the United States of America.
1787: the American Constitution establishes a federal government.
1789: George Washington becomes the first President of the United States. In the following years, Federalists (in favour of a strong central government) and Republicans (in favour of individual states being given more power) will alternate as presidents.
1791: Bill of Rights* : ten amendments are added to the Constitution in order to guarantee freedom of speech, freedom of the press and freedom of worship.

stamped paper: *du papier timbré*; **to board:** *monter à l'abordage*; **to back:** *soutenir*; **the Bill of Rights:** *la déclaration des droits*

Expansion

1803: Louisiana purchased* from France. It is a huge tract* of land which doubles the size of the United States. Beginning of the movement westward, to settle on virgin* and still uncharted* land. The 'frontier' (the limit between civilized and wild

territories) will gradually move westward until 1890. This will be accompanied by many fights and treaties with the Indians who live on the land.
1804-6: The Lewis & Clarke expedition explores the West and reaches the Pacific Ocean.
1808: Congress bans* the importation of slaves.
1812: War with Britain
1819: Florida purchased from Spain
1823: The Monroe doctrine: President Monroe opposes European colonization on the American continent and declares that the United States will not interfere in the affairs of European states.
1830: Indian Removal Act to relocate* Indians west of the Mississippi River: in the decade which follows, Indians are pushed further back in order to make way for the white settlers. In 1838, for example, the Cherokees who lived in Georgia are deported to Oklahoma. This is referred to as "The Trail of Tears"*.
1844: First message sent by telegraph from Baltimore to Washington.
1848: Texas, New Mexico and California are won after the war with Mexico.
1849: California Gold Rush*: it encourages the movement westward. The idea of "Manifest Destiny" appears.
1845-1855: First large wave of immigration, mainly from Ireland and central Europe.

to purchase: *acheter*; **a tract:** *une étendue*; **virgin land:** *la terre vierge*; **uncharted:** *non exploré*; **to ban:** *interdire*; **to relocate:** *transférer*; **the Trail of Tears:** *le sentier des larmes*; **the gold rush:** *la ruée vers l'or*; **Manifest Destiny:** *la destinée manifeste*

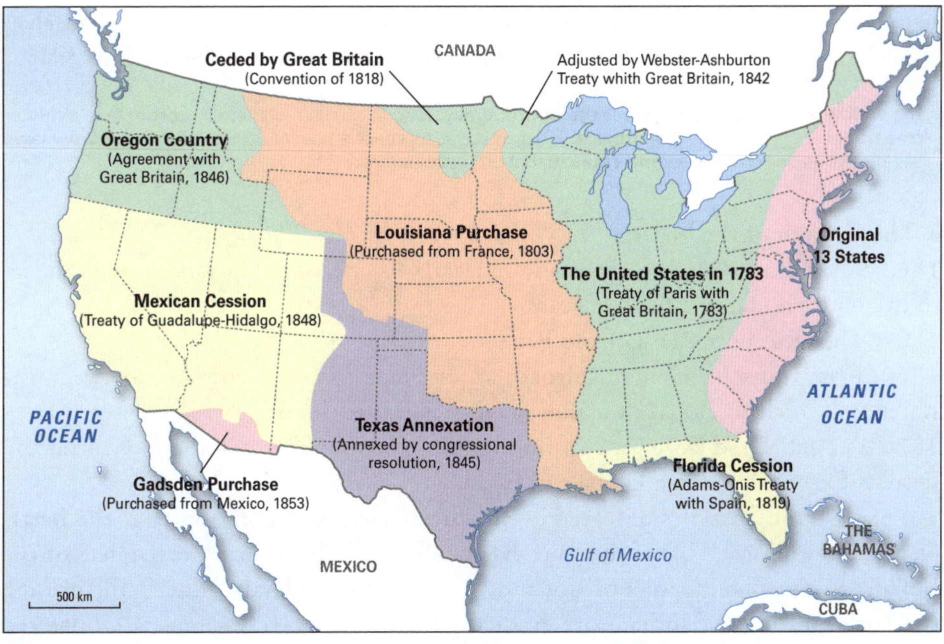

■ The Civil War*

1860: Abraham Lincoln becomes President.
1861-1865: Civil War: 11 Southern states (the Confederate States) secede* in order to keep slavery, which they consider necessary to farm the extensive lands of their cotton, tobacco and rice plantations. They choose Jefferson Davis as their president. The northern states, on the contrary, with their industries based on free labour, are abolitionist (in favour of abolishing slavery). The north and the south also have different economic interests, the former wishing to protect their industrial production, the latter desiring free trade*. Lincoln is against secession and leads the war between the Union (the north) and the Confederacy* (the South).
1863: Emancipation Proclamation: President Lincoln declares that all slaves are free. The British and the French side with the Union.
1865: The north wins the war and a 13th amendment is added to the Constitution, abolishing slavery. President Lincoln is assassinated by a supporter of the former Confederacy.
1865-1877: Reconstruction: The term applies to the rebuilding of the South, which has been ruined by the war. Congress forces the Southern states to accept a programme of military reconstruction and to give all black people full citizenship. When the federal troops leave in 1877, there is a lot of resentment* on the part of Southern whites and many dishonest speculators try to take advantage of the situation. Although the 15th amendment gave black people voting rights in 1870, the South in fact enacts* a series of laws, called Jim Crow laws*, to encourage racial segregation: in schools, buses, and other public places, black people find themselves second-rate citizens*. This is encouraged by secret societies like the Ku Klux Klan.

the Civil War: *la guerre de Sécession*; **the Confederacy:** *la confédération sudiste*; **to secede:** *faire sécession*; **free trade:** *le libre-échange*; **resentment:** *le ressentiment*; **to enact a law:** *promulger une loi*; **Jim Crow laws:** *des lois ségrégationnistes*; **a second-rate citizen:** *un citoyen inférieur*

■ The Growth of the Nation

1862: The Homestead Act* gives any settler 160 acres of public land if he promises to live on it and farm it for five years.
1867: The USA buys Alaska from Russia.
1869: First transcontinental railroad, which helps to create cohesion between the states and which accelerates the movement westward.
1870-1920: Second large wave of immigration, mainly from Southern, Central and Eastern Europe, and from China and Japan.
1876: General Custer is defeated by the Sioux (led by Sitting Bull) at the Battle of Little Big Horn. This is just one event reflecting the growing resistance of the Indians to their conditions of life and the loss of their lands. Indeed all through the 19th century, the Indians are gradually forced into reservations, administered

by the Bureau of Indian Affairs, where they are not allowed to develop their own culture.
1879: Edison invents the electric light bulb*. The last decades of the century (called The Gilded* Age) are marked by industrial growth, and the emergence of some captains of industry who accumulate enormous fortunes (e.g. Rockefeller, Carnegie), often using part of their money to fund* educational or artistic programmes. The United States becomes increasingly urbanised.
1886: Creation of the American Federation of Labor, a union* made necessary by the rapid growth of industry and big business during the last two decades of the century.
1890: Indians massacred at Wounded Knee. This marks the end of their resistance. 1890 is also the year when the frontier is officially closed.
1901-1917: The Progressive Era: Under the presidencies of Theodore Roosevelt and Woodrow Wilson, reforms are introduced aimed at fighting social inequalities, developing higher education, regulating big business, and preserving natural sites.
1903: First flight of the Wright brothers.
1908: Ford starts producing his Model T car and develops efficient plants* with assembly-lines* increasing the output*.
1917: After US ships are sunk by German submarines, the USA enters WWI. It helps win the war, but over 100,000 American soldiers lose their lives in the conflict. The United States becomes a major power internationally.

the Homestead Act: *la loi agraire*; **the electric light bulb:** *l'ampoule électrique*; **gilded:** *doré*; **to fund:** *financer*; **a union:** *un syndicat*; **a plant:** *une usine*; **an assembly-line:** *une chaîne de montage*; **the output:** *le rendement*.

■ Between two world wars

1920: Women get voting rights. Prohibition (making or selling alcohol is prohibited) leads to bootlegging*.
1920-1929: The Jazz Age (also called The Roaring Twenties*). This decade is a period of prosperity, during which consumerism reaches a climax : electrical appliances*, cars, the radio, advertising become extremely popular. This is reflected in literature in the writings of the Lost Generation* (Fitzgerald, Hemingway, Dos Passos) who expose* the concern with materialism. Corruption and bootlegging add to the decline of morals.
1924: Indian Citizenship Act (the Indians are given American citizenship).
1927: Lindbergh flies across the Atlantic Ocean.
1929: Increasing speculation leads to the collapse* of the Stock Exchange or Wall Street Crash (Black Thursday). Beginning of the depression years, when many banks and businesses go bankrupt* and millions become unemployed.
1932: Roosevelt's New Deal* to boost* the economy, create jobs, thanks to a programme of public works, and help the poor and the unemployed. Roosevelt's reforms are also economic (The Agricultural Adjustment Act, to help farmers with subsidies*; the Tennessee Valley Authority, to use water for agriculture; the Banking

Act) and they are social (the right of workers to belong to a union; social security). All these measures will be effective although unemployment will remain high until the United States enters the war against Germany.

bootlegging: *la fabrication et la vente illicites d'alcool*; **the Roaring Twenties:** *les années folles*; **electrical appliances:** *les appareils électriques*; **the Lost Generation:** *la génération perdue*; **to expose:** *dénoncer*; **the Stock Exchange collapse:** *l'effondrement de la Bourse*; **to go bankrupt:** *faire faillite*; **the New Deal:** *le programme de réformes de Roosevelt*; **to boost:** *redonner du tonus à*; **subsidies:** *des subventions*

■ World War II

1933: Many German Jewish refugees start arriving in America.
1941: The USA (which has so far maintained an isolationist policy) enters the war after the bombing of Pearl Harbor (a US navy base) by the Japanese. America starts mass-producing tanks, planes and all kinds of military equipment.
1944: The allied forces land in Europe (on June 6, D-Day*).
1945: Germany surrenders (VE-day). The US drops atom bombs on Hiroshima and Nagasaki; Japan surrenders (VJ-day). Altogether, over 400,000 Americans have been killed in the conflict. The United Nations Organization (UNO*), is created as an international organization to prevent future conflicts.

D-Day: *le Jour J, le jour du débarquement*; **UNO:** *ONU*

■ The Cold War

1947: The Marshall Plan brings financial and material help to countries fighting communism. The relationship between the USA and the USSR becomes increasingly tense*. This will lead to the Cold War in the 1950s.
1949: creation of NATO* (North Atlantic Treaty Organization) – an alliance between the US and Western European countries in case of Soviet aggression.
1950-3: Korean War, between North Korea (communist and helped by the USSR) and South Korea (helped by the Americans).
1952: McCarthyism: Senator McCarthy leads a witch-hunt* against communists in America. Many like Arthur Miller see a parallel with the trials for witchcraft* in Puritan New England. (See his play *The Crucible*). An atmosphere of paranoia takes hold of America, with denunciations, trials and even executions, as in the case of Julius and Ethel Rosenberg, accused of spying for the USSR.

tense: *tendu*; **NATO:** *l'OTAN*; **a witch-hunt:** *une chasse aux sorcières*; **a trial for witchcraft:** *un procès en sorcellerie*

■ Civil Rights and the Vietnam War

1954: Segregation in public schools becomes unconstitutional.
1956: Montgomery bus boycott (black people protest against segregation on buses). It will lead to the desegregation of buses.

1960-1963: Kennedy President. He starts a social policy called "the New Frontier": its aim is to put an end to segregation and help the poorest in the country through welfare measures*.
1961: Kennedy tries to invade Cuba and overthrow* Castro, but fails. The following year, Soviet missiles are found in Cuba, which leads to a new crisis.
1963: Johnson becomes president after Kennedy is assassinated. He introduces extensive reforms to fight poverty, including Health insurance and aid to education.
1963: Martin Luther King leads a Civil Rights march on Washington to protest against segregation and inequality.
1964: The Civil Rights*Act abolishes segregation.
1965: In spite of the Civil Rights Act, riots* erupt in a number of larger cities.

With God On Our Side (Bob Dylan)

Oh my name it is nothin'
My age it means less
The country I come from
Is called the Midwest
I's taught and brought up there
The laws to abide*
And that land that I live in
Has God on its side.

Oh the history books tell it
They tell it so well
The cavalries charged
The Indians fell
The cavalries charged
The Indians died
Oh the country was young
With God on its side.

I've learned to hate the Russians
All through my whole life
If another war starts
It's them we must fight
To hate them and fear them
To run and to hide
And accept it all bravely
With God on my side.

But now we got weapons
Of chemical dust
If fire them we're forced to
Then fire them we must
One push of the button
And a shot the world wide
And you never ask questions
When God's on your side

A few stanzas from a popular 1960s anti-war song by Bob Dylan, who, in 2016, was awarded the Nobel Prize in literature.

to abide by a law: *respecter une loi*

1964-1973: The Vietnam War, between the North (communist) and the South, helped by the Americans. Almost 60,000 American soldiers are killed and the United States finally has to retreat after growing dissatisfaction at home (anti-war demonstrations, draft dodgers*).

a POW: a prisoner of war – KIA: Killed in Action – MIA: Missing in Action – PTSD: Post Traumatic Stress Disorder

1968: Martin Luther King assassinated.
1969: First man on the moon.
1972: President Nixon signs the strategic Arms Limitation Treaty with the USSR.
1974: Nixon resigns* after the Watergate scandal (He had ordered that the headquarters of the Democratic Party be broken into*).

> **welfare measures:** *des mesures d'aide sociale*; **to overthrow:** *renverser*; **civil rights:** *les droits civils*; **a riot:** *une émeute*; **a draft dodger:** *quelqu'un qui essaie d'échapper à la conscription*; **to resign:** *démissionner*; **to break into:** *entrer par effraction dans*

Recent times

1980-1988: Presidency of Ronald Reagan, who introduces conservative and liberal policies.

> **Reaganomics**
> The economic policies of President Reagan, which mainly consisted of tax cuts for companies in order to boost production, cuts in government spending and social welfare, and fewer federal regulations.

1989: Fall of the Berlin Wall. End of the Cold War.
1991: Gulf War against Iraq. The United States forces Iraq to withdraw from* Kuwait, which they had invaded. It is the starting point of the New World Order: the United States polices the world.
1992-2000: Presidency of Bill Clinton, who initiates social reforms and reduces the deficit as well as unemployment.
2000: George W. Bush is elected President.
2001: Terrorist attacks against the USA: on September 11, the Twin Towers of the World Trade Center are destroyed, and the Pentagon is damaged by hi-jacked* airplanes. Almost three thousand people are killed.
Senate approves US Patriot Act, to give the government increased powers to detain suspected terrorists, eavesdrop on communications and counter money-laundering.
2002: "Axis of Evil": In his State of the Union address*, President Bush said that countries like North Korea, Iran and Iraq «constitute an axis of evil*, arming to threaten the peace of the world." President Bush thus pledged* to disarm these countries and help Iraq become a «free and peaceful nation».
2003: War against Iraq, which the United States believes to possess weapons of mass destruction.

> **The war on Iraq**
> First meant as a pre-emptive strike* against a country which was said to have weapons of mass destruction, the war against Iraq was at first supported by a large majority of Americans, who believed that the military campaign would be

short and vindicate* the coalition's decision. Although it did not have the approval of NATO, it was particularly encouraged by Donald Rumsfeld, the Secretary of Defence and the "neo-conservatives", the members of the Bush administration who believed that America's role was to reshape* the world and bring democracy to the Middle East. But the failure to find banned weapons of mass destruction (meaning the US went to war on flawed information), evidence* showing the abuse* of Iraqi prisoners in US custody, and casualties* among US troops led to growing disapproval of America's engagement in Iraq. In 2009, President Barack Obama announced the withdrawal of most US troops by the end of August 2010.

2004: George W. Bush wins a second term.

2005: Hurricane Katrina causes severe destruction along the Gulf Coast and in New Orleans.

2006: Democrats take control of Congress in mid-term elections.

2007: President Bush vetoes a bill setting a timetable to pull American troops out of Iraq.

2008: Investment bank Lehman Brothers collapses; beginning of the worst financial crisis since the Great Depression.

Democratic senator Barack Obama becomes the first black president of the United States.

2009: «Tea Party» rally (the first of many) held in protest at Obama administration's plans to bail out banks and introduce healthcare reform. President Obama is awarded the Nobel Peace Prize for his foreign policy vision, based on multilateralism (i.e. gaining the support of the UN or other nations).

2010: Oil spill disaster in Gulf of Mexico; the Senate votes in favour of repealing Don't Ask, Don't Tell, the Clinton-era military policy that forbids openly gay men and women from serving in the military.

2012: President Obama wins a second term.

Barack Obama's legacy

Barack Obama, the first African-American president, won the presidency in 2008 and again in 2012, backed mainly by young voters and minorities. Several of his intended reforms were overturned after 2010, when Democrats lost control of Congress, but his main achievements were:

– Healthcare reform : thanks to the Affordable Care Act ('Obamacare'), the percentage of Americans without insurance dropped from 15.7% in 2011 to to 9.1% in 2015 .

– Environmental legislation : The United States signed the Paris climate agreement (to cut greenhouse gas emissions) and limited coal mining as well as oil and gas drilling.

– The Economy: when President Obama took office, the economy was plummeting*, with high unemployment, a fall in house prices and the financial industry on the verge of collapse. Eight years later the economy was stable again thanks to a stimulus package for industry, financial reform, and the Home Affordable Refinance Program, to rescue millions of US homeowners facing foreclosure*.
– Foreign relations: Barack Obama's presidency was marked by co-operation with allies and improved relations between the US and two former antagonists : normalised relations with Cuba and the Iran nuclear deal. He also scaled down* US troop commitments in Afghanistan and Iraq.
– Criminal Justice reform: President Obama demanded accountability* for police violence, backed a series of sentencing reforms as well as a few gun-control executive actions, but any further new gun-control policy was thwarted* by the National Rifle Association's powerful lobbying.
– Immigration: Mr Obama took a series of executive actions to give normalised status to undocumented immigrants who entered the US as children. He also deported more undocumented immigrants than ever, especially those who had been convicted of some criminal offence.
– The defence of LGBT rights.
– By occupying the White House, something that would have seemed impossible for a black man one or two decades earlier, Barack Obama also set an example and gave hope to thousands of black Americans.
But he was not a good party builder and the Democrats lost many seats during his presidency. As he left office, the Republican Party controlled the White House, both houses of Congress, a large majority of governorships and state legislative houses.

to plummet: *dégringoler*; **foreclosure:** *la saisie d'un bien hypothéqué*; **to scale down:** *réduire*; **accountability:** *responsabilité*; **to thwart:** *contrecarrer*

2013: Edward Snowden releases classified documents concerning mass surveillance by the NSA.
2014: After four years of Republican opposition, protests and legal challenges, the Patient Protection and Affordable Care Act, also known as "Obamacare", begins to be implemented*.
2015: Same-sex marriage is legalized in all fifty states.
2016: Donald Trump is elected president, while the Republicans also regain the majority in both the House and the Senate.

Donald Trump's legacy

One of the first presidents elected without having held an elected office before, Donald Trump was chosen by staunch Republicans, but also by many among the poor and the working class who felt they had been neglected by the Washington establishment and decided to elect someone who flouted* convention and did not symbolize governance, expertise and bureaucracy.

→ Many of Trump's decisions reflect the priorities of the Republican Party:
– The appointment of conservative Supreme Court and federal judges, and a support for pro-lifers.
– Massive tax cuts for corporations to give a boost to the economy, which led to record low unemployment. All this was swept away by the pandemic, which left America with huge unemployment and national debt. But America also succeeded in developing coronavirus vaccines in a matter of months.
– A curb* on regulations to protect the environment and America's withdrawal from the Paris agreement to combat climate change.
– Tougher curbs on illegal immigration, separating children from their parents in the process (and erecting some 500 miles of barrier along the U.S.-Mexico border); a travel ban on several of Muslim-majority nations.
– 'American First': a surrender of global leadership, replaced by a fortress-like mentality. Hence Donald Trump's questioning the NATO alliance, his withdrawal from the Paris accord on climate change, from the UN Human Rights Council, and from the agreement to stop Iran's nuclear program (unilaterally imposing sanctions on countries doing business with Iran).
Donald Trump also reduced U.S. forces in conflict zones such as Afghanistan, Iraq and Syria, confronted China over unfair trade practices, while seeming to get on well with leaders like North Korea's Kim Jong Un and Russia's Vladimir Putin.
– But Donald Trump failed to repeal Barack Obama's Affordable Care Act.

→ But his governance has also been called 'dysfunctional' by Republicans and Democrats alike, in particular:
– His close relationship with the 'alt-right' (for alternative right, a loosely connected far-right, white nationalist movement) ; his encouragement of conspiracy theories and support for QAnon's rambling theories , and support for those who refused the electoral College vote and stormed* the US Capitol.
At the end of his tenure*, Trump left America more fragmented and polarized than ever.
– His refusal to make his tax returns public.
– The fact that he put democracy to the test by advancing misinformation (also called 'alternative facts', which go much beyond spin, for example his false claims of a stolen election or his downplaying* the severity of the Covid pandemic). Donald Trump also used social media to transmit such ideas directly to his followers, which led to his banishment from social-media platforms in 2021.

to withdraw from: *se retirer de*; **to hi-jack:** *détourner*; **the state of the union address:** *le discours annuel du président, en janvier, pour présenter son programme à venir*; **the axis of evil:** *l'axe du mal*; **to pledge:** *jurer, promettre*; **a pre-emptive strike:** *une frappe préventive*; **to vindicate:** *justifier*; **to reshape:** *réorganiser*; **evidence:** *des preuves*; **prisoner abuse:** *les mauvais traitements infligés aux prisonniers*; **casualties:** *morts et blessés*; **to implement:** *mettre en œuvre*; **to flout:** *se moquer de*; **a curb:** *un frein*; **to storm:** *prendre d'assaut*; **his tenure:** *son mandat*; **to downplay:** *minimiser l'importance de...*

2017 : The White House denies allegations of collusion between Donald Trump's election campaign and the Russian authorities. In the wake of the #MeToo movement, Harvey Weinstein is found guilty of rape and sexual assault.
An estimated 49,000 Americans die of opioid overdoses during the year.
2019-2020: After it emerged that Donald Trump leaned on Ukraine to discredit the Democratic front-runner, the House of Representatives starts an impeachment inquiry. Mr Trump is acquitted after the Republicans decide not to call any witnesses.
2020: Covid-19 quickly spreads in America. It leads to a market crash. Congress votes to provide relief to businesses and households. Some states go into lockdown* but Donald Trump does not take the pandemic seriously at first and prefers relaxing restrictions to help the economy. By April, The US has more reported infections than any other country. Over 600 000 people have died from Covid by the end of 2020. But over 90,000 Americans have also died from drug abuse (including opioids) in 2020.
Three vaccines against Covid-19 are developed by US laboratories (Pfizer – co-produced with a German laboratory, Moderna, Johnson and Johnson).
Peaceful protests as well as riots and looting spread across the US after the death of George Floyd, a black American who died after a policeman knelt on his neck (in 2021 he was eventually convicted of murder). This leads to a surge of support for 'Black Lives Matter'. In several states, protesters begin toppling statues representing personalities linked to racism in the past. The Confederate battle flag disappears from official regalia.
In the American election, Joe Biden and Kamala Harris, his running-mate, pass the required 270 electoral-college votes. Donald Trump refuses to concede defeat claiming that the vote was fraudulent, and hinders the smooth transfer of power.
2021: Joe Biden's win is confirmed by Congress in spite of Donald Trump inciting supporters to storm the Capitol building. For the second time Donald Trump is impeached for inciting such an attack. But the vote in the Senate failed to reach the two-thirds majority required to convict the former president.
President Biden's presidency is marked by a radical change. He overturns several previous decisions such as the ban on travel from some Muslim countries, re-joins the Paris accord on climate change, and relaxes Donald Trump's strict immigration rules. American troops will pull out of Afghanistan by September. The focus is on union rather than division under Trump's presidency.
The House of representatives approves a $1.9 trillion stimulus bill to help all Americans, with extra help for poorer families and those on unemployment benefit.

President Biden says he will support an effort to suspend patents for Covid-19 vaccines in order to help countries like India to produce their own doses. But there are still restrictions on the export of vaccines.
August 2021 : emboldened by Joe Biden's decision that US troops will leave Afghanistan by September, the Talibans capture most cities, including the capital Kabul. The Afghan army is too weak to fight back and the US and Western countries start evacuating their personnel and Afghan associates amid chaos.
September: The UK, US and Australia sign a historic security pact in the Indo-Pacific (AUKUS), in an effort to counter China's influence there. Australia abandons a contract for conventional submarines with France in favour of a nuclear submarine program with the US.
This decision, as well as the sudden withdrawal of American forces from Afghanistan, confirms Biden's intention to put 'America first' but also earns him criticism for lack of consultation with America's allies.

repeal : *abroger*; **lockdown:** *confinement*; **a patent:** *un brevet d'invention*

The UK, US and Australia sign a historic security pact in the Indo-Pacific (AUKUS), in an effort to counter China's influence there. Australia abandons a contract with France for conventional submarines in favour of a nuclear submarine program with the US.

(A site devoted to American history)
liennathan.fr/yj22i6

(An archive of politically significant audio material (e.g. political speeches))
liennathan.fr/8y3a2q

(The historical collections of the Library of Congress)
liennathan.fr/aau966

4 EIGHT DATES WHICH SHAPED AMERICA

1776: The Declaration of Independence

Mainly drafted* by Thomas Jefferson, the Declaration of Independence was adopted by Congress on July 4th 1776 (July 4th is now a public holiday.) Here are its main points:
– The preamble* declares that men have natural rights ("life, liberty and the pursuit of happiness") and that people are entitled* to replace a government which does not protect these rights.
– It then condemns the tyranny imposed by the British government and the king over the colonies.
– Following Locke's ideas, the declaration concludes that the people are justified in overturning* a government which does not respect the will of the majority of the people.

IN CONGRESS, July 4, 1776.
The unanimous Declaration of the thirteen united States of America,

When in the Course of human events, it becomes necessary for one people to dissolve the political bands* which have connected them with another, and to assume among the powers of the earth, the separate and equal station* to which the Laws of Nature and of Nature's God entitle them, a decent respect to the opinions of mankind requires that they should declare the causes which impel* them to the separation.

We hold these truths to be self-evident, that all men are created equal, that they are endowed* by their Creator with certain unalienable Rights, that among these are Life, Liberty and the pursuit* of Happiness.

The first paragraphs of the Declaration of Independence

to draft: *rédiger*; **a preamble:** *une préambule*; **to be entitled to:** *avoir droit à*; **to overturn:** *renverser*; **bands = bonds:** *des contrats, des liens*; **station:** *la condition, le rang*; **to impel:** *obliger, pousser*; **to endow:** *doter*; **the pursuit:** *la quête*

■ 1787-8: The Constitution

It was inspired by
– the writings of the English philosopher Locke (1632-1704), who advocated* a 'compact' or social contract between people and their government, in order to guarantee their natural rights (life, liberty, property),
– Montesquieu's ideas about the separation of powers.
– The British Magna Carta and the Habeas Corpus Act.

The Constitution drafted by the delegates to the Continental Congress (among whom were Washington, Franklin, Hamilton and Madison) guaranteed the rights of the citizens against the abuses of government, and established a system of balance* between the three branches of government.

The main principles which form the basis of the Constitution are:

1. Separation of powers

– The legislative branch (Congress, with the House of Representatives and the Senate)
– The executive branch (the President and Vice-President)
– The judicial branch (the Supreme Court)

Each branch has some control over the other two, which creates a system of checks and balances*.

2. Representation of the people by direct suffrage in a republic.

3. Federalism

It creates a balance between the powers and rights of the federal government (which is responsible for foreign affairs and the relations between states) and those of the states. Each state is equally represented in the Senate, but the representation is proportional to the state's population in the House of Representatives.

4. The defence of individual rights

It is enshrined* in the Bill of Rights*.

to advocate: *préconiser*; **balance:** *équilibre*; **checks and balances:** *l'équilibre des pouvoirs*; **enshrined:** *assuré, garanti*; **the Bill of Rights:** *la Déclaration des droits*

■ **1791: The Bill of Rights**

Ten amendments, called The Bill of Rights, were added to the constitution in 1791 to defend the citizens against the excessive power of a centralized government. Here are some of the most important ones:

First Amendment: it guarantees freedom of speech, of religion and of the press. It contains the Establishment Clause, which states the separation of Church and State.

Second Amendment: it guarantees the right to keep and bear arms.

Fourth Amendment: it deals with the right to privacy*: a citizen's home cannot be searched* without a warrant*.

Fifth Amendment: it guarantees the right to remain silent (that is to say, not to testify* against oneself) when accused of a crime, and states that someone cannot be tried* twice on the same charge*.

Eighth Amendment: it protects the individual against "cruel and unusual" punishment (and is therefore called upon by those who are against the death penalty).

Tenth Amendment: it states that all powers not given to the federal government in the Constitution reside with the States.

Other amendments were later added but are not part of the Bill of Rights. For an amendment to be ratified there must be a two-thirds majority in both Houses and the bill must then be passed in three-quarters of the states' legislatures.

the right to privacy: *le respect de la vie privée*; **to search:** *fouiller*; **a warrant:** *un mandat de perquisition*; **to testify:** *témoigner*; **to try so:** *juger quelqu'un*; **a charge:** *une inculpation*

■ **1865: The Thirteenth Amendment** made slavery illegal. Southern States were required* to approve of the amendment in order to re-enter the Union.

to require: *exiger*

■ **1920: The Nineteenth Amendment** gave the right to vote to every citizen, including women.

■ **1954: Brown v. Board of Education of Topeka** was a Supreme Court decision which reversed the 1896 "separate but equal" principle and paved the way for* desegregation.

to pave the way for: *préparer le terrain pour*

■ **1964: The Civil Rights Act** defended the rights of black people, guaranteeing the right to vote and the right to Equal Employment Opportunity, and protected them against discrimination in housing.

- **1973: Roe v. Wade** was a Supreme Court decision which legalized abortion*

abortion: *l'avortement.*

(a site devoted to the American constitution)
liennathan.fr/8c8cu8

CONTROVERSIAL ISSUES

- **The USA Patriot Act**

Passed in 2001, in the month that followed the 9/11 attacks, and partly prompted* by the fear of biological attacks, the law increases the powers of investigators over citizens and immigrants, although such powers do not conform to the Constitution's Bill of Rights. It extends surveillance (cameras, bugged* telephones, monitored* e-mails, searching a suspect's house without informing him for weeks, accessing records: libraries, credits cards...), targets* immigrants, mainly those who are Arab or Muslim, and makes it possible to hold prisoners from Afghanistan at Guantanamo Bay, indefinitely and without any charge*, beyond the reach of American courts, simply labelling* them 'enemy combatants'.
The USA Patriot Act has been much criticized by those who say that the balance between personal liberty and security is shifting in favour of the latter.

Here are some arguments for and against.

For	Against
With terrorists, information has to be found before they strike. This may mean embarrassing innocent people (by revealing some hidden business dealings or strange reading habits) but that is a small price to pay for saving lives.	Civil libertarians* are concerned that it gives the authorities too much power to look into the lives of innocent people and encroach on* their freedom and privacy.

to prompt: *pousser, entraîner*; **to bug:** *brancher sur table d'écoute*; **to monitor:** *contrôler*; **to target:** *viser*; **a charge:** *une inculpation*; **to label:** *étiqueter*; **a civil libertarian:** *un défenseur des libertés civiques*; **to encroach on:** *mordre, rogner sur*

5 CHECKS AND BALANCES

The constitution is based on the separation of powers – legislative, executive, judiciary – each being able to limit the powers of the others and prevent any misuse* of them. This is called a system of **checks and balances***.

Executive power
= the President & Vice-President

The President is the head of the executive and the commander-in-chief of armed forces. He suggests new legislation to Congress but may veto the bills* which were not voted for by two-thirds of the Representatives. He appoints* Supreme Court Judges and the Secretaries of State.

The President and Vice-President are elected for four years on the same ticket*. If the President is ill or resigns* before the end of his term*, the Vice-President takes over. The President can be re-elected once only.

Legislative power = Congress

Congress puts forward laws and votes to pass them. It also controls the executive (controls the budget, taxation, the military, and can, with a two-thirds majority, override* the President's veto of a bill, can impeach* the President.)

Congress is made up of:

– The House of Representatives (with the number of representatives proportional to the population of each state.) It consists of 435 members, elected for 2 years. They represent the interests of individuals. The House of Representatives is presided over by the "speaker of the House", a member of the majority party.

– The Senate: 100 elected senators (two Senators for each state). They are elected for 6 years, with one third of Senate renewed every two years.) They represent the interests of the state.

The Judiciary
= The Supreme Court

The highest court of justice. It checks that the laws (both federal and state laws) are constitutional and it interprets acts of Congress.

The Supreme Court is made up of 9 members, appointed by the President for life, but their nomination must be approved by the Senate.
(→ p. 162)

a misuse: *une mauvaise utilisation*; **checks and balances:** *l'équilibre des pouvoirs*; **a bill:** *un projet de loi*; **to appoint:** *nommer*; **the ticket:** *la liste électorale portant le nom du président et du vice-président*; **to resign:** *démissionner*; **a term:** *un mandat*; **to override:** *annuler, passer outre*; **to impeach:** *mettre en accusation*

WHAT THE CONSTITUTION CREATED

The Constitution's Framers set out to design a government in which no person or branch of government could become all-powerful. Thus, they carefully divided the powers of government among lawmakers, judges, and a chief executive, and they made it possible for each group to balance and check each other's powers. What major powers does the Constitution assign to each branch of government? How can each branch check the powers of the other two branches? The charts on this page provide clear answers.

THREE GOVERNMENT BRANCHES, EACH WITH SEPARATE POWERS...

CHIEF POWERS OF THE LEGISLATIVE BRANCH (Congress)

1. Passes federal laws
2. Raises taxes
3. Regulates foreign and interstate commerce
4. Declares war
5. Raises and funds the military
6. May borrow money by issuing bonds for sale

CHIEF POWERS OF THE EXECUTIVE BRANCH (The President)

1. Commander-in-Chief of the military
2. Makes treaties with other countries
3. Appoints ambassadors, federal judges, Supreme Court Justices, thousands of other federal officials
4. Administers U.S. laws
5. Acts as head of state

CHIEF POWERS OF THE JUDICIAL BRANCH (Supreme Court)

1. Makes final review of lower federal court rulings and appeals from state courts when they involve federal law or Constitutional issues
2. Is first and final court to hear cases involving foreign ambassadors
3. Rules on disputes between states

CONGRESS'S CHECKING POWER

Over the President

- May override President's veto.
- May impeach the President.
- Senate must ratify treaties President makes.
- Senate must approve President's nominees for ambassador, other high level jobs.
- Controls spending; can reject President's budget requests, including military funds.
- May investigate, reorganize Executive Branch departments.

Over the Supreme Court

- May propose amendments to the Constitution to override a Supreme Court ruling.
- Senate must approve Court nominees.
- May impeach federal judges.
- Decides jurisdiction of courts.
- May change size of Supreme Court.
- May create new, shut down old federal courts below Supreme Court level.

PRESIDENT'S CHECKING POWER

Over the Supreme Court

- Nominates Supreme Court Justices and lower federal court judges.
- May grant pardons to persons convicted of violating federal laws.
- May refuse to enforce a federal court order.

Over the Congress

- May veto laws passed by Congress.
- May order special sessions of Congress.
- As leader of political party, may pressure members of the party to vote a certain way.*
- May appeal directly to citizens to pressure their representatives in Congress to vote a certain way.*

SUPREME COURT'S CHECKING POWER

Over the President

- May rule that the President, other members of Executive Branch have acted unconstitutionally, exceeded their authority under law.
- May interpret treaties signed by President.

Over the Congress

- May rule that laws passed by Congress and signed by the President are unconstitutional and therefore illegal.

...AND THE ABILITY TO CHECK EACH OTHER

Though not defined by the Constitution, these powers evolved over time.

(The official site of the US Executive Branch)
liennathan.fr/3kb3s3

(An official site about US Courts)
liennathan.fr/73p8dc

(An official website of the United States government)
liennathan.fr/99z3gh

6 STATES VS FEDERAL GOVERNMENT

■ **The Federal government** is responsible for foreign policy, the armed forces, the FBI*, the printing of money.

■ **States** are responsible for all other matters concerning them (e.g. education, transport, health...). Each state has, like the country as a whole, a constitution, a governor (gubernatorial elections* take place every four years in most states, usually on non-presidential election years, so that electors are not influenced by national politics), a House of Representatives and a Senate and its own courts. Different states often have very different laws (the age at which you can drive, the death penalty, the educational system), but any law passed by the federal government must be applied by each state.

FBI = Federal Bureau of Investigation: *service de police judiciaire et de renseignement intérieur*; **a gubernatorial election:** *une élection du gouverneur*

■ **The executive** consists of fourteen departments headed by secretaries*.
Here are some of the main departments:
The State Department*
The Treasury*
The Interior Department*
The Defence Department*
The Justice Department, headed by the Attorney general*

There are also Federal Agencies to control various specific areas, for example NASA or the CIA*. In 2002, in the wake of* 9/11, a new Department of Homeland Security was created to coordinate the work of the FBI, the CIA, Immigration Services and Customs, and try to prevent terrorist attacks.

a Secretary: *un ministre*; **the State Department:** *le ministère des Affaires étrangères*; **the Treasury:** *le ministère des Finances*; **the Interior Department:** *le ministère de l'Intérieur*; **the Defence Department:** *le ministère des Armées*; **the Attorney general:** *le ministre de la Justice*; **CIA = Central Intelligence Agency:** *la surveillance du territoire*; **in the wake of:** *à la suite de*

■ **Laws** can be passed at the federal level (they then apply to all states) or at the level of a particular state (as long as they do not contradict federal law). In both cases, the procedure is the same:
• A bill is introduced by a member of the Senate or House of Representatives, and is then discussed in a committee.
• Public hearings* are held and various pressure groups are heard, after which some changes may be made to the bill.
• The bill is discussed in one house, changes are sometimes made, and if the bill is approved, it is sent to the other house, which may make changes (which need to be accepted by the first house), before accepting or rejecting the bill.

• The President must then sign the bill, but he can also veto it. In the latter case, the bill will still become law if it is approved by two-thirds of Congress.

Many legal battles take place when new state laws might violate federal law, as in the case of same-sex marriages, which several states (like Massachusetts and California) have legalised, while others want a constitutional amendment to define marriage as a union between a man and a woman and thus a constitutional ban on gay marriage.

a public hearing: *une séance publique de discussion*

CONTROVERSIAL ISSUES

▪ Big government conservatism

The expression sounds like an oxymoron* since most Republican and conservative governments (like President Trump's) wish to curb* the powers of central government, believing that the fewer regulations there are the better. President Bush's government, however, considerably increased government spending, mostly in order to promote conservative ideas. The federal government was thus given more power to set standards of education (teaching the value of abstinence and marriage, warning of the dangers of drugs), to extend Medicare, to ensure homeland security. This is why President Bush's two terms in office increased the powers both of the federal government and of the President. The Covid-19 crisis similarly led to a massive government intervention to reduce the economic impact of quarantine. President Trump's huge stimulus was met with little resistance.

an oxymoron: *un oxymore*; **to curb:** *limiter*

7 PARTIES & ELECTIONS

▪ A two-party system

A split soon appeared among the framers of the American Constitution*, some, like Hamilton, being in favour of a strong federal government (they became the Federalist Party, which disappeared a few decades later), others, like Jefferson, argued for more autonomous states. The latter formed the Democratic-Republicans, which later split into two parties, which developed into the present two-party system.

– The Republicans (= the GOP, Grand Old Party). Their emblem is the elephant. It is a more conservative party on the side of big business, in favour of economic liberalism and defending the rights of individuals against too powerful a central government. The Republicans pride themselves on Lincoln's fight against slavery and on helping pass the law that gave women the vote in 1920.

– The Democrats. Their emblem is the donkey*. They are traditionally more in favour of state intervention in economic and social affairs and closer to the minorities. Democratic presidents in the past tended to have more social programmes, Roosevelt with his New Deal, Kennedy and Johnson with their Civil Rights and Voting Rights Acts, Clinton with education and health reforms, Obama with 'Obamacare'.

Since 2009, the Tea-Party movement has been on the fringe of the Republican Party. Named after the Boston Tea Party of 1773, when colonists protested against a British tax on tea, it is a loose, decentralized association of local groups which share a number of libertarian and populist ideas: limiting the size of the federal government, reducing government spending (hence their opposition to Obama's PACA) and curbing tax increases.

a framer of the Constitution : *un artisan de la Constitution*; **a donkey:** *un âne*

The elections

The President is not elected directly but by an electoral college, itself elected by the people. In each state, it is the candidate with the largest number of votes who gets all the votes in the electoral college.

This system makes it difficult for a smaller party to be more than a pressure group*.

ELECTING THE US PRESIDENT

When does an election take place?

The President and Vice-President are elected every four years. The election takes place in November, on the Tuesday following the first Monday. The President can be elected for a second term*, but not for a third one (Roosevelt being the exception).

Who can run for* President?

The candidates must be native-born US citizens, have resided in the United States for at least 14 years, and be at least 35 years of age.

How are the candidates of each party chosen?

First each party selects delegates:

– either in "primary elections" held in the states by secret ballot* of party members

– or in "caucuses" in other states, where delegates are chosen after a series of meetings at county, then district, then state levels.

Some delegates can also be chosen because they are prominent party members.

During the summer which precedes each November election, political parties hold conventions, which are very large meetings attended by the delegates.

A majority of delegate votes is needed for a candidate to win the party's nomination. He/she becomes the party's "nominee"*. Usually, the delegates let the chosen presidential candidate select a vice-presidential candidate.

The "ticket"

The candidates for President and Vice-President (also called the President's "running mate") "run" together on a "ticket": they will win together or lose together; Americans cannot vote for one of the two and not the other.

The electoral college

The American presidential election is not a direct one. In November, elections are held in each of the 50 states and in the District of Columbia, where the voters choose "electors"* who promise to vote for one of the tickets. These electors form the "Electoral College".
Each state has the same number of electors as it has senators (two for each state) and representatives (the number is proportional to the population of the state.) The District of Columbia (Washington) has three electors. There are therefore 538 electors (435 + 100 + 3).

The result of the vote

In most states the "winner-take-all" system* prevails, which is to say that the ticket which receives the largest number of votes in the state gets all the electors of the state. (The exceptions are Maine and Nebraska, where the electors are chosen by district.)This means that it is possible for a President to be elected although he had fewer popular votes than his/her rival.

Voting for the President

The Electoral College then votes for the President and Vice-President, each elector being given one vote. Normally, one of the tickets receives a majority of votes (at least 270), so that the President and Vice-President are elected. If there is no majority, it is the House of Representatives which then chooses the President from the three candidates who received the largest number of votes in the Electoral College. It is the Senate which would then choose the Vice-President.

The incumbent president* remains in office until the official inauguration of the new president, who is sworn into office* in January.

a pressure group: *un groupe de pression*; **a term:** *un mandat*; **to run for:** *être candidat à*; **a secret ballot:** *un vote à bulletin secret*; **the nominee:** *le candidat désigné, choisi par un parti*; **an elector:** *un grand électeur*; **the winner-take-all system:** *le système électoral où toutes les voix vont au vainqueur*; **the incumbent president:** *le président sortant, le président en exercice*; **to be sworn into office:** *prêter serment*.

The Presidents of the United States

1789 George WASHINGTON
1792 “
1796 John ADAMS
1800 Thomas JEFFERSON
1804 “
1808 James MADISON
1812 “
1816 James MONROE
1820 “
1824 John Quincy ADAMS
1828 Andrew JACKSON
1832 “
1836 Martin VAN BUREN
1840 William H. HARRISON
1841 John TYLER
1844 James K. POLK
1848 Zachary TAYLOR
1850 Millard FILLMORE
1852 Franklin PIERCE (D)
1856 James BUCHANAN (D)
1860 Abraham LINCOLN (R)
1864 “
1865 Andrew JOHNSON (D)
1868 Ulysses S. GRANT (R)
1872 “
1876 Rutherford B. HAYES (R)
1880 James A. GARFIELD (R)
1881 Chester A. ARTHUR (R)
1884 Grover CLEVELAND (D)
1888 Benjamin HARRISON (R)
1892 Grover CLEVELAND (D)
1896 William McKINLEY (R)
1900 “
1901 Theodore ROOSEVELT (R)
1904 “
1908 William H. TAFT (R)
1912 Woodrow WILSON (D)
1916 “
1920 Warren G. HARDING (R)
1923 Calvin COOLIDGE (R)
1924 “
1928 Herbert C. HOOVER (R)
1932 Franklin D. ROOSEVELT (D)
1936 “
1940 “
1944 “
1945 Harry S. TRUMAN (D)
1948 “
1952 Dwight D. EISENHOWER (R)
1956 “
1960 John F. KENNEDY (D)
1963 Lyndon B. JOHNSON (D)
1964 “
1968 Richard M. NIXON (R)
1972 “
1974 Gerald R. FORD (R)
1976 James E. CARTER, Jr, (D)
1980 Ronald W. REAGAN (R)
1984 “
1988 George H. BUSH (R)
1992 William J. CLINTON (D)
2000 George W. BUSH (R)
2004 “
2008 Barack OBAMA (D)
2012 “
2016 Donald TRUMP (R)
2020 Joe BIDEN (D)

(D) = Democratic; (R) = Republican

(The official site of the Republican Party)
liennathan.fr/tf69u5

(The official site of the Democratic Party)
liennathan.fr/t6f43a

(A site with information about the US presidential elections)
liennathan.fr/3r8n6g

(A White House site giving information about all the American Presidents)
liennathan.fr/4y7u9r

8 POPULATION & IMMIGRATION

The United States' population reached 332, 915 073 inhabitants in 2021.
The United States is a Nation of Immigrants. In the 19th century particularly, the population grew rapidly, with the arrival of two main waves of immigrants fleeing* religious persecution and/or poverty:
– in the early years of the century, many Irish, English, Germans, Austrians and Scandinavians came to America. The reasons were mainly economic: loss of jobs in England, the potato famine in Ireland.
– in the last decades of the century, many immigrants arrived from central and southern Europe (Germans, Italians, Greeks, Armenians, Jews, Poles...). The reasons were economic, but also political (e.g. the 1848 revolutions in France and Germany).
In the twentieth century, the new immigrants mainly came from central Europe (fleeing Nazi Germany), from Asia (China, Japan, the Philippines...) and from Cuba, Mexico and South America.

For most of these people, the United States represented a land of freedom and opportunity, the possibility of a new departure after severing* their links with the mother country. Between 1892 and 1954, the new immigrants arrived at Ellis Island in New York harbor*, where they were inspected and either refused or accepted.

Regulating the tide of immigrants

Here are the key dates in the attempt to regulate or stem the tide* of immigrants to the USA.
1819: The Steerage* Act limits the number of passengers arriving on each ship.
1879-1943: A number of laws restrict the immigration of Asian people, particularly of Chinese immigrants, who provided cheap labour in California and kept wages low.
1891: The Immigration Act bars a number of people (e.g. those considered immoral, those with contagious diseases) from entering the United States. Ellis Island opens the following year.
1924: The National Origins Act creates quotas and privileges immigrants from Northern and Western Europe as well as from Central America.
In 1929, the total number of these immigrants is limited to about 150,000 a year.
1965: The Immigration and Nationality Act repeals* the 1924 Act, creates different ceilings for different groups and favours qualified immigrants, thus increasing the brain drain* from Europe.
1980-2000: The annual ceilings rise from 300,000 a year to 700,000 during this period. Skilled and qualified immigrants are still being favoured.
2001: After 9/11, The Patriot Act is passed to help the deportation, or prevent the immigration, of possible terrorists.

In spite of stringent laws* and penalties against illegal immigrants, it is believed that up to a million enter the United States every year. One of President Trump's campaign promises was to deport illegal immigrants and ban Muslims from entering the US.

Originally, the newly arrived immigrants aimed at merging into* the American culture. America would be a "melting pot"*. The expression comes from a play by Israel Zangwill, *The Melting Pot* (1908), a modern version of *Romeo and Juliet.*

"Understand that America is God's Crucible*, the great Melting-Pot where all the races of Europe are melting and reforming! A fig for* your feuds* and vendettas! Germans and Frenchmen, Irishmen and Englishmen, Jews and Russians – into the Crucible with you all! God is making the American."

The immigrants would thus lose their national identities as they became Americans and shared the English language. Indeed, laws passed in a number of states in the late 19th century encouraged linguistic assimilation.

But as several communities felt excluded from the dominant WASP* culture, they began to reassert* their roots*and show pride in their origins and cultural differences. The new aim was no longer a melting pot but a "mosaic" or a "salad bowl" in which the different elements remained identifiable. Americans who wish to assert their ethnic origins call themselves Afro-Americans, Chinese-Americans or Hispano-Americans, that is to say hyphenated Americans, the hyphen* showing that neither of the two identities is superior to the other.

Recently however, the growing use of Spanish, and the potential conflicts between communities that live in separate cultural enclaves, have led to a backlash* and to several movements defending the use of English only.

Although the United States remains a land of opportunity, there is still a great deal of poverty, which mainly affects Blacks, Hispanics and single-parent families. There are also a great many illegal immigrants, many of them crossing the 2000-mile long US-Mexican border.

The United States population remains deeply divided between liberals and conservatives on a number of issues, being for instance the country from which the MeToo movement started, but also the one in which a number of states have recently passed bills to make abortion illegal.

to flee: *fuir*; **to sever:** *couper*; **New York harbor:** *le port de New York*; **to stem the tide:** *endiguer le flot*; **steerage:** *l'entrepont*; **to repeal:** *annuler*; **the brain drain:** *la fuite des cerveaux*; **stringent laws:** *des lois strictes*; **to merge into:** *se fondre dans*; **a melting pot:** *un creuset*; **a crucible:** *un creuset*; **a fig for...:** *au diable...*; **a feud:** *une querelle*; **WASP = White Anglo-Saxon Protestant; to reassert:** *réaffirmer*; **a root:** *une racine*; **a hyphen:** *un trait d'union*; **a backlash:** *une réaction*

(The homepage of the US Census Bureau)
liennathan.fr/x6yu55

(US citizenship and immigration services)
liennathan.fr/ec89g8

Is the United States still a meritocracy?

The idea that the United States is a meritocracy, that there are opportunities for everyone depending on their abilities, not on family background, is still deeply anchored* in American mentality. The idea is embodied* in the novels of Horatio Algers (1832-1899), which are rags to riches* stories of poor boys succeeding through sheer determination and hard work.
However that view is now being challenged by a number of facts.
– According to the OECD, in 2020, income inequality in the U.S. was the highest of all the G7 nations. In 2018, households in the top fifth of earners (with incomes of $130,001 or more) brought in 52% of all U.S. income. The gap between the richest and the poorest families has doubled from 1989 to 2016.
– The political elites seem to perpetuate themselves, all coming from rich families and having benefited from a select education (private school, Yale, Harvard...). Parental income is one of the best ways of predicting how well a child will do.
– According to the Economic Policy Institute, social mobility has even declined.
– A study of the correlation between the incomes of fathers and sons shows that it is higher in the United States than in other rich countries like Canada or Germany.
America thus seems to be turning into a class society. As *The Economist* put it in 2005, the American social ladder is getting both "higher" and "stickier".

Why?
– Education, which largely determines social mobility, very much depends on class. 75% of students in the top 146 colleges come from the richest socio-economic 20%. Where Affirmative Action takes place, it does not help since it helps on the basis of race rather than social disadvantage. Besides, many colleges give preference to students whose parents attended the college, and such students are already socially advantaged.
– What with outsourcing*, contracting* out and increased competition, there is little employee stability in large companies, which makes it increasingly difficult for someone to move up the company hierarchy.
– Information technology has increased the demand for the very highly skilled, who have profited from the new global audience and seen their productivity rocket*.

America remains a socially mobile country, though not as much as it used to be.

anchored: *ancré*; **is embodied:** *est exprimé, concrétisé par*; **from rags to riches:** *de la misère à la richesse*; **outsourcing:** *la délocalisation*; **to contract out:** *sous-traiter*; **to rocket:** *monter en flèche*

Immigration policies

A country born of immigration, the United States is now becoming increasingly protectionist and less eager to attract new talents from abroad. The reason is both fear of terrorism and the threat posed by illegal immigration.
Around a million new immigrants cross the United States border* illegally every year, most of them from Mexico. Many others die in the attempt. There were about 10.5 million unauthorized immigrants in the U.S. in 2017, 80% of them Latino. Though the border with Mexico is patrolled* to stop them entering, little has been done so far to cope with the problem. It is a thorny issue* which divides Americans.

There are obvious objections to illegal immigration:
- It undermines the rule of law since it is illegal.
- It might bring terrorists in.
- It takes the jobs or brings down the salaries of unskilled Americans.
- It might lead to the "Mexification" of American culture.

But there are also strong arguments in favour of letting them stay:
- They take the jobs Americans refuse to take.
- They are good for the economy.
- Most illegal immigrants are hard-working and their only wish is to become full American citizens.

The need to overhaul* America's immigration laws has recently led to a number of proposals and bills, none of which has so far been successful.

Here is a range of proposals aired* during the recent debates:

The more restrictive proposals:
- Build a wall along the border with Mexico (as has already been done in some areas) in order to tighten* the border. That is what Donald Trump pledged to do during his campaign.
- Increase border security with the help of better equipment (there are already volunteer "Minutemen" stationed along the Arizona border to deter would-be illegal immigrants).
- Repatriate captured illegal immigrants to their hometowns. It was another of Donald Trump's promises.
- Punish them, those who help them, and their employers, with prison sentences. Make sure that the law is properly enforced*.

Towards legalization:
- Foreign workers might be given identity cards with biometric data on them.
- Illegals who want to stay in America would pay a fine*, learn English, keep working and be allowed to apply for citizenship after several years, although they would have

to wait in line* behind those who have applied to enter legally. Illegals might also have to return to their countries of origin in order to apply for legal entry.

• Other illegals could be given temporary cards as "guest-workers" to satisfy the demand for labour*.

In 2014, the influx of thousands of child migrants from Central America (El Salvador, Honduras, Guatemala), fleeing gang violence and domestic abuse, created a 'humanitarian situation' along the border between the United States and Mexico. They hoped to be allowed to stay in the United States, believing rumours that might have been spread by people-smugglers. In 2012 Barack Obama created DACA, a program aimed at giving temporary protection to undocumented migrants who arrived in the US as children (also known as 'Dreamers').

This is how the Official site of the White House described President's Obama's immigration policies (2014):

Barack Obama lowered the cap on the number of refugees to 15,000 but also removed a large number of undocumented immigrants. Donald Trump aimed at reforming immigration and creating a decade-long path to citizenship for the 'Dreamers' in return for lower immigration and money to build a wall. As for President Biden he has lowered the number of deportations and arrests of illegal immigrants (prioritizing those recently arrived and those who posed a threat to national security, while promising a path to legalization for those who have a job and are integrated within a community) and raised the cap on the number of refugees to 62,500 for 2021.

In 2021 the DACA programme for children brought to the US illegally was brought to an end for new applicants.

'America's immigration system is broken. Too many employers game the system* by hiring undocumented workers and there are 11 million people living in the shadows. Neither is good for the economy or the country.

Together we can build a fair, effective and common sense immigration system that lives up to our heritage as a nation of laws and a nation of immigrants.

The President's plan builds a smart, effective immigration system that continues efforts to secure our borders and cracks down on* employers who hire undocumented immigrants. It's a plan that requires anyone who's undocumented to get right with the law by paying their taxes and a penalty, learning English, and undergoing background checks before they can be eligible to earn citizenship. It requires every business and every worker to play by the same set of rules.'

to cross a border: *passer une frontière*; **to patrol:** *patrouiller*; **a thorny issue:** *un problème épineux*; **to overhaul:** *réviser*; **enforcement:** *la mise en vigueur, l'application (d'une loi)*; **to air (proposals, views):** *suggérer*; **to tighten:** *renforcer*; **to enforce a law:** *appliquer, faire respecter une loi*; **a fine:** *une amende*; **to be in line:** *faire la queue*; **labour:** *le travail*; **game the system:** *profitent du système*; **crack down on:** *prendre des mesures contre*

• #MeToo

In the fall of 2017 *The New York Times* and *The New Yorker magazine* won the Pulitzer Prize for revealing allegations of sexual harassment against the Hollywood film producer Harvey Weinstein. Within weeks the #MeToo hashtag became a global movement, with women all over the world sharing personal stories of violence, promises of career advancement in exchange for sexual favours, and the naming of perpetrators.

Weinstein was charged with rape and sexual assault and in 2020 sentenced to 23 years in prison. Nine members of Congress have also resigned or failed to run for re-election after facing such charges. Andrew Cuomo said he would resign as governor of New York after allegations of sexual harassment.

Although #MeToo has increased awareness and empowered many women who decided to come forward after years of silence, mentalities are slow to change. A 2018 poll in the US showed that 1 in 8 bosses considered that they were owed sex from their employees, and there was little reaction when President Trump was accused of sexual misconduct.

(US census facts about women, 2020)
liennathan.fr/4h2ct5

9 ETHNIC MINORITIES

■ The Native Americans (formerly called Indians) (2.09%, 2021)

The Indian tribes and clans which lived in America before the arrival of the settlers* lived close to nature, depending on fishing and hunting for their survival and believing in supernatural forces and spirits. The new settlers on the American continent believed it was their destiny to move westward and occupy the land, an idea which was foreign to the Native Americans, who believed that the land could not be possessed. The movement westward in the 19th century was accompanied by massacres and brought about the destruction of most of these native cultures. A series of treaties allocated reduced areas of land to the tribes and confined them in reservations. Many still live there today, as American citizens (they were given American citizenship in 1924) but with a special status which allows them to regulate their own affairs. In the 20th century, unemployment, disease, violence and alcoholism became rampant* in the Indian communities.

a settler: *un colon*; **to become rampant:** *régner, sévir*

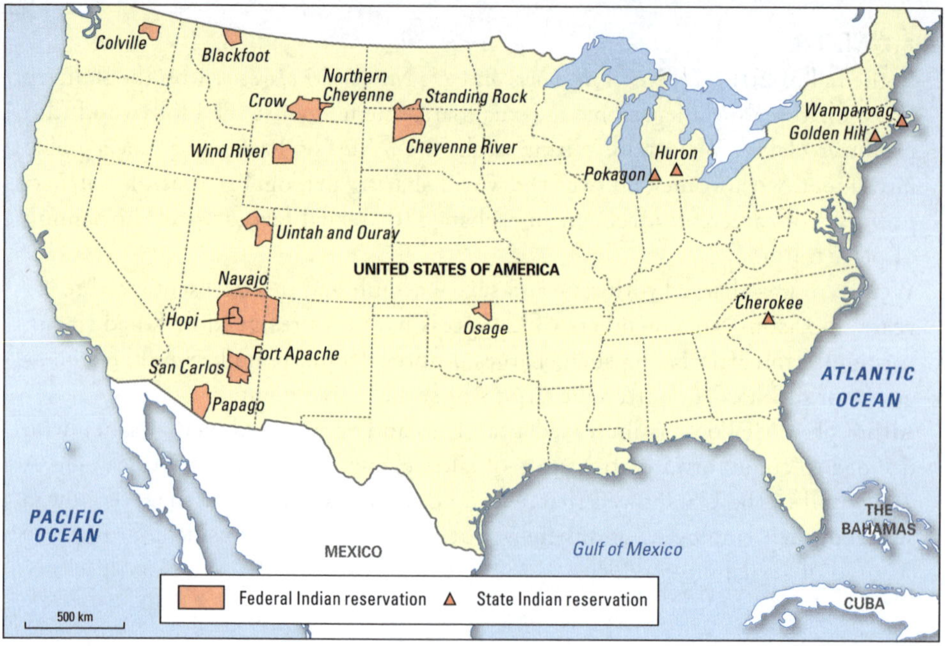

■ African Americans (12.2%, 2021)

Slavery

By the time slavery was abolished, in 1865, some 15 million black people had been brought from Africa to become slaves on the Southern plantations, a process known as the Black Ivory Trade*. On the plantations, they and their children became the property of the white owners, who made them work in the cotton, tobacco and rice fields, often using violence, and could sell them to other owners. In the early 19th century, many northern states abolished slavery, and these became a destination for runaway slaves*, with many abolitionists organizing escape routes for them. Harriet Tubman, a black woman who had fled north, thus led hundreds of slaves north through the Underground Railroad*.

Emancipation

The Civil War set the industrial North, which was against slavery (which it did not need), against the agrarian South, which needed a lot of hands* to work the land. After the victory of the north, slavery was outlawed* and all slaves were freed in 1865 (13th Amendment to the Constitution), became American citizens in 1868 (14th Amendment) and gained the right to vote in 1870.

From segregation to the Civil Rights Act

In the Southern states, however, black people were often denied the right to vote and a policy of overt* segregation ("separate but equal") or discrimination was gradually enforced*with so-called Jim Crow Laws*. Such a situation was encouraged by racist

groups like the Ku Klux Klan, which believed in the supremacy of the white race and maintained a climate of terror. By the end of the 19th century, segregation had become virtually legal in the South, with different schools for blacks and whites, different seats in restaurants, cinemas and buses.
Many black people migrated to northern cities, where they lived in ghettos. Several solutions to the problem were considered in the first half of the century, from separation (an independent black state?) to going back to Africa, or to the fight for civil rights through legal battles (the NAACP, National Association for the Advancement of Colored People).
But mentalities gradually changed, particularly after World War II, when black soldiers fought alongside white ones. In 1954, the Supreme Court declared school segregation illegal. In 1955, Rosa Parks, a black militant woman, refused to give her seat to a white man in the bus (in Montgomery, Alabama), which led to a bus boycott and eventually to the end of segregation on public transport. The next ten years were marked by the Civil Rights movement*, led by Martin Luther King (1929-1968), who, influenced by Christianity and Gandhi's principles, encouraged non-violent protest in favour of equal rights for blacks and whites. This took the form of marches, boycotts and sit-ins*. Martin Luther King became president of the SCLC (Southern Christian Leadership Conference) and organized a huge march on Washington in 1963. Criticized by some for his non-violent approach, he was assassinated in 1968.

I say to you today, my friends, so even though we face the difficulties of today and tomorrow, I still have a dream. It is a dream deeply rooted in the American dream.
I have a dream that one day this nation will rise up and live out the true meaning of its creed: "We hold these truths to be self-evident: that all men are created equal."
I have a dream that one day on the red hills of Georgia the sons of former slaves and the sons of former slave owners will be able to sit down together at the table of brotherhood.
I have a dream that one day even the state of Mississippi, a state sweltering with the heat of injustice, sweltering with the heat of oppression, will be transformed into an oasis of freedom and justice.
I have a dream that my four little children will one day live in a nation where they will not be judged by the color of their skin but by the content of their character.
I have a dream today.

Martin Luther King, March on Washington, 1963

The 1964 Civil Rights Act finally put an end to discrimination, while the 1965 Voting Rights Act ensured* that black people could vote.

The fight for social and economic equality
But the law which brought political equality did not radically change the situation

of most black people overnight. They were still economically and culturally at a disadvantage.

Several movements and trends appeared as a consequence, for example:

– The Black Panthers, and the Black Muslims, who in the 1960s and 1970s, were in favour of more violent methods. The Black Muslims' best-known representative was Malcom X, who refused non-violence and integration, calling instead for the establishment of a black nation within the United States.

– Affirmative Action*, an attempt to take legal steps to reduce inequalities, for example by creating quotas of black workers in certain jobs or businesses (12% of the employees, the same percentage as that of black people in the whole US population) or by bussing* black children to white schools.

– Critical race theory (CRT), an academic concept developed in the 1970s, has recently become highly divisive, particularly where state and local school curriculums are concerned. According to CRT, racism is systemic, stemming not from individual prejudice but from legal and political policies which, over the years have shaped decisions concerning criminal justice, housing or school curriculum. Should CRT be part of the way the American past is taught ? Progressives believe it should, as children should be aware of all aspects of history. But Conservatives consider it would be un-American, revisionist, and a betrayal of the founding principles of the United States. Twenty-six states have currently introduced bills to limit the teaching of CRT in public schools.

Nowadays, black people still live mainly in the south of the United States as well as in large cities. Although they are slowly becoming integrated, and there is a significant black middle-class, their average income* is still much lower than that of white people and there is a large and growing black underclass. The unemployment rate among black people is more than twice that among white people.

Black culture has been enormously popular and influential, particularly in the realm of music, with:

– **negro spirituals:** probably derived from Methodist hymns, they reflect humility, religious faith, the belief in a heavenly life to come, but also the misery of slavery.

– **blues:** secular songs of lament for solo voices

– **jazz:** mainly improvised music, which appeared at the beginning of the 20th century in the poor districts of New Orleans; it was influenced by ragtime (dance music with a syncopated rhythm) and the blues. It quickly spread north, where it took on a number of forms: swing, bebop, bop, rap, etc.

Many black writers have also contributed to American literature (the Harlem Renaissance, James Baldwin, Richard Wright, Toni Morrison).

the Black Ivory Trade: *le commerce de l'ivoire noir*; **a runaway slave:** *un esclave fugitif*; **the Underground Railroad:** *la filière clandestine pour quitter le Sud*; **hands:** *la main-d'œuvre*; **to outlaw:** *rendre illégal*; **to enforce:** *appliquer*; **overt:** *déclaré, non déguisé*; **Jim Crow Laws:** *lois racistes*; **the Civil Rights movement:** *la campagne pour les droits civils*; **a sit-in:** *une occupation de locaux*; **to ensure:** *garantir*: **affirmative action:** *discrimination positive*: **bussing:** *une mesure de déségrégation qui consiste à transporter des enfants par autobus vers certaines écoles*; **an income:** *un revenu*

Hispanic Americans (18.5%, 2021)

Most Hispanic-Americans immigrated to the United States in the 20th century, coming from Mexico, Cuba and Puerto Rico for economic or political reasons. Most of them have settled in the South (California, Texas, Florida), although there is also a large Puerto Rican population (Puerto Ricans are American citizens) in New York City. Another influx* of immigrants later came from Nicaragua, the Dominican Republic and Colombia. Latinos now represent the largest ethnic community in America, being now more numerous than African Americans. This is why Spanish is so widely spoken in the United States. Hispanics often take low-paid, seasonal* jobs and their rate of unemployment is higher than that of white people. They are under-represented in politics. Many Latinos being conservative and Roman Catholic, they have influenced the religious right.

→ Population & Immigration

an influx: *un afflux*; **a seasonal job:** *un travail saisonnier*

Asian Americans (5.6%, 2021)

Coming from China, Japan, Vietnam and Korea, they have mostly settled on the west coast. Because they represent an educated minority, they have integrated more easily.

(The official site of the US Census Bureau)
liennathan.fr/x6yu55

(A site devoted to African Americans)
liennathan.fr/76if5b

(The official site of the Department of the Interior, which is responsible for the Bureau of Indian Affairs)
liennathan.fr/32z5se

CONTROVERSIAL ISSUES

For or against Affirmative Action?

Affirmative action* is a policy which consists in giving racial preference in employment or university admissions in order to facilitate the promotion and social integration of minorities (Hispanics, Blacks, women, Vietnam veterans...). It amounts to establishing racial quotas to redress* what is seen as decades of disadvantage for such groups. Ideally, the proportion of minority employees or students should be the same as the proportion of the group in American society. But the policy has proved controversial, and led to numerous lawsuits filed* by people who felt wronged* if a less competent person was selected because he/she belonged to a minority group.

In the 1990s, quotas and the choice of employees or candidates on the basis of race or sex were increasingly challenged and several states passed laws forbidding such policies. In 1996, for example, California amended its constitution to include Proposition 209:

"The state shall not discriminate against, or grant* preferential treatment to, any individual or group on the basis of race, sex, color, ethnicity, or national origin, in the operation of public employment, public education, or public contracting*."

Several other states followed suit.*

For university admissions, for example, Affirmative Action is allowed but not required. About 20% of 4-year colleges and universities engage in it.

A few arguments for and against Affirmative Action:

For	Against
– Affirmative Action is a way of making up for* the difficult background of minorities (poor schooling, poor housing,...) who cannot compete with* white people on an equal footing*. – It helps to make up for* intended or unintended bias* or institutional racism or sexism*. – People from different backgrounds become less prejudiced when they are educated together or work together.	– AA is racially discriminatory; it is reverse discrimination* since people are judged by the colour of their skin. Indeed some have even sued* universities for refusing white applicants of more merit in order to give preference to racial minorities (a number of universities have admission policies which award 20 points for a student's skin colour, but only 12 for the best possible SAT score.). – AA perpetuates the idea that Blacks cannot succeed on their own but must be helped. It therefore undermines* people's belief in the myth of the self-made man. – It reduces black people's incentive* to strive* for excellence. – Black students recruited with lower academic scores are more likely than white students to drop out of college because they find it difficult to cope. – It causes people to see themselves as part of a group and not as individual Americans.

affirmative action: *la discrimination positive*; **to redress:** *corriger*; **to file a lawsuit:** *intenter un procès*; **to wrong:** *traiter injustement*; **to grant:** *accorder*; **contracting:** *la sous-traitance*; **to follow suit:** *faire de même*; **to make up for:** *compenser*; **to compete with:** *rivaliser avec*; **on an equal footing:** *sur un pied d'égalité*; **reverse discrimination:** *discrimination à l'envers*; **a bias:** *un préjugé*; **institutional racism or sexism:** *racisme ou sexisme inhérent à l'institution*; **to sue:** *poursuivre en justice*; **to undermine:** *miner, saper*; **an incentive:** *une motivation*; **to strive:** *s'efforcer*

African Americans today

There have been huge steps forward in racial attitudes and in 2021 90% of Americans said they approved of mixed marriages. When Barack Obama's presidency was followed by that of Donald Trump many white Americans became aware that racism was widespread and partly explained differences in income, housing and jobs.

There have also been huge gains in legal and political Rights since the Civil rights Act of 1964. There is a thriving black middle class, with many black Americans represented in politics (as mayors of large cities or Congressmen or women) and in business (as chief executives of large firms), and a large upper class. Yet there are still areas of concentrated poverty and deprivation where, generation after generation, there is little future for a black child. Downward mobility is the rule, although black girls fare a little better. Poverty tends to be concentrated in city centres, many white Americans and middle-class black Americans having left for residential suburbs. In such inner-city black neighbourhoods there are few jobs available, and schools are difficult to integrate, resulting in poor academic achievements. There is violence and drugs (the death rate from an overdose of opioids has tripled among black Americans since 2014) and many black Americans find themselves behind bars. One of the causes of this violence is the breakdown of the black family. In 2018 7 out of 10 children were illegitimate and grew up in a one-parent families.

Black Lives Matter

In May 2020, George Floyd, an unarmed African American, was killed by a police officer who knelt on his throat. This was the start of civil-rights protests in the US and around the world to denounce police brutality and racism. It gave new life to a former movement created in 2013 after the death of a teenager, Black Lives Matter.

As in Britain one of the consequences of the movement was the toppling of statues of controversial figures. In New Orleans, for instance, the statues of Confederate figures of the Civil War (such as Robert E. Lee and Jefferson Davis) were removed. In 2013 the statue of 'Silent Sam'(who symbolized a Confederate soldier) was pulled down by protesters at the University of North Carolina.

This has to be seen in the broader context of cancel culture or call-out culture, which consists in boycotting or shunning a powerful figure or company for their controversial actions or words. For example an ABC journalist resigned after having defended someone who, on old photos, was seen attending an Old South antebellum party. In France, Agatha Christie 's novel *Ten Little Niggers* (later renamed *And Then There Were None*) was changed to *Ils étaient dix* in 2020 in order to avoid the n-word *Dix petits nègres* in the original translation, even though that title was based on a 19th century rhyme. And in 2020, the San Francisco school board voted to remove a number of names from public schools, considering them unworthy of the honour. Among them were the names of Washington and Jefferson (because they were slave owners) and of Lincoln (because of the way he treated first nation people).

Such cancel culture has often been criticized for polarizing society and some have seen it as reminiscent of the Salem witch trials.

The impact of the Black Lives Matter movement was also felt in other areas, as shown by the following examples:
– In 2021, Chicago Mayor Lori Lightfoot announced that for the second anniversary of her inauguration she was offering sit-down interviews exclusively to reporters of colour, her way of fighting for diversity and inclusion at a time when Chicago reporters were mainly male and white.
– Instances of racial injustice and police brutality have recently sparked a wave of protests, some spontaneous, others organised by black activist groups and often supported by centre-left activists. This in turn has led to several proposals to make the police more accountable: banning chokeholds, creating an office to look into deaths caused by police officers, limiting qualified immunity (which shields officers from civil liability), creating a database of officer misconduct or requiring police to wear cameras.
– Black Lives Matter have also recently focused on elections: too few polling stations, too few volunteers and antiquated voting machines often mean long queues, which can dissuade people from voting, which is particularly the case among non-white Americans.
– In 2021 Congress declared that Juneteenth (a portmanteau word for June 19th) would be a federal holiday to celebrate the end of legal enslavement of Black Americans. Juneteenth had already been chosen by many organisations and States to celebrate the abolition of slavery).

■ English vs Spanish

Spanish is often spoken at home by over 28 million Americans. In New Mexico, California, Texas and Arizona, about 30% or more of the population speak Spanish, although most have some knowledge of English. And the constant influx* of immigrants seems to guarantee that Spanish will survive as a second language in the United States. When it comes to politics, many candidates insist on using Spanish in their speeches or broadcasts in order to win part of the huge Latino vote. There is however a parallel movement towards assimilation, as the children and grandchildren of immigrants gradually come to consider English as their main, then as their only language and become completely anglicized. Although the government and states use both English and Spanish for most official documents, the use of some English is essential for naturalization, as well as for legal and professional purposes.
A number of movements and tendencies have appeared concerning the use of English or Spanish.
– The English-Only Movement argues in favour of English as the only official language in the United States. Many supporters of the movement fear that with

the spread of Spanish, the United States might lose its national identity. Besides, it would not encourage assimilation.
– Integrated schools teach Hispanic pupils in Spanish while providing them with intensive classes to learn English.
– Other schools have opted for immersion, Hispanic children attending regular classes with English-speaking children. In 1998, Proposition 227 was passed in California, mandating* that children be taught mostly in English through immersion programs lasting one year. It thus eliminated most bilingual education.
The portmanteau word* Spanglish (Spanish + English) refers to a number of speech characteristics deriving from the close contact of Spanish and English in certain communities (for example, using some English words influenced by Spanish or the reverse, reproducing the syntax of Spanish in English or the reverse, switching* from one language to the other in the middle of a sentence).

an influx: *un afflux, une arrivée*; **to mandate:** *rendre obligatoire*; **a portmanteau word:** *un mot-valise*; **to switch from... to...:** *passer de... à...*

10 EDUCATION

The Constitution makes no mention of free and compulsory education and each state is therefore free to organise education as it wishes.

■ Schools

Before the age of 5: nursery school or kindergarten
– Age 5 to age 11: Elementary School or Grade School: first to 6th grades
– Age 11 to age18: High School
- 11-15: Junior High School (or Middle School): 6th to 9th grades
- 15-18: Senior High School: 9th to 12th grades

Education from kindergarten to twelfth grade is referred to as K-12.

Pupils need to have a certain number of credits to graduate* from High School: some credits are compulsory (English, mathematics...), others optional with a wide variety of subjects including non-academic ones like Home economics, Photography... There is also a stronger emphasis than in France on patriotic and civic values: all students recite the Pledge of Allegiance* every day.

At the end of the 12th grade, students receive their High School Diploma. They graduate from High School*. Public education has a poor academic record* and many parents choose to send their children to private schools, often religious ones.

The federal government provides guidelines and sets standards but most decisions concerning curriculum* and the way schools are run are taken by the Department of Education of each state and by school boards* for each school district.

American children still have quite poor scores* in the 3 Rs* and several experiments have recently been tried at state or federal levels to remedy the problem.

– Magnet schools are specialised in a particular subject (for example music or languages) in order to attract students.

– Charter schools, which are independent of state regulations and non-sectarian*, are open to all and funded* according to enrolments*, and must remain successful in order to survive.

– Vouchers* are given to parents, who can use them as they wish (sending their children to schools inside or outside the catchment area*, public or private).

– Since 2002 NCLB Act (No Child Left Behind Act) aimed at ensuring that all pupils were proficient in "reading, mathematics and science" by 2013-14. Schools in poor areas were provided with money as long as they showed progress in annual tests. If too many children failed the tests in a given school, parents then had the right to move them elsewhere.

About 4% of children are home-schooled.

to graduate: *obtenir son diplôme*; **to graduate from High School:** *équivalent de passer son baccalauréat*; **the Pledge of Allegiance:** *le serment d'allégeance*; **the academic record:** *le niveau, les résultats*; **to fund:** *financer*; **enrolments:** *les inscriptions*; **a voucher:** *un bon*; **a curriculum (pl: curricula), :** *un programme*; **a school board:** *un conseil d'administration élu*; **poor scores:** *de mauvais résultats*; **the 3 Rs = Reading, wRiting, aRithmetic; non sectarian:** *non religieux*; **a catchment area:** *un secteur de recrutement scolaire*

■ Higher education

To enter a university, you have to sit for a Scholastic Aptitude Test (SAT), a test of ability and academic achievement . Students apply for* different universities and, depending on their results, are accepted or refused. There is a wide range of levels in the United States, from Junior colleges (also called Community Colleges, with two-year programs specializing in professional needs), to well-known and very expensive universities such as Harvard or Berkeley. Although the tuition fees* are very high (and can reach as much as $50,000 a year for a residential four-year degree in elite private colleges), many students are awarded grants*.

There can be 'back door' ways of entering highly selective universities, for example if students are relatives of alumni (they are called 'legacies'), if their parents have made large donations to the university or even funded a new building, or if you are a particularly gifted athlete. Indeed, between 2009 and 2016, a student with excellent grades had a 25% probability of being admitted to Harvard if (s)he came from a low-income family, but it rose to 55% if he/she was the son or daughter of alumni, and to 80% if he was a top athlete.

The Ivy League is a group of old and prestigious universities: Brown, Columbia, Cornell, Dartmouth, Harvard, Princeton, Yale, University of Pennsylvania.
The Seven Sisters is a group of seven highly respected colleges for women: Vassar, Wellesley, Smith, Bryn Mawr, Barnard, Radcliffe, Mount Holyoke.

College: 2- or 4-year cycles.
1st year = freshman year
2nd year = sophomore year
3rd year = junior year
4th year = senior year
= leading to a Bachelor's Degree.

University: like colleges, they prepare students for a Bachelor's Degree, but also offer post-graduate studies*, leading to a Master's Degree, then PHD.

With growing pressure to get a degree and even post-graduate qualifications in order to ensure a good job, there is increasing competition between universities to obtain a top slot in the international rankings. US and UK universities tend to do best in the Shanghai rankings, which mainly take research into consideration. Now that competition is international, many countries also try to get excellent US universities to set up campuses in their countries. NYU, for instance, has a campus in Shanghai.

to apply for: *poser sa candidature*; **tuition fees:** *les frais de scolarité*; **a grant:** *une bourse*; **post-graduate studies:** *le troisième cycle universitaire*

(The US Department of Education website)
liennathan.fr/4gan94

(Education statistics)
liennathan.fr/v968zi

CONTROVERSIAL ISSUES

Evolutionism vs Creationism

In 1925, John Scopes, a biology teacher from Tennessee, challenged the state's law which outlawed* the teaching of Darwinian theories. He was tried and lost the case, but the trial had enormous repercussions and discredited the defenders of Divine creation. Today, however, Darwin's theory that human beings gradually evolved until they reached their present form is still widely challenged in the United States, where people refuse the idea that mankind evolved in an unplanned and random* way, depending on the survival of the fittest* rather than divine guidance. Instead, about half the population believe in creationism, that is to say the idea that God created man and all living things directly as they are now - a literal interpretation of the Book of Genesis. Many Boards of Education, particularly in the South, will allow the teaching of evolutionism only if creationism is mentioned along with it.

Intelligent design

Intelligent Design* (ID) is another theory defended by the neoconservatives and supported by President Bush. According to them, the beauty and complexity of human and animal life are such that they could not possibly be the result of natural selection over millenia, but must have been conceived by an intelligent designer* – God. Although its opponents say there is no scientific evidence to support this view, which can only point to weaknesses in evolutionary theory and cannot be tested by experiment, the theory of intelligent design is seen by many as having more scientific respectability than creationism. A number of Boards of Education have already recommended the mention of intelligent design in secondary school textbooks.

to outlaw: *proscrire*; **random:** *au hasard*; **the survival of the fittest:** *la lutte pour la vie*; **a design:** *un dessein*; **a designer:** *un créateur*

■ Education without segregation?

The 1954 *Brown vs Board of Education* Supreme Court ruling banning 'separate but equal' schools, then the Civil Rights Act of 1964 made the desegregation of schools mandatory. But it was only in the 1970s, when the *de facto* situation had barely changed, that busing (transporting pupils to certain schools in order to redress racial imbalances) began to be used. The practice was controversial, criticised for eroding community spirit and for sending white children to more dangerous neighbourhoods. In the 1990s, government efforts to integrate schools and to create race-conscious programs made bussing increasingly unnecessary. In 2007 the Supreme Court prohibited the use of racial classifications in any student assignment in order to maintain racial balance. As a result, the trend has recently been towards the re-segregation of many public schools.

11 RELIGION

Religion still plays an important part in the United States where, in 2020, 63% of the population said they believed in God. However membership of any faith is plummeting and only 47% of milleniums have signed up to a church, synagogue or mosque, down more than 20 points from 2000. Although church and state are separated, religion is omnipresent in political and everyday life : the President has to swear* on the Bible when he takes office ; the motto* which appears on US coins is 'In God We Trust'; there are some 200 Christian television channels and 1,500 Christian radio stations. Yet there is no official religion and the freedom of religion is enshrined* in the Constitution; this means that the State should be neutral and not favour one religion above another. The relationship between state and church has led to numberless court cases, the courts sometimes issuing contradictory rulings*, for example allowing public funds to be given to some religious schools while not allowing the Ten Commandments to be posted in a Court of Justice.

The Puritan religion of the early settlers has been enormously influential in encouraging hard work and in promoting* the idea that wealth and material success are not shameful* but are a sign of salvation* and of God's blessing*.
Along with multiculturalism, immigration has brought a great variety of denominations* to the United States.

to swear: *prêter serment*; **a motto:** *une devise*; **enshrined:** *inscrit*; **a ruling:** *un jugement*; **to promote:** *promouvoir*; **shameful:** *honteux*; **salvation:** *le salut*; **blessing:** *la grâce, la bénédiction*; **a denomination:** *un culte, une confession*

Major Religious Traditions in the U.S. (Among all adults, in %) 2021

Christian 70.6%	Muslim 0.9%
Evangelical Protestant 25.4%	Buddhist 0.7%
Mainline Protestant 14.7%	Hindu 0.7%
Historically Black Protestant 6.5%	Other world religions 0.3%
Catholic 20.8%	Other Faiths 1.5%
Mormon 1.6%	
Orthodox Christian 0.5%	**Unaffiliated (religious 'nones')** 22.8%
Jehovah's Witness 0.8%	Atheist 3.1%
Other Christian 0.4%	Agnostic 4.0%
	Nothing in particular 15.8%
Non-Christian Faiths 5.9%	
Jewish 1.9%	**Don't know** 0.6%

What is striking in these 2021 figures is that an increasing number of Americans declare they do not belong to a church and are religiously unaffiliated. A growing number say they believe in 'nothing in particular'. They are not atheist or agnostics but refuse to be defined or labelled.
Fewer Americans as well declare themselves as Christians. It may be that not identifying as such is now more acceptable than it ever was; it might also be because many feel left out, both economically and socially.

A few specifically American churches:

- **The QUAKERS**: The Quakers (also called The Society of Friends) were established in Pennsylvania by William Penn in the 17th century. They believe in the "inner light" of Jesus Christ in the soul, and reject such things as ornaments and sacraments. Their social commitment* is very strong: throughout history they have been active against slavery, violence and war, and in favour of prison reform and social justice.

- **The MORMONS**: Also called The Church of Jesus Christ of Latter-Day Saints, and founded by Joseph Smith in 1830. They believe that Jesus Christ was revealed to early immigrants and will found a new Jerusalem in the United States. Conversion comes through baptism and can be undergone vicariously* for the dead. Mormons do not drink alcohol or coffee, do not smoke, practise sexual abstinence and give two years' free service to the church. Their earlier habits of polygamy have now been abandoned. Many of them live in Salt Lake City, Utah.

■ **The AMISH**: The Amish are a Mennonite community who settled in Pennsylvania in the 18th century. They reject all forms of industrialisation and modernity, refusing radios, televisions, cars and fridges, and dressing in very strict and simple clothes. The **evangelical 'born again' movement** (someone is 'born again' when he/she has recovered his/her faith after a spiritual experience) has been steadily growing, linked to moral crusades and fundamentalist beliefs in a literal interpretation of the Bible as the word of God. A movement like this is in the tradition of the Great Awakening* of colonial times, when religious revival* was linked to the fear of sin*, the importance of conversion, and the need to spread the word of God. Fundamentalists oppose homosexuality, abortion, and sex outside marriage. Televangelists like Pat Robertson (and, until recently, Jeremy Falwell and Billy Graham) organize impressive religious services on television to broadcast their conservative ideas. Many born-again Christians also believe in creationism, refusing the Darwinian theory of evolution and defending the creation of the universe as it is told in the Book of Genesis.
59% of evangelicals supported the Trump administration.

a social commitment: *un engagement social*; **vicariously:** *indirectement*; **an awakening:** *(littéralement), un réveil*; **a revival:** *un renouveau*; **sin:** *le péché*

(The website of the Quakers)
liennathan.fr/z4ex63

(The website of the Mormons)
liennathan.fr/cr787u

CONTROVERSIAL ISSUES

■ Stem cell research*

The use of federal funding* for reproductive human cloning* is banned in the USA, as it is almost everywhere in the world. As for therapeutic cloning (to treat diseases), it is controversial.
Many religious groups oppose as unethical* the use of embryos for research on cloning and stem cells, since it implies the killing of human life. Scientists, however, argue that this might help save very many lives – something which is still hypothetical since there is still a long way to go and not enough eggs to carry out proper experiments. In many countries (as in Britain), only embryos left after fertility treatment* are used – and those would have been killed anyway. In 2001, President Bush banned the federal funding* of stem-cell research*, except where existing work on embryonic stem cells* had already begun.

stem cell research: *la recherche sur les cellules souches*; **reproductive human cloning:** *le clonage humain reproductif*; **unethical:** *contraire à l'éthique*; **a fertility treatment:** *un traitement contre la stérilité*; **to fund:** *financer*; **embryonic stem cells:** *les cellules souches embryonnaires*

■ The religious right

(Kevin Kallaugher, *The Economist*, November 6th 2004, p. 7)

At the very end of the 20th century, the United States was in the grip of* a fundamentalist Christian revival*, a moral trend which helped re-elect President Bush – himself a born-again Christian – in 2004. Indeed evangelical Protestants actively campaigned for the Republican party, particularly in the South, and strongly supported President Trump, particularly because he appointed conservative justices to the Supreme Court.

White Evangelicals, who believe in a literal interpretation of the Scriptures*, make up about one fourth of the population.
Most right-wing Christians share the same views, believing in creationism, in family values, in education for abstinence in order to fight AIDS, and opposing same-sex marriages, abortion and stem-cell research.
America is becoming increasingly polarized along religious lines. Liberals even speak of a move towards a theocracy. This dynamism of the religious right may partly be ascribed to a reaction against the excessive liberalism of the 1970s.
The success of Evangelical churches may also have resulted from the fact that many of them are organized like businesses, with chief executives, management teams, and parishioners* seen as consumers. Everything is geared to* the needs of these consumers: affinity groups, child care, counselling, sport, psychological or business advice... With their "pastorpreneurs", some of these mega-churches attract huge numbers of people and have become powerful businesses. Some indeed seem more like religious theme parks than churches.

in the grip of: *en proie à*; **a revival:** *un renouveau de la foi*; **the Scriptures:** *les Saintes Écritures*; **a parishioner:** *un paroissien*; **geared to:** *fait pour satisfaire*

■ Abortion

In 1973, the *Roe v Wade* Supreme Court ruling declared that abortion was a constitutional right. But the ruling has remained highly controversial. Encouraged by Donald Trump's pro-life statements as well as his appointment of conservative Supreme Court justices, several conservative states have passed bills (called 'heartbeat bills') making abortion illegal if a heartbeat is detectable. In 2019 the Alabama Senate passed a bill making any abortion a felony*. Such bills usually never go further since *Roe v Wade* is a federal law, but some pro-life activists keep pushing for such bills which might have a better chance with the new conservative Supreme Court. Indeed, in 2021, the Supreme Court ruled 5-4 against blocking a controversial new law in Texas which bans termination if a heartbeat can be heard.
EMILY's list, a political action committee founded in 1985, aims at electing Democratic pro-choice women (women in favour of abortion rights) to office.

a felony: *un crime*

12 JUSTICE, LAW & ORDER

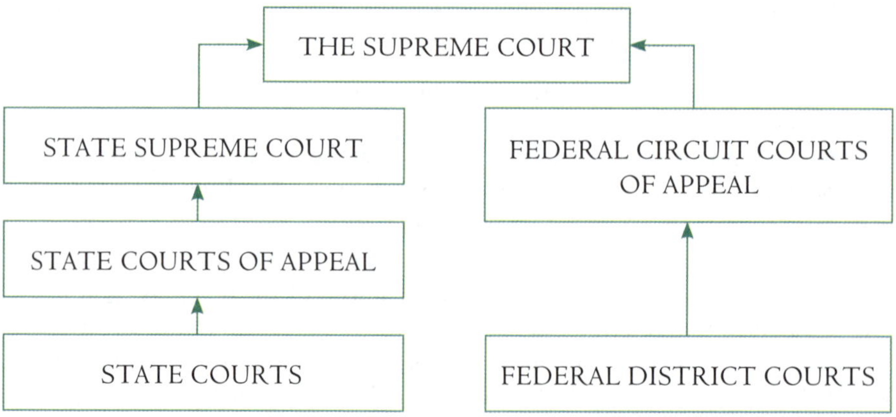

(Different courts such as Police Courts, County Courts, Family Courts... to deal with minor offences, divorce, financial disputes... Superior courts deal with more serious cases* and crimes.)

(Cases which have to do with federal law such as welfare, civil rights, international trade disputes, or which concern several states.)

Each state has its own legal system determined by the state constitution. However, the overall organization is the same:

■ **The Supreme Court** is the final court of appeal but only hears cases involving federal law, constitutional issues or foreign nations. It will, for example, decide whether or not a state law constitutes a violation of the Constitution.
It is made up of 9 justices*, who are appointed* for life by the President, but the Senate must confirm their nomination. Their appointment usually reflects the political leanings* of the President who appoints them. Any new nomination (when one of the judges dies or resigns*) is therefore closely scrutinized and much discussed in the Senate since it may alter* the political coloring of the Court as a whole.
Donald Trump consolidated the Courts' conservative bent* by appointing 3 Supreme Court judges, 54 federal appellate judges and 174 US District Court judges during his administration. At the end of his tenure, the Supreme Court had a 6-3 majority of Republican nominees, the most unbalanced proportion in a century.

a case: *une affaire judiciaire*; **a justice:** *un juge de la Cour Suprême*; **to appoint:** *nommer*; **a leaning:** *une tendance*; **to resign:** *donner sa démission*; **to alter:** *changer*; **bent:** *penchant*

■ **The legal system** is based on:
1. Common law* (precedent, judicial decisions)
2. Statutes* (written laws) passed by Congress
3. The constitution (both federal and state - the former having precedence over the latter)

common law: *le droit coutumier*; **a statute:** *une loi*

■ **The legal profession**
– Judges are appointed or elected for various terms of office*, depending on which state they are in.
– Lawyers advise and defend their clients. The profession is a lucrative one in a country where people go to court for all sorts of reasons, suing* schools, hospitals, services whenever they hope to gain some profit from doing so. As many lawyers only get paid if the plaintiff* wins the case (the "no win-no fee*" principle), there is little risk in starting a lawsuit*, which explains why litigation* is so common in the United States.
– District Attorneys* decide whether there is enough evidence to prosecute* people and are responsible for the prosecution in court. The Attorney-General* is at the head of the Department of Justice.

the term of office: *la durée du mandat*; **to sue:** *poursuivre en justice*; **a plaintiff:** *un plaignant*; **a fee:** *des honoraires*; **a lawsuit:** *un procès*; **litigation:** *les litiges*; **to prosecute:** *engager des poursuites judiciaires contre*; **a District Attorney:** *un procureur*; **the Attorney General:** *le procureur général*

■ **A jury trial**
Here are the different stages of such a trial, which is presided over by a judge.
– Some jurors* are selected at random*.
– Both the defence attorney* and the prosecuting attorney* question jurors in order to select the final jury.

– Witnesses* are heard and cross-examined* by both attorneys.
– The two attorneys sum up their arguments for the jury.
– The judge sums up the case.
– The jury deliberates.
– The jury returns a verdict* of guilty or not guilty.
– The judge decides what the penalty or sentence will be.

a juror: *un juré*; **at random:** *au hasard*; **the defence attorney:** *l'avocat de la défense*; **the prosecuting attorney:** *l'avocat général*; **a witness:** *un témoin*; **to cross-examine:** *faire subir un contre-interrogatoire*; **to return a verdict:** *rendre un verdict*

■ The fight against criminality

Until the early 1990s, criminality was rampant* in American cities, particularly in inner cities* abandoned by the well-to-do* middle-class population who had fled* to the suburbs. The situation grew worse, as these poor districts generated* little tax revenue* but saw rocketing costs in policing and social services. In the 1990s, an attempt to change direction led to a tightening* of the fight against offences of all kinds, including minor ones such as littering*, fare-dodging* or the writing of graffiti. This was accompanied by a crackdown on* illegal weapons and in some cities by welfare-to-work policies. Such a 'zero tolerance' approach was implemented in several major cities like New York (thanks to Rudolph Giuliani, its mayor) or Boston, thus drastically bringing down the crime statistics.

to be rampant: *sévir*; **inner city:** *le quartier souvent pauvre du centre des villes*; **well-to-do:** *aisé*; **to flee, fled, fled:** *fuir*; **to generate:** *engendrer*; **tax revenue:** *recettes fiscales*; **to tighten:** *renforcer*; **to litter:** *jeter des papiers/détritus par terre*; **fare-dodging:** *le fait de resquiller*; **to implement:** *appliquer*; **to crackdown on:** *prendre des mesures de répression contre*

(The site of the US Department of justice)
liennathan.fr/32fn2m

CONTROVERSIAL ISSUES

■ Guantanamo Bay

When the US launched* its war on terror after the 9/11 attacks against New York and Washington, it decided to use its naval base in Cuba as a prison camp for the suspected supporters of Al-Qa'eda. Its location would mean both security and freedom from the rules guaranteeing certain rights to prisoners in the United States. Inmates* there were not considered as prisoners of war (POWs), not treated according to the rules of the Geneva Conventions – an infringement* of their civil liberties*. This meant they could be kept there indefinitely without being allowed a fair

trial* or released*. The conditions of detention, in small cells, with no privacy* and no visits allowed, not to mention allegations of abuse*, were also much criticized by organisations such as the Red Cross and Amnesty International.
The US government justified such treatment by the need to keep its citizens safe and the hope of preventing further attacks thanks to intelligence* gathered from some of the detainees*.
In spite of President Obama's pledge to close the compound*, there were still 40 prisoners at Guantanamo Bay in 2019. During his campaign Donald Trump said that he would keep the detention facility* open.

to launch: *lancer*; **an inmate:** *un détenu*; **infringement:** *la violation*; **civil liberties:** *les droits individuels*; **a fair trial:** *un procès équitable*; **to release:** *libérer*; **privacy:** *intimité*; **abuse:** *des sévices*; **intelligence:** *des renseignements*; **a detainee:** *un détenu*; **the compound:** *le complexe*; **facility:** *installation, infrastructure*

Three Strikes and You're Out

"Three strikes* and you're out" is the familiar name of a law passed in about half the US states, mandating* prison sentences of 25 years or more for anyone offending for the third time after two serious or violent felony* convictions*.
Arguments for and against:

For	Against
– It is a strong deterrent* against re-offending.	– Originally meant for violent crimes only, the law is now applied in all cases, for instance stealing, in some states like California. This often makes the punishment disproportionate to the crime. – Crime rates have not fallen more rapidly in states with the three-strikes law.

a strike: *un coup, donc un crime*; **to mandate:** *rendre obligatoire*; **a felony:** *un crime*; **conviction:** *condamnation*; **a deterrent:** *une loi, une décision... qui a un effect de dissuasion*

The Death Penalty

The death penalty is still legal and used in 24 states, including, Kansas, Indiana, Virginia and Texas. Three others, Pennsylvania, California and Oregon have Governor imposed moratorium, which is a suspension of a law until deemed worthy again. Washington state is the last state to have abolished the death penalty (in 2018), finding it 'arbitrary and racially biased.' Thirty-one states use capital punishment* today, but one third of the executions have taken place in Texas since 1976. In 1972, it was made illegal, because seen as "cruel and unusual punishment", something not allowed by the Constitution. But four years

later, the Supreme Court reinstated* it as a legal means of punishment. In 2005, a federal law made it illegal for crimes committed by offenders under the age of eighteen. Since prisoners can appeal to higher courts against a death sentence (first to State courts, then to the Federal courts), many remain for years on death row*, and a stay of execution* or pardon can be granted* by the state governor or the President right up until the execution itself takes place.
There are different methods of execution in different states: the electric chair*, lethal injection*(the most widely-used method), the gas chamber*, the firing squad* and hanging*. In 2014, after several botched* lethal injections, a number of executions were postponed, pending* a review of the methods used.
Here are the most common arguments put forward for and against:

For	Against
– It is normal that someone who has killed and is too dangerous to live in society should be killed. – A majority of American citizens are in favour of the death penalty. – The victim's family have a right to some form of revenge. – The death penalty is mentioned in the Bible (Genesis, 9:6).	– It is "cruel and unusual punishment", something unthinkable in a modern civilized society. – Mistakes do occur and they cannot be corrected. Indeed, over the years, several death-row inmates* have been proved innocent. – It has not been proved to act as a deterrent*. – We should aim at forgiveness, not revenge. – A majority of inmates* on death row are black and poor, and have not been able to afford good lawyers – a fact which should be contrasted with the case of O.J. Simpson.

Both opponents and advocates of the death penalty use the argument of race, the former saying that it is mostly black people who are executed, while the latter argue that a higher proportion of white people are executed in relation to the number of crimes committed.

capital punishment: *la peine de mort*; **to reinstate:** *rétablir*; **death row:** *le couloir de la mort*; **a stay of execution:** *un sursis à l'exécution*; **to grant:** *accorder*; **the electric chair:** *la chaise électrique*; **a lethal injection:** *une injection mortelle*; **the gas chamber:** *la chambre à gaz*; **a firing squad:** *un peloton d'exécution*; **a hanging:** *une pendaison*; **pending:** *en attendant*; **botched:** *raté*; **to act as a deterrent:** *avoir un effet dissuasif*; **an inmate:** *un prisonnier*

Gun control

The right to bear arms is enshrined* in the constitution (Second Amendment) and goes back to pioneering times, when men had to fight in order to defend their freedom and property. For many Americans, it symbolizes the idea of self-reliance*. The idea is encouraged by the NRA (National Rifle Association), a gun lobby* which appeared after the Civil War and is still extremely powerful today, thwarting* all attempts by Congress to control the use of guns. They find most of their supporters among Republicans, but an increasing number of Americans, mostly women, across the political spectrum are now asking for a whole range of anti-gun legislation (banning assault weapons, a wider blacklist* of people who should not buy guns, fitting guns with child-proof* locks...). They are particularly concerned by children using guns. The only timid step yet taken towards gun control is the obligation for dealers to verify the buyers' identity and check a computerized criminal data base system before selling a handgun.

In the past two years, however, and as a consequence of recent mass-shootings and soaring homicides, several states have adopted more radical stances, passing 'permitless-carry' laws, which make it easier for anyone to carry a gun without any checks or training. Texas even wants to be declared a 'Second Amendment sanctuary state'.

Both sides in this divisive issue are adamant*: a case in point* is that of school violence. After the 1999 Columbine massacre and after over 30 students died at Virginia Tech in 2007, a double reaction was heard:

– Those in favour of gun control said that it is too easy for anyone - including adolescents - to obtain guns, and then to pull the trigger* on the spur of the moment*. Besides, individuals carrying arms have rarely interrupted a mass shooting.

– Others, on the contrary, argued that if the teachers had been armed too, they could have prevented the massacres. Carrying guns, they say, thus boosts public safety. They add that the government should not interfere in what is an individual decision.

enshrined in: *garanti par*; **self-reliance:** *l'indépendance*; **a lobby:** *un groupe de pression*; **to thwart:** *contrecarrer*; **a blacklist:** *une liste noire*; **childproof:** *sans danger pour les enfants, qui ne peut être utilisé par les enfants*; **a spate of:** *une série de*; **to be adamant:** *rester sur ses positions*; **a case in point:** *un bon example*; **to pull the trigger:** *tirer sur la gâchette*; **on the spur of the moment:** *sur un coup de tête, sans réfléchir*

13 THE MEDIA

The freedom of the press is guaranteed by the first amendment to the Constitution: "Congress shall make no law respecting an establishment of religion, or prohibiting the free exercise thereof; or abridging the freedom of speech, or of the press..."

The media are all-powerful in the United States, as was shown when *The Washington Post* revealed the Watergate scandal, which led to the impeachment* of President Nixon.

There are a few national papers (*The New York Times, The Wall Street Journal, USA Today, The Washington Post, The Los Angeles Times, The Boston Globe, The Chicago Tribune*) but even these are not always available all over the different states. Newspapers tend to contain both local news and syndicated columns* which appear in different newspapers all over the country.

News magazines include *Time*, *Newsweek*, *US News and World Report* and *Fortune*.

Because of their broad appeal, most of these newspapers and magazines tend to be politically centrist.

Newspaper	Circulation (print and digital paid subscriptions, 2019)
1. *The Wall Street Journal*	786,599
2. *USA Today*	726,906
3. *New York Post*	426,129
4. *The New York Times*	362,763
5. *The Los Angeles Times*	164,845
6. *The Washington Post*	180,159
7. *The Chicago Tribune*	118,572

America's largest newspaper brands have switched much of their focus to building up digital subscription businesses in recent years – a trend that has become more pronounced over the past 18 months because of the pandemic. Over 80% of Americans now get their news from digital devices. But print remains an important source of revenue for the industry, both for circulation and advertising income.

A few TV statistics (2019)

The average American watches over 3 hours and 35 minutes of TV a day.
The average American household* has 2.3 sets.
95.9% of households have at least one TV set.
65% of households possess 3 or more TV sets.
35% of Americans watch TV while eating dinner.
Kids ages 6-11 spend about 28 hours a week in front of the TV.
By the time a child is 12, he has watched some 8,000 murders on TV.
30% of news broadcast time is spent on advertising.

Source: BLS American Time Use Survey

The medium is the message.

Marshall McLuhan

I find television to be very educating. Every time somebody turns on the set, I go in the other room and read a book.

Groucho Marx

Politics will eventually be replaced by imagery. The politician will be only too happy to abdicate in favor of his image, because the image will be much more powerful than he could ever be.

Marshall McLuhan

Television: chewing gum for the eyes.

Frank Lloyd Wright

There are thousands of radio stations and over 1,500 TV stations for example:
ABC (American Broadcasting Corporation)
CBS (Columbia Broadcasting System)
NBC (National Broadcasting Company)
PBS (Public Broadcasting Service) is a non-profit enterprise which offers quality programs (children's programs, documentaries).
CBN (The Christian Broadcasting Network) is a Christian television station (founded by the televangelist Pat Robertson).
CNN (Cable News Network) is a 24-hour news channel.
Discovery Channel, broadcasting all over the world, specializes in science, nature and history.
The Federal Communication Commission is the government agency which grants broadcast licences*, ensures* that there is no monopoly, and decides whether programmes should be considered obscene.

The Cambridge Analytica scandal

In 2018 it was revealed that Cambridge Analytica, a Cambridge consulting firm, harvested the personal data of millions of Facebook users (without their consent) for political advertising. Psychological profiles were used to help Donald Trump's 2016 campaign and influence the Brexit referendum. The scandal caused outrage and led to heightened awareness about privacy and the possible influence of social media on politics.

impeachment: *la mise en accusation*; **syndicated columns:** *des articles de journalistes d'agence*; **a household:** *un ménage*; **a licence:** *un permis*; **to ensure:** *s'assurer*

(The New York Times online)
liennathan.fr/7n52sm

14 SOCIAL SECURITY & HEALTH CARE

SOCIAL SECURITY*

Social Security in the United States is a federal system of insurance (paid by both employer and employee) which provides pensions for workers, family aid (for maternity, child care, dependants) and disability benefits*. In 1996, President Clinton's Workfare was designed to help people off benefits and back to work by limiting the number of years during which one can benefit from welfare assistance.

Social Security: *les prestations sociales*; **benefits:** *allocations*

HEALTH CARE

Not all Americans have full health coverage*.

▪ The federal government provides two main types of health programs:
– Medicaid (created in 1965) is a health care programme for poor people who cannot afford medical care. It is financed jointly by the federal government and the states.
– Medicare (also created in 1965) is a federal health care scheme for elderly people (aged 65 or more) and those with long-term disabilities. It is not entirely free since people pay taxes then a premium* to benefit from Medicare. It provides doctors' services, hospitalization and, since 2003, a prescription-drug entitlement*.

▪ There are also a number of programmes at the level of each state, for instance the State Children's Health Insurance Program which is aimed at children, whose parents have no health care insurance.

▪ Many Americans are also insured through their employers, in return for a monthly premium.

▪ Others are insured privately.

This means that there are still many Americans (about a sixth of the population) who find themselves without health insurance, because they are not yet 65, because they are not eligible for* Medicaid, because they cannot have health care coverage through their employers, or because they have lost their jobs and cannot pay the high premiums of a private insurance. They can still be treated in hospitals but may not get preventive care.

▪ 'Obamacare'
Several Senators had already tried, but failed, to obtain a comprehensive* reform of the healthcare system. It was during the 2009 presidential campaign that Healthcare reform became a major issue. Senator Obama presented it as one of his top four priorities if he was elected. It eventually led to the Patient Protection and Affordable Care Act, more commonly called ACA (Affordable Care Act) or 'Obamacare'. Its aim is to control healthcare costs, and expand coverage* through public and private insurance: broader Medicaid eligibility and Medicare coverage, and subsidized, regulated private insurance.

The ACA took effect on January 1, 2014.
Here are some of its main provisions:
– It expands Medicaid eligibility, and reforms the Medicare payment system.
– Any individual who is not covered by an employer's insurance, by Medicaid, Medicare or any other plan is required to take out a private-insurance policy. This is mandatory* but there are subsidies for people with low incomes.
– Insurers cannot deny coverage to people because of their pre-existing health problems.

– Insurance policies will have to conform with minimum standards and people will be able to compare policies in each state through health insurance exchanges.
– Businesses with more than 50 full-time employees are required to offer health insurance.
America's most serious problem is now deaths from opiod overdoses, which kill about 70,000 Americans every year (soaring by 30% to 93,331 in 2020), more than guns and more than AIDS ever did at the height of the epidemic.
One of President Trump's major promises was to repeal* the Affordable Care Act and replace it later with another health care plan.

health coverage: *la couverture sociale*; **a premium:** *une prime d'assurance*; **entitlement:** *le droit à quelque chose*; **to be eligible for:** *avoir droit à*; **comprehensive:** *vaste, complet*; **coverage:** *couverture*; **mandatory:** *obligatoire*; **to repeal:** *abroger*

(The home page of the US Department of Health and Human Services)
liennathan.fr/46bg3d

CONTROVERSIAL ISSUES

▪ Health care litigation

America is *the* country of litigation*, where suing* for compensation is something quite common. This is particularly true in the world of medicine. Doctors – obstetricians and gynaecologists in particular - have to pay huge premiums to be insured against malpractice lawsuits*. Not only does it cost doctors a great deal, but it also leads to their asking for unnecessary tests and checks – just to be on the safe side. Health care costs are spiralling* out of control as a result, with the consequence that more and more people are unable to afford health coverage.

litigation: *les procès*; **to sue:** *poursuivre en justice*; **a malpractice lawsuit:** *un procès pour faute professionnelle*; **to spiral:** *monter en flèche*

15 AMERICAN LITERATURE: MAJOR TRENDS AND WRITERS

The early Puritan settlers admired the arts as long as they promoted* the Puritan cause and the way of life it entailed*. The main genres favoured at the time were therefore sermons, religious works, autobiographies and diaries, historical works and poetry.

to promote: *favoriser, encourager*; **to entail:** *entraîner*

THE LITERATURE OF THE NEW REPUBLIC: 1770-1865

At the very end of the 18th century, the ideals of the Enlightenment* are reflected in an interest in balance, order and clarity. The dramatic events which led to independence gave rise to many political writings and journals: **Thomas Paine**'s *Common Sense* (1776) is a convincingly argued pamphlet which urges separation from England; **Benjamin Franklin**'s *Autobiography* (1793) shows how hard work, frugality and moral concerns can lead to the improvement of the self and of society.

Romanticism and the **American Renaissance**

If **John de Crèvecoeur**'s *Letters from an American Farmer* (1782, showing an idealized vision of America as a nation of free, self-reliant* citizens), already announces romanticism, the movement is only truly felt after 1820.

■ **The Knickerbockers** combine conventional methods and American themes: **James Fenimore Cooper**'s novels (*The Pioneers*, 1823, *The Prairie*, 1827) are romances set in the American wilderness and lamenting the destruction of its purity by civilization. **Washington Irving**'s *Sketch Book* adapts Gothic German tales (imbued with* a sense of mystery and the supernatural) to America (*The Legend of Sleepy Hollow*, 1819-20).

■ **Transcendentalism** is an extremely influential philosophical movement in the mid 19th century. Transcendentalists believed that all beings were divine, that Man, God and nature shared the same soul, the "Oversoul." Men should therefore trust the divinity within them, follow their own intuitions and be self-reliant. Such individualism played an important part in the spirit of the frontier. The best-known figures of the movement are **Emerson** (*Self-Reliance*, 1841) and **Thoreau** (*Walden*, 1854, an account of the months Thoreau spent alone living in the wild, observing the changes in nature through the seasons and recording the spiritual experience it gave rise to.)

■ The **American Renaissance** is the name given to the 1840s and early 1850s, when some highly imaginative and symbolic works were published:

• **Edgar Allan Poe**'s tales of terror and mystery (*Tales of the Grotesque and Arabesque*, 1840)

• The sombre novels of **Nathaniel Hawthorne** are "allegories of the heart", romances set in the Puritan past of New England and exploring sin, guilt and moral conflicts (*The Scarlet Letter*, 1850)

• **Melville's** *Moby Dick* (1851) is about Captain Ahab's hunting of the whale which cost him a leg. His quest* takes on mythic dimensions, evoking the frontier spirit and the fight between good and evil, and exploring themes such as madness, obsession and hubris.

– In poetry, the period is dominated by the figure of **Walt Whitman**, whose *Leaves of Grass* (1855-1892) shocked most Americans but was gradually seen as deeply influential. The poems are written in free verse and are a celebration of the self, of sexuality, of the potentialities of all Americans. They are deeply nationalistic, praising the beauty and the democratic spirit of America.

the Enlightenment: *le siècle des Lumières*; **self-reliant:** *indépendant*; **imbued with:** *imprégné de*; **a quest:** *une quête*

REALISM: 1865-1915

Increasingly, as the end of the century approached, idealization gave way to a more faithful description of rural and urban America, then to the criticism of the evils brought about by capitalism.
• The novels of **Mark Twain** are set on the Mississippi River. *The Adventures of Tom Sawyer* (1876) and *The Adventures of Huckleberry Finn* (1884) are **novels of initiation** in which the young, innocent hero is confronted with all forms of dishonesty and evil.
• In the novels of **Stephen Crane** (*The Red Badge of Courage*, 1895), **Frank Norris** (*The Octopus*, 1901), **Theodore Dreiser** (*Sister Carrie*, 1900) and **Jack London** (*The Call of the Wild*, 1903), realism becomes bleaker and turns to **naturalism**, showing lives determined by their environment.

Inner realism

• **Henry James**'s realism is psychological. He contrasts the values of America (innocence, energy, materialism) and those of Europe (corruption, decadence, art), through the portrayal* of characters whose moral conflicts we follow as they become "centres of consciousness": *The Portrait of a Lady*, 1881; *What Maisie Knew*, 1897; *The Turn of the Screw*, 1898.
• **Edith Wharton**'s novels expose the artificiality, immorality and corruption of the well-to-do* society of her time (*The Age of Innocence*, 1920).
• The highly personal poetry of **Emily Dickinson** is about nature, love, and death, and explores the tension between conformity and rebellion, Puritanism and the rejection of conventional morality.

the portrayal: *la peinture, la représentation*; **well-to-do:** *aisé, riche*

BETWEEN TWO WORLD WARS (1915-1945)

The Lost Generation and the Modernists

The sense of disillusion and loss which followed the first World War is reflected through the new literary forms and experiments of the 1920s.
– Although conventional in form, the poetry of **Robert Frost** and **Carl Sandburg** shows ironic detachment and scepticism.

– **William Carlos Williams, e.e. cummings, Wallace Stevens** and **Marianne Moore** all experimented with form. The poem which best symbolizes its age is probably *The Waste Land* (1922), by the Anglo-American poet **T.S. Eliot**, who uses collage, allusions, and multiple voices to convey the chaos and fragmentation of modern society.

– Several American novelists came to live in Paris after World War I and experimented with new forms. They are often referred to as The Lost Generation.

• **Ernest Hemingway**'s clear, terse and controlled prose is used to portray stoic heroes whose only way of facing death and nihilism is to respect a code of honour and loyalty (*A Farewell to Arms*, 1929).

• **John Dos Passos**' *USA* is an epic trilogy using collage, multiple voices, fragmentation and cinematic techniques to paint a social portrait of America.

• As for **Francis Scott Fitzgerald**, he exposes the moral vacuity of the Jazz Age and its vain attempts to achieve the American Dream (*The Great Gatsby*, 1925).

• The narrow-mindedness, philistinism and conformism of small-town America is exposed in the novels of **Sinclair Lewis** (*Babbitt*, 1922); the short stories of **Sherwood Anderson** (*Winesburg*, Ohio, 1919) focus on the secrets and repression that hide behind the façade of the same small towns.

■ Social Concerns

After the 1929 crash, the search for new techniques gave way to a concern for the plight* of the poor, the unemployed, and all the victims of society. **John Steinbeck**'s novels, for instance, praise the virtues of love and solidarity in the face of hardships such as displacement, unfair labour practices and poverty (*The Grapes of Wrath* (1939)).

a plight: *une situation difficile*

■ New identities

It was in the 1920s that a number of black writers asserted their pride and cultural heritage. This literary movement was called **The Harlem Renaissance** (e.g. the poetry of **Langston Hughes**). In the 1930s, the mood of optimism was replaced by class-consciousness and revolt. This is clear in **Richard Wright**'s novels (*Black Boy*, 1945), political and naturalistic works which show how the environment of the ghetto can only lead to violence.

Carrying a burden* of guilt after the Civil War and Reconstruction, the Southern States, too, needed to redefine their identity. In the novels of **William Faulkner**, their best representative, the characters are often violent and degenerate, grotesque even, typical of what will be called **Southern Gothic**. The novels make use of multiple voices, stream of consciousness and temporal dislocation (*The Sound and the Fury*, 1929).

a burden: *un fardeau*

The Theatre

It was in the 1920s that the American theatre came into its own*, with the plays of **Eugene O'Neill**, influenced by Greek tragedy, the theories of Freud, and Ibsen. They unite realism and expressionism, social concerns and symbolism (*Mourning Becomes Electra*, 1931).

to come into its own: *se révéler*

FROM WORLD WAR II TO THE PRESENT DAY

The Beat Generation

The sense of alienation and loss which resulted from World War II led a number of writers to rebel against authority, the Establishment and the materialism of society. Instead they turned to the exploration of the self by means of drugs or oriental meditation. Indeed the word "beat" refers to the rhythm or *beat* of jazz, the search for *beat*itude, and a generation which is *beat*en.
The Beats wrote works of both poetry (**Allen Ginsberg, Lawrence Ferlinghetti**) and fiction (**Jack Kerouac**, *On the Road*, 1957).

Confessional poets

After the experimentations of modernist poets like T.S. Eliot, a reaction set in, reflecting the desire to express one's emotions and feelings directly. This is to be found in the poetry of **Robert Lowell, Sylvia Plath, Elizabeth Bishop** and **Adrienne Rich**.

The theatre

Two major playwrights dominate the 1950s and 1960s:
• **Tennessee Williams**' s plays show frustrated individuals, whose failure leads to neurosis and a world of illusion. The message is brought home by symbolism and expressionistic devices. (*A Streetcar Named Desire*, 1947).
• **Arthur Miller** is more concerned with social problems and the conflict between ordinary, private lives and public issues. In *The Crucible* (1953), for example, Miller links the Salem witch hunts of the late 17th century to McCarthyism in the 1950s.

Southern literature

The decadence of the South, conveyed by Baroque and Gothic themes, still haunts the novels of **Carson Mc Cullers** (*The Heart is a Lonely Hunter*, 1940), **Eudora Welty** (*A Curtain of Green, short stories*, 1941), **William Styron** (*The Confessions of Nat Turner*, 1967), **Harper Lee** (*To Kill a Mockingbird*, 1960)), **Flannery O'Connor** (*A Good Man is Hard to Find*, 1955 - stories), **Truman Capote** (*In Cold Blood*, 1966), and **Joyce Carol Oates** (*Bellefleur*, 1980), **Cormac McCarthy** (*The Road*, 2006).

■ **The voices of minorities**

Many of these voices express estrangement and a desire for recognition.

– Black American voices record the experience of suffering and alienation: **Ralph Ellison** (*Invisible Man*, 1952), **James Baldwin** (*Go Tell it on the Mountain*, 1953), **Alice Walker** (*The Color Purple*, 1982), **Maya Angelou**'s poems, **Toni Morrison** (*Beloved*, 1987).

– Women's voices: **Joyce Carol Oates, Grace Paley** (*The Little Disturbances of Man*, 1959).

– Jewish American voices, describing the conflict between the scars of the past, the Holocaust, and the wish to become part of the American Dream: **Saul Bellow** (*Herzog*, 1964), **Bernard Malamud** (*The Assistant*, 1957), **Philip Roth** (*The Human Stain*, 2000).

– Chicano voices: **Rudolfo Anaya**'s novels show the influence of Mexican and Aztec traditions (*Bless Me, Ultima*, 1971)

– Indian American voices: **Louise Erdrich** (*Love Medicine*, 1984) and **N. Scott Momaday** (*House Made of Dawn*, 1968).

■ **New Journalism**

Several writers attempted to unite journalism and fiction, facts and the subjectivity of the narrator, which resulted in a technique that can be called "**neorealism**": **Truman Capote** (*In Cold Blood*,1966), **Norman Mailer** (*The Armies of the Night*, 1968), **Tom Wolfe** (*The Bonfire of the Vanities*, 1987).

Many of **Gore Vidal**'s works are historical fiction (*Lincoln*, 1984) or essays about American society.

■ **The novel of manners**

Often satirical, these novels describe the relationships within a community; they often imply the belief in ethical values: **J.D. Salinger** (*The Catcher in the Rye*, 1951), **John Updike** (*Rabbit, Run*, 1960), **Raymond Carver** (short stories), **Joyce Carol Oates** (*Bellefleur*, 1980), **Russell Banks** (*Continental Drift*, 1985), **Grace Paley** (*The Little Disturbances of Man*, 1985).

■ **Postmodernism and the literature of the absurd**

Another way of conveying the chaos and complexity of society is to reject the conventions of plot and realism and to use burlesque, farce, dislocation and collage in order to create an effect of defamiliarization: **Vladimir Nabokov** (*Lolita*, 1955), **Joseph Heller** (*Catch-22*, 1961), **Kurt Vonnegut** (*Slaughterhouse-Five*, 1969), **Thomas Pynchon** (*The Crying of Lot 49*, 1966), **Richard Brautigan** (*Trout Fishing in America*, 1967), **Paul Auster** (*The New York Trilogy*, 1985-86), **Don DeLillo** (*White Noise*, 1985).

The theatre of the Absurd is represented by the plays of **Edward Albee** (*Who's Afraid of Virginia Woolf?*, 1962) and **Sam Shepard** (*Fool for Love*, 1983).

16 AMERICAN PAINTING: MAJOR MOVEMENTS AND ARTISTS

THE COLONIAL AGE (1650-1765)

Not considered serious enough for the Puritans, painting was not a major art in colonial America. It mainly consisted of fairly lifeless portraits, showing the influence of Elizabethan miniatures or of Dutch painting. The first native group of painters were **the Patroon Painters**, whose portraits include vivid colours and a pastoral background. In the first half of the 18th century, **John Smibert**'s studio in Boston became a centre for the arts, and paintings became more complex in their composition.

PAINTING IN THE NEW NATION (1765-1880)

■ Historical paintings

The American Revolution and the birth of the new nation explain the popularity of historical portraits and scenes inspired by classical or American events. They are mostly didactic, moralizing and dramatic, as with West's *Death of General Wolfe*. The main representatives are **Benjamin West, John Singleton Copley, John Trumbull, Charles Willson Peale** and **Gilbert Stuart**.

■ Landscape painting

Under the influence of romanticism and as the new country began to expand westward, landscape painting became a truly American art, reflecting the beauty of the land and the pride it inspired. Huge panoramic and dramatic landscapes symbolized the grandeur of the land and the Divine spirit, which, according to the Trancendentalists, animated both men and nature. This is mainly to be found in the paintings of the **Hudson River painters** (**Asher B. Durand, Thomas Cole, Albert Bierstadt**), and in the very dramatic landscapes of **Frederick Church**.

The Luminists (**John Frederick Kensett, Martin J. Heade, Fitz Hugh Lane**) preferred more melancholy scenes of lakes and woods in half-light, with a particular interest in light effects.

As for **John J. Audubon**, he was a naturalist who made a detailed study of American birds, which he painted in their natural habitats and with great aesthetic sensitivity.

■ Genre painting

Another consequence of nationalism was an interest in everyday life, in country scenes and pictures of frontier life, as in the paintings of **William Sidney Mount** and **George Caleb Bingham**.

THE AGE OF REALISM (1880-1915)

▪ The Expatriates

At the end of the 19th century, several artists chose to work abroad, particularly in Paris – an artistic hotbed* at the time. They were influenced by Impressionism, Japanese prints and the 'art for art's sake' movement.

George Innes's landscapes show the influence of the Barbizon School.

Whistler's landscapes and portraits create harmonies in muted* colours and show the influence of Japanese painting.

Mary Cassatt specializes in domestic scenes, often with mother and children seen from unusual angles.

a hotbed: *un foyer*; **muted:** *sourde, atténuée (couleur)*

▪ Realism

Winslow Homer renders movement and vitality in the wild and in outdoor scenes: man fighting against the elements or scenes of battle. **Thomas Eakins** specializes in realistic portraits or scenes reflecting his interest in the human body and anatomy (surgeons operating, men bathing).

▪ The Ash Can School

At the beginning of the 20th century, a group of artist (**Robert Henri, John Sloan**) rejected conventions and turned to the urban environment and the depiction of ordinary people.

THE MODERN AGE: 1915-1945

In 1913, America discovered modern art with the New York Armory Show, in which cubist and neo-impressionist paintings were exhibited. It both shocked and profoundly influenced American artists.

▪ The Modernists

The paintings and photographs of **Man Ray** reflect the **Surrealist movement**.

Georgia O' Keeffe's paintings (often close-ups*) of flowers, bones, and New Mexico buildings are very powerful and intense with their bright colours and clear lines, and show the influence of Abstraction.

Joseph Stella's and **Stuart Davis**'s paintings of the city are full of vitality with their bright colours and their composition inspired by futurism and cubism.

a close-up: *un gros plan*

▪ Painting American life

The Precisionists: **Charles Demuth** and **Charles Sheeler** used modernist techniques (geometric forms) to paint the industrial age, its machines and factories.

Edward Hopper's paintings show lonely beings in ordinary urban settings such as restaurants or hotel rooms which are made very powerful by their dramatic lighting and convey a sense of alienation.
Ben Shahn is one of the painters of the Great Depression: he uses distortion and exaggeration, as in German expressionism, to convey the distress of the people he depicts.
Hart Benton and **Grant Wood** are **regionalists**, whose paintings depict rural scenes – farmers, village life, small towns – often using distorted lines or near caricature.

THE MODERN AGE: 1945-2000

Realism

The main representative of this trend is **Andrew Wyeth**, who paints New England landscapes in subdued* tones and with meticulous precision. His paintings, often depicting barren landscapes or disabled people, evoke loneliness and nostalgia.

subdued tones: *des tons doux*

Abstraction

Abstract expressionism, that is to say the use of abstract art to convey profound emotion, is best represented in the 1950s by **Jackson Pollock** and **Willem de Kooning**, also called **Action Painters**. The fluid lines and swirls* of the brushstroke* have an intense kinetic effect on the viewer.
Color-Field Painting: The term applies to vast canvases*, with only a few simple shapes creating fields of pure colour, as in the paintings of **Barnett Newman** and **Mark Rothko**.
Minimal Painting: Artists such as **Kenneth Noland** and **Frank Stella** reduce painting to geometrical shapes and even optical illusions in order to divest the painting of any emotion or meaning.
Op Art: The paintings of **Larry Poons** rely on optical effects to make the viewer participate and try to make out a design or pattern in the picture.
Pop Art: This 1960s movement was a reaction against the banal, the commercial and the vulgar in mass culture. In an attempt to "fill the gap between art and life", a number of artists stuck real objects onto their canvases (**Robert Rauschenberg**), painted ordinary objects (**Jasper Johns**), used collage (**James Rosenquist**), Ben Day dots (**Roy Lichtenstein**), or images from advertising or pop culture (like Marilyn Monroe) repeated over and over (**Andy Warhol**).

a swirl: *tourbillon*; **a brushstroke:** *un trait de pinceau*; **a canvas:** *une toile*

"Hollywood is where if you don't have happiness you send out for it."
Rex Reed

The history of the American cinema is dominated by Hollywood and a hugely successful industry which evokes both glamour and cheap commercial culture.

FROM SILENT FILMS TO THE TALKIES

It was soon after 1910 that the first studios (Universal, Metro-Goldwyn-Mayer, Warner Brothers, Twentieth Century Fox) settled in Hollywood, attracted by the good weather all the year round (which meant shooting* all through the year) but also escaping from having to pay fees to Thomas Edison's studios in the east. Many silent films were produced and went on being produced until the late 20s:
– Large-scale **documentaries** and didactic films with D.W. Griffiths'*Birth of a Nation* (1914) about the Civil War, or *Intolerance* (1916) or von Stroheim's *Greed* (1925), a whole survey of money as the root of all evil.
– **Comedies** with Charlie Chaplin (*The Kid* (1921), *The Gold Rush* (1935), *Modern Times* (1936)) and Buster Keaton (*The General* (1926).
Hugely successful studios like Universal Studios and United Artists were created, and with them the star system appeared.
With the first colour films in the early 20s and the first talkies* in the late 20s, the cinema became hugely popular. Some stars became very famous (Mary Pickford, Greta Garbo, Marlene Dietrich, Rudolph Valentino...) and many European directors such as Fritz Lang, Alfred Hitchcock (*Strangers on a Train*, 1951, *Rear Window*, 1954) or Jean Renoir came to America.

to shoot: *tourner (un film)*; **the talkies:** *le cinema parlant*

THE 1930s AND 1940s: THE GOLDEN AGE OF HOLLYWOOD

This was the heyday of the film industry, when many types of films were produced: **westerns** like Ford's *Stagecoach* (1939) or *Fort Apache* (1948); **social documentaries** inspired by the Great Depression, like John Ford's *The Grapes of Wrath* (1940) or *Tobacco Road* (1941) – both adaptations of novels by Steinbeck and Caldwell. Orson Welles's *Citizen Kane* (1941), which shows that money is not everything, is part of the same social criticism. Another popular adaptation from a novel by Margaret Mitchell was Fleming's *Gone With the Wind* (1939) with Clark Gable and Vivien Leigh. There were also **thrillers*** (John Huston's *The Maltese Falcon*, 1936) and **spy thrillers*** inspired by WWII, like Michael Curtiz's *Casablanca*, **slapstick comedies***,

like Frank Capra's, those with Laurel and Hardy or the Marx Brothers. **Musicals***, **animated cartoons***, **cliffhangers*** or **tear-jerkers*** were very successful as well as adaptations from literature.
They often reflected deep-rooted American themes: the lonesome cowboy, or a character taking the law into his own hands, the triumph of good over evil, or violence.

Most Hollywood films were then produced under the studio system: each studio had its own actors, directors, and writers as well as movie theaters in which the films were shown all over the country. These years also witnessed the rise of the star system. Famous film stars like John Wayne, Clark Gable, Henry Fonda, Humphrey Bogart, Gregory Peck, Kirk Douglas, Erol Flynn, Bette Davis, and Katharine Hepburn became world famous. Well-known directors included Fritz Lang, Michael Curtiz, Orson Welles, and John Ford.

a thriller: *un film à suspense*; **a spy thriller:** *un film d'espionnage*; **slapstick comedy:** *de la grosse farce*; **a musical:** *une comédie musicale*; **an animated cartoon:** *un dessin animé*; **a cliffhanger:** *film à suspense*; **a tear-jerker:** *film sentimental*

"POST-CLASSICAL" CINEMA: THE 1950s AND 1960s

By the end of the 1930s, some 300 to 400 films were produced every year in Hollywood.
But the competition from television and the end of the studio system, as anti-trust laws came into effect, brought a radical change in the film industry. Although many films belonging to the genres mentioned above were produced, the cost of production soared, and film-makers focused on new approaches.
One such trend was to develop the cinema as an art form, using a variety of techniques such as jumbled* chronology, and putting an end to the Manichean vision of earlier films. More and more films also reflected America's multi-cultural society (*In the Heat of the Night* (1967), *West Side Story* (1961)), as well as its obsession with sex, violence and rebellion (*Rebel without a Cause* (1955), *Bonnie and Clyde* (1967), *Easy Rider* (1969)).
Stars such as Marilyn Monroe and James Dean preserved the popularity of the art.

jumbled: *brouillé, dans le désordre*

NEW HOLLYWOOD: THE 1980s AND AFTER

In the late 1970s, Hollywood underwent another revolution as its studios were bought by large media companies, which started specializing in the production of expensive blockbusters* – epic spectacles with rising stars like Meryl Streep, Tom Hanks and Leonardo DiCaprio. For example, Steven Spielberg's *Jaws* (1975), *E.T.* (1982), *Jurassic Park* (1993), *Schindler's List* and *Saving Private Ryan* (1998), George

Lucas's *Star Wars* (1977), James Cameron's *Titanic* (1997), Zemeckis's *Forrest Gump* (1994), and Clint Eastwood's *Million Dollar Baby* (2004), *The Star Wars* series, James Cameron's *Avatar* (2009), to name only a few, were enormous box-office hits*, hyped* in order to attract a large world audience.

More original films still keep being produced: Woody Allen's comic satires of modern life (*Hannah and her Sisters* (1986), *Husbands and Wives* (1992) or Stanley Kubrick's controversial cult films (*Lolita* (1962), *Dr Strangelove* (1964), *A Clockwork Orange* (1971), *Full Metal Jacket* (1987), *Eyes Wide Shut* (1999), David Lynch's *Mulholland Drive* (2001).

The independent smaller-budget productions of directors like Spike Lee, Quentin Tarantino (*Reservoir Dogs*, 1992) or Michael Moore (*Fahrenheit 9/11*, 2004) are often innovative and critical of mainstream America.

a blockbuster: *une superproduction*; **a hit:** *un gros succès*; **to hype:** *faire du battage publicitaire*

18 A FEW KEYWORDS IN AMERICAN CULTURE

A

Abortion*: Although the Supreme Court ruled* in favour of abortion in 1973 (*Roe vs. Wade*), it is still a highly divisive* issue in the United States, where attacks against abortion clinics or doctors are not uncommon. Pro-choice campaigners defend a woman's right to choose whether or not to have a child, whereas pro-life supporters argue that the unborn child has a right to life. Each state now has its own policy concerning abortion.

Academy Awards: The Oscar film awards given every year in Los Angeles for 'Best Actor/Actress', 'Best Picture', etc.

AFL-CIO: The largest workers' union* in the United States (American Federation of Labor - Congress of Industrial Organizations).

Alma Mater: Someone's former school or university.

American Dream, The: The cornerstone* of American society, it is the dream of a promised land of liberty and equality and it has attracted many immigrants to America. The early Puritans wanted to build a "City upon a Hill", then the dream became a political one with the huge waves of immigrants fleeing war and poverty in the 19th and 20th centuries. It is also the idea that, through courage, hard work and education, any American can go up the social ladder and succeed. (cf. Self-made man) Over the years, poverty, racism and the lack of universal health-care insurance have sometimes turned the dream into mere illusion.

abortion: *l'avortement*; **to rule:** *décider, déclarer*; **divisive:** *sujet à controverse*; **a union:** *un syndicat*; **the cornerstone:** *le fondement, la pierre angulaire*

B

Babbitt: The eponymous hero of Sinclair Lewis's novel (1922), he stands for narrow-mindedness* and philistinism.

Baseball: Baseball is the national pastime in America. It is played by two teams of nine players on a large field, divided into four bases forming a diamond*. Its outlines* show the way a runner must run to score. A ball is thrown by a pitcher* and hit by a batter* in the opposite team. The latter tries to throw it back as far as possible to give him time to run a complete circuit around the bases. There are nine innings* in a game.

Bible Belt, The: The Southeast of the United States, where there is a high proportion of Christians, and particularly of fundamentalists.

Boston Brahmin: Someone who belongs to an old, wealthy and influential Boston family. Many live in the fashionable Beacon Hill district of Boston.

Broadway: A New York street which is famous for its theatres; the word symbolises show business in New York. The shows there are mainly commercial so that smaller theatres in New York are said to be off-Broadway, and more experimental productions are off-off Broadway.

Bussing: Taking children by bus to a school outside their district in order to encourage racial integration. Bussing was widely used in the 70s and 80s but is now more controversial.

narrow-mindedness: *l'étroitesse d'esprit*; **a diamond:** *un losange*; **an outline:** *un contour*; **the pitcher:** *le lanceur*; **the batter:** *le batteur*; **an inning:** *une manche*

C

Capitol, the: The building in Washington where Congress meets. It is built on Capitol Hill, and the words Capitol Hill or the Hill are often used metonymically for Congress.

CIA (Central Intelligence Agency): The government organization which gathers information about foreign countries.

Corn Belt, the: The name given to the Midwest states (e.g. Illinois, Indiana, Iowa) where corn is grown extensively.

D

Deep South, The: The Deep South is the name given to the southern states (for instance, Alabama, Mississippi, Louisiana, South Carolina, Georgia) which formed the Confederacy defeated in the Civil War. They are deeply religious. See Bible Belt.

Dinkie: A word formed with the first letters of the expression "double income, no kids" and referring to a couple who are well off because they have two salaries and no children.

Dixie: A familiar word for the Southern states.

Dow-Jones Index (or Dow-Jones Average): The average price of shares* of certain companies published every day by the New York Stock Exchange. It gives an idea of how well the US stock market is doing.

a share: *une action (en Bourse)*

E

Ellis Island: From 1892 to 1943, Ellis Island (in New York harbour) was the place where the newly-arrived immigrants went through the necessary immigration procedures before entering the United States. There, their health was checked and they were questioned about their destination and profession before being given a landing card*. Ellis Island is now a museum.

Emmy Awards: Awards given annually for excellence in television, programming, production, and performance.

ERA: Equal Rights Amendment, a proposal for an amendment to the Constitution giving women and men equal rights. Not enough states had given their approval by the 1982 deadline*, so that the proposal never became a law.

Euthanasia: Euthanasia is illegal in the United States, except in Oregon where doctor-assisted suicide is possible if a terminally-ill patient requests it.

a landing card: *une carte de débarquement*; **a deadline:** *une date limite*

F

FBI (Federal Bureau of Investigation): The government organization responsible for national security and dealing with both crime and terrorism.

Flag Day: June 14th, when everyone flies the US flag*.

Four Freedoms, The: The four essential freedoms defined and promised by Roosevelt: freedom of speech, freedom of worship, freedom from want, freedom from fear.

Fourth Estate: The media, which is said to represent the fourth power after the government, the law and religion.

Fraternity: A social organization for male or female students in most colleges. Students belonging to a fraternity live in the same house. Fraternities have Greek names, like Phi Beta Kappa, a well-known fraternity for the brightest students.

Frontier, The: The limit between the civilized, settled land and the "wilderness". The frontier gradually moved westward in the 19th century, encouraged by the 1848 California Gold Rush and by the Homestead Act (1862), which granted* 160 acres of land to any man ready to farm it. The movement westward can be summed up by Horace Greeley's well-known saying: "Go West, young man, and grow up with the country!" The spirit of the frontier has come to symbolise the American spirit: it is synonymous with individualism, courage, resilience* and the search for opportunity.

to fly the flag: *pavoiser*; **to grant:** *accorder*; **resilience:** *le ressort, l'élasticité*

G

Gated communities*: Communities where the entry gates are locked to prevent outsiders from entering. Such communities have their own security systems and are often exclusive, providing a large range of services for their members. They also contribute to a certain segregation since some are mainly for white people, others for black people, others for the elderly.

Gay marriage: Should marriage be regulated by federal law? The constitution mentions marriage but does not say whether it is between a man and a woman. Some states (like Massachusetts or California) have allowed gay marriages, while others have passed "defence of marriage acts", which define marriage as a union between a man and a woman. Those who oppose gay marriages are therefore in favour of a constitutional ban to stop same-sex marriage everywhere in the United States. This would still make it possible for states to allow civil unions (granting homosexuals some legal rights and benefits).

G8: see p. 97

God Bless America: A very popular song and unofficial national anthem.

God bless America, land that I love.
Stand beside her, and guide her
Thru* the night with a light from above.
From the mountains, to the prairies
To the oceans, white with foam*
God bless America, my home sweet home.
From the mountains, to the prairies
To the oceans, white with foam
God bless America, my home sweet home!
God bless America, my home sweet home!

a gated community: *une résidence sécurisée*; **thru: through; foam:** *l'écume*

H

Halloween: The night of October 31, when it was believed that ghosts and witches* could be seen. Children now celebrate Halloween by putting lights inside jack'o lanterns (hollowed pumpkins*), dressing up as witches and going from door to door, asking "Trick or treat?" (a treat*, for instance candy, otherwise, they will play a trick* on you.)

Harlem: The district of upper Manhattan where many African Americans settled in the 1920s and 1930s when they left the Southern states. It is still a mainly black district today.

a witch: *une sorcière*; **a treat:** *un cadeau*; **to play a trick on:** *jouer un tour à*; **a hollowed pumpkin:** *une citrouille vidée*

I

Independence Day: On July 4th, Americans celebrate the anniversary of their Declaration of Independence (July 4th 1776).

Inner cities: the central parts of cities, often more derelict* and with more social problems than in the wealthier suburbs. For years, the middle and upper classes left inner cities to move to the suburbs. There is, nowadays, an attempt to put the clock back*.

derelict: *abandonné*; **to put the clock back:** *revenir en arrière*

L

Labor Day: A national holiday in the United States (on the first Monday in September) to honour all workers.

Land of Opportunity, The idea that the United States is a country where anyone can climb up the social ladder and become rich through hard work.

Lobbies: Lobbies are pressure groups which try to influence members of Congress to vote for or against certain bills. The right to lobby is guaranteed by the first amendment to the Constitution:

Congress shall make no law respecting an establishment of religion, or prohibiting the free exercise thereof; or abridging the freedom of speech, or of the press; or the right of the people peaceably to assemble, and to petition* the government for a redress of grievances*.

Some lobbies are highly influential, for example:

• The National Rifle Association (which defends the free sale of firearms)

• The NAACP: National Association for the Advancement of Colored People, which defends the rights of black people

• NOW: National Organization of Women

• CFA, the Consumer Federation of America, and Public Citizen, which are very active in defending the rights of consumers

Lobbies have often been accused of indirectly financing electoral campaigns through gifts and donations to groups or organizations that support them.

to petition: *envoyer une pétition à*; **a redress of grievances:** *une réparation de torts*

M

Main Street: The expression metonymically refers to the attitudes (often seen as narrow-minded) of small-town America.

Manifest Destiny*: The idea, expressed by John L. O'Sullivan that the United States has a natural right to expand and "overspread the continent allotted by Providence for the development of our yearly multiplying millions" (1845). The expansion of America was thus seen as God's will.

Mason-Dixon Line: During the Civil War, this was the boundary* between the Southern States (the Confederacy) and the Northern States. The term is still used to refer to the division between the North and the South.

Melting Pot*, The: Millions of people immigrated to the United States in the 19th and 20th centuries, fleeing* poverty, political or religious persecution. The idea was originally that in the United States they would merge into a single race, with their differences erased*. But many people today want to keep their ethnic identities. They prefer speaking of a "salad bowl", a mosaic, a patchwork, or of ethnic pluralism.

Moral Majority, The: Religious, conservative, right-wing forces in American politics.

Manifest Destiny: *la Destinée manifeste*; **a boundary:** *une frontière*; **a melting pot:** *un creuset*; **to flee:** *fuir*; **to erase:** *effacer*

N

National Book Award: An American award given each year. There are categories for fiction, poetry, non fiction and children's literature.

New Economy, The: A term which applies to the American economy of the 1990s and 2000s, an economy which was no longer based on heavy industry, but derived from information technology.

New World Order: The American foreign policy after the fall of the Berlin Wall and the Gulf War, according to which America sees itself as policeman to the world.

O

Oscars: Oscars are US Academy Awards presented every year to the best films and actors.

P

PEN/Faulkner Award: A prize given every year to the best novel by an American writer.

Pentagon: The huge building near Washington which is the headquarters of the US department of defence and which therefore symbolizes the US military power. Together with the twin towers in New York, it was the target of terrorist attacks in 2001.

Pledge of Allegiance: a pledge* of loyalty to the US flag: "I pledge allegiance to the flag of the United States of America and to the republic for which it stands, one nation, under God, indivisible, for liberty and justice for all." The pledge is still recited daily in many American schools.

Political correctness (PC): A rejection, in the wake of* the Civil Rights Movement of the 1960s, of a culture seen as dominated by dead white European males and insensitive to minorities. PC took the form of curricula* favouring the works of women and minorities; but it also attempted to reform language by avoiding words which might be considered as offensive by certain groups of people because of their gender, race or physical condition. It is thus better to say "a chairperson" rather than "a chairman" and "senior citizens" rather than "the elderly". Many object to the abuses of political correctness, which they think endanger free speech.

A few examples of politically-incorrect words and their replacements:

Negro → African American	blind → visually impaired
Indian → native American	short → vertically challenged
policeman → police officer	boyfriend, girlfriend → partner
woman, women → womyn or wimmin	black coffee → coffee without milk
disabled → physically challenged	perverted → sexually dysfunctional

Protestant Work Ethic: The idea that hard work is a way of serving God.

Pulitzer Prize: A US prize awarded every year in a number of fields such as literature, journalism, and history.

a pledge: *un gage, un engagement, une promesse*; **in the wake of:** *à la suite de*; **a curriculum:** *un programme scolaire ou universitaire*

R

'Rags to Riches*': An expression which sums up the possibility of climbing up the social ladder through hard work and will power. It is illustrated by the novels of Horatio Alger (1832-1899),

Rust* Belt: a number of states around the Great Lakes, where the decline of traditional heavy industry has led to economic problems.

from rags to riches: *mot à mot: des haillons à la richesse*; **rust:** *la rouille*

S

Self-made man: If the American Dream is possible, then you can start from poverty and work your way up to wealth and/or a higher social position. You have then become a self-made man, or you can say that you have gone "from rags to riches". The idea is clearly developed in Benjamin Franklin's *Autobiography*, which shows how industry* and prudence help you to improve yourself and society. The lives of Lincoln, Carnegie and Rockefeller are good examples of success stories.

Abraham Lincoln (1809-1865) was born in a log cabin*, in Kentucky, and spent his youth working on the family farm. He ran a store, was captain of a militia unit, then postmaster*, before he entered the state legislature in 1832. He then studied law by himself and became a lawyer in 1837. This was the starting point of his political career: he was first elected to the House of Representatives in 1846, and then became President in 1861. He led the war against the Confederacy, signed the Emancipation Proclamation, and was re-elected, but shot by a supporter of the Confederacy the next year.

Andrew Carnegie started as a poor immigrant boy and worked his way up, ending as the leading American steel manufacturer. He believed in the "Gospel of Wealth", a mixture of Protestant belief in hard work and of Darwinism, with the rich better at surviving and thus having a responsibility to help the poor. Carnegie's money was used for a large number of philanthropic activities.

John D. Rockefeller (1839-1937) began working as an accountant, then entered the oil business at the end of the Civil War and consolidated the oil refineries by eliminating competitors. The richest man in America at the end of the 1890s, he was deeply religious, saying "God gave me the money", and devoted much of his money to various philanthropic activities.

Self-reliance*: The typically American idea that man should rely on* himself, on his intellectual and physical abilities, to survive and prosper, just as America should rely on its own resources rather than perpetuate European traditions. The idea is developed in Emerson's essay *Self-Reliance* (1841).

Silicon Valley: an area close to San Francisco specialized in high technology.

Spanglish: a portmanteau word* describing the mixture of Spanish and English spoken in some bilingual areas of the United States.

Statue of Liberty: The statue which stands at the entrance to New York harbor, on Liberty Island. The work of the French sculptor Bartholdi, it symbolizes both liberty and all the immigrants who have arrived in America to find that liberty.

A few lines from a poem by Emma Lazarus are written on its pedestal:

Give me your tired, your poor,
Your huddled* masses yearning* to be free,
The wretched* refuse* of your teeming* shore,
Send these, the homeless, tempest-tost*, to me.
I lift my lamp beside the golden door!

Sun Belt, The: the name given to the Southern and Western States, with their hot climate.

industry: *l'application*; **a log cabin:** *une cabine en rondins*; **postmaster:** *receveur des postes*; **self-reliance:** *l'indépendance*; **to rely on:** *compter sur*; **a portmanteau word:** *un mot-valise*; **huddled:** *blotti*; **to yearn:** *aspirer à*; **wretched:** *misérable*; **refuse:** *des détritus, ce dont on ne veut pas*; **to teem:** *fourmiller*; **tempest-tost = tempest-tossed:** *secoué par la tempête*

T

Thanksgiving: On the 4th Thursday in November, people celebrate the arrival of the first pilgrims in America on the Mayflower. It is traditional to have a large family meal with turkey* and cranberry jelly*, sweet potatoes* and pumpkin pie*.

Transcendentalism: A mid-nineteenth century movement, best reflected in the works of Thoreau and Emerson. In a reaction against the Puritans' view of predestination, the Transcendentalists believed in a divine immanence within man and nature, thus making all men truly divine and equal.

a turkey: *une dinde*; **cranberry jelly:** *de la gelée aux airelles*; **sweet potatoes:** *des patates*; **a pumpkin pie:** *une tarte à la citrouille*

U

Uncle Sam: The symbol of the United States. He was invented by cartoonists in the 19th century and usually resembles Abraham Lincoln, with a goatee*, and a star-spangled hat reminiscent of the American flag.

Uncle Tom: A kind and courageous black slave in Harriet Beecher Stowe's novel *Uncle Tom's Cabin* (1852). The name has become synonymous with humble cooperation with the whites and is used pejoratively to describe servile black Americans.

a goatee: *une barbiche*

W

Wall Street: The New York street where the New York Stock Exchange is situated.

WASP: The abbreviation of White Anglo-Saxon Protestant. Influential and wealthy white Americans, whose families have been in America for several generations.

World Trade Center: The twin towers of the World Trade Center were the highest buildings on the New York skyline until they were destroyed in the terrorist attacks of 9/11, in 2001.

the Stock Exchange: *la Bourse*

Y

Yankee: Originally a pejorative term used by Southerners to describe an American on the side of the Union during the Civil War. The word is still pejorative and refers to a typical American from New England.

Yuppies (Young urban professional persons): Young professional people living in cities, with high incomes* and a fashionable lifestyle.

an income: *un revenu*

INDEX

Dépôt légal : janvier 2022 - N° de projet : 10277541
Achevé d'imprimer en France, en décembre 2021
sur les presses de l'imprimerie Chirat - N° 202111.0268